I0130542

SENSORY AFFECT, LEARNING SPACES, AND DESIGN EDUCATION

Through the lens of sensory affect, this book offers a new way of thinking about day-to-day teaching and student engagement within learning spaces in design education.

The book examines the definitions, concepts, ideas, and overlaps of a repertoire of learning spaces prevalent in higher education and addresses the pedagogical gap that exists between broader learning structures and spaces, and the requirements of specialist design education. Recognising that mainstream teaching environments impact upon design studio learning and student engagement, the book positions creative learning spaces at the heart of practice-based learning. It defines the underlying pedagogical philosophy of a creative learning space in design education and reports on how practical strategies incorporating sensory affect may be implemented by educators to foster better student engagement in these spaces within higher education.

Bringing much-needed attention to specialist design teaching and learning spaces in higher education, this book will be of interest to educators, researchers, and post-graduate students immersed in design education, pedagogy, and learning spaces more broadly.

Lorraine Marshalsey is currently Senior Lecturer and the Curriculum Lead for Design and Technologies in Education (Education Futures) at the University of South Australia in Adelaide, Australia. She originally trained in design and applied arts and then moved into teaching design and design research in a variety of further and higher education universities in the UK and Australia. She completed her PhD in Design (Education) at Glasgow School of Art in 2018. She is a Senior Fellow of the Higher Education Academy (SFHEA) and a member of NSEAD (The National Society for Education in Art and Design). Lorraine is an Editorial Board Member of the Q1 journal, the *International Journal of Art and Design Education* (iJade). She is also a founding Convenor and Member of the *Studio Matters* design education research community, which hosts members from the US, Sweden, the UK, Australia, and the Netherlands, among others. She has published widely on the studio as a site for innovative learning, as a learning space (physical and online), and on sensory affect in educational environments.

SENSORY AFFECT, LEARNING SPACES, AND DESIGN EDUCATION

Strategies for Reflective Teaching and Student Engagement in Higher Education

Lorraine Marshalsey

Routledge
Taylor & Francis Group

LONDON AND NEW YORK

Designed cover image: 'Cover image: © Lorraine Marshalsey'

First published 2023
by Routledge
4 Park Square, Milton Park, Abingdon, Oxon OX14 4RN

and by Routledge
605 Third Avenue, New York, NY 10158

Routledge is an imprint of the Taylor & Francis Group, an informa business

© 2023 Lorraine Marshalsey

The right of Lorraine Marshalsey to be identified as author of this work
has been asserted in accordance with sections 77 and 78 of the Copyright,
Designs and Patents Act 1988.

All rights reserved. No part of this book may be reprinted or reproduced or
utilised in any form or by any electronic, mechanical, or other means, now
known or hereafter invented, including photocopying and recording, or in
any information storage or retrieval system, without permission in writing
from the publishers.

Trademark notice: Product or corporate names may be trademarks or
registered trademarks, and are used only for identification and explanation
without intent to infringe.

British Library Cataloguing-in-Publication Data
A catalogue record for this book is available from the British Library

Library of Congress Cataloging-in-Publication Data
Names: Marshalsey, Lorraine, author.
Title: Sensory affect, learning spaces, and design education : sensory affect,
    learning spaces and design education / Lorraine Marshalsey.
Description: Abingdon, Oxon ; New York, NY : Routledge, 2023. |
    Includes bibliographical references and index.
Identifiers: LCCN 2022046532 | ISBN 9781032008288 (hardback) |
    ISBN 9781032008264 (paperback) | ISBN 9781003175988 (ebook)
Subjects: LCSH: Classroom environment—Psychological aspects. |
    Education, Higher—Psychological aspects. | Instructional systems—
    Design. | Learning strategies. | Sensory stimulation.
Classification: LCC LB3013 .M347 2023 | DDC 371.102/4—dc23/
    eng/20221107
LC record available at https://lccn.loc.gov/2022046532

ISBN: 978-1-032-00828-8 (hbk)
ISBN: 978-1-032-00826-4 (pbk)
ISBN: 978-1-003-17598-8 (ebk)

DOI: 10.4324/9781003175988

Typeset in Bembo
by Apex CoVantage, LLC

To Maddy Sclater and Steve Rigley, who started this sensory affect journey with me at Glasgow School of Art.

To my Mum, Dad, Sean, and Andy, who are always alongside me no matter where I go or what I decide to do next.

CONTENTS

FIGURES

TABLES

FOREWORD

Sensory affect, learning spaces, and design education

Given the events of the past few years, it is particularly fitting that this book on sensory affect and learning spaces in design education has been published. The global pandemic has had a significant effect on teaching and learning communities around the world and the impact on higher education is still being processed. In design education, the most obvious consequence was the loss of access to, and lack of physical proximity afforded by, design studio learning spaces because of campus closures and other insurmountable restrictions on accessing specialised resources. These rapid changes necessitated a complete severance of physical engagement to learning spaces, social interactions, and the making of material artefacts. Instead, design educators embraced remote learning platforms, online communication, and distance instruction in almost all institutions (Marshalsey and Sclater, 2020). What followed was at least partly predictable: a lack of hands-on experiential teaching and learning within a specialised community of practice and the challenges this brings. However, this pivot was accompanied by the realisation that other affordances offered by a physical nearness to peers, specialised spaces and resources are just as, if not more, important to design education.

Within hours and days of the pandemic, design educators and students realised just how easy it was to take for granted those basic and specialised aspects offered by design studio learning as a material, visible, present community of practice. The 'little things' became visible, for those who chose to look, and quickly turned out to be essential to how design is predominantly taught (Jones, 2021). The specialised learning spaces we use as 'studio' are much more than functional places and do more than simply contain people and materials: housing moments of discovery and serendipity; fostering unique atmospheres of individual and collective studio learning; cultivating rhythms and cycles of design activity; nurturing networks of social learning and comparison with peers. When these entities are removed, we experience, often viscerally, the loss of basic affordances of embodiment and sensory affect in design education.

I have a disclosure to make here: my institution teaches design entirely at a distance and online. Hence, you might wonder why I should be writing a foreword to a book on *Sensory Affect, Learning Spaces, and Design Education*. To understand this, you only have to read the first chapter of this book to realise that human experience is necessarily embodied in *all* face-to-face, blended, and distance education settings. Without sensory and embodied cognition our ability to experience design and design education is significantly limited. Without embodiment in its various manifestations, we are simply unable to practice or to 'be'. In all realities we remain embodied in our thinking and processes, projecting our sensory affect into the world as much as we receive it. The very embodied nature of cognition – of thinking, doing, and being – also allows me, as a distance and online educator, to create successful learning in design education. Ironically, what people assume is lost in the move from physical to distance learning, becomes the central catalyst for learning design: experiences. Hence, we, as educators, design learning experiences that deliberately engage students with the material, affective, and existential worlds around them. Without an understanding of sensory affect, we would not be able to teach design at a distance.

Which brings us back to this book: *Sensory Affect, Learning Spaces, and Design Education*. The challenges faced during the pandemic highlighted that, whilst we may rely on sensory affect as an unconscious influence in education, we have an incomplete working knowledge (beyond a few examples) of how sensory affect supports processes of teaching and learning. Hence, having an expert like Marshalsey present her work in this area is so important and timely.

Design education scholarship and research are now starting to reach a maturity built on its own knowledge base and is not simply a consequence of work explored in other areas of higher education. This book builds on and adds to this knowledge base, a testament to how the discipline is maturing. And particularly, when it is easy to look at the design studio and the practices taking place, and think that what transpires there is simple, trivial, and even irrelevant to education. Such a view comes from thinking that specialised design education can be understood by only looking at it objectively from the outside in. What design educators, students, and practitioners know is that the design studio is understood through experiencing it; that its essential nature is one of human activity and being. The notion of foregrounding an awareness of sensory affect comes across clearly in this book because the author, Lorraine Marshalsey, is an experiential and experienced design studio educator and colleague, supported by an academic background and significant knowledge in this field of study.

I encourage you to open this books pages, feel the paper, read and to employ the suggested approaches, methods, and strategies. I encourage you to dynamically embrace sensory affect in experiential learning, learning spaces, and design education, and lastly, enjoy *Sensory Affect, Learning Spaces, and Design Education*.

Derek Jones

Senior Lecturer in Design, The Open University

Education SIG Convenor, Design Research Society.

References

Jones, D. (2021) 'Making little things visible', *Design and Technology Education*, 26(1), 8–11.

Marshalsey, L. and Sclater, M. (2020) 'Together but apart: Creating and supporting online learning communities in an era of distributed studio education', *International Journal of Art & Design Education*, 39(4), 826–840.

1

WHICH WAY FORWARD? DESIGN EDUCATION TODAY

Introduction

> *There is no way in which to understand the world without first detecting it through the radar-net of our senses.*
>
> Ackerman (1992: xv)

To begin, my son, in 2 years of his primary education in the UK, experienced two very different approaches to learning in the classroom, which influenced my interest in sensory affect as a tool for engagement within learning spaces. In one approach, the educator encouraged the students to sit still, whisper, quietly focus while learning mathematics and, although this method may suit a degree of school-age learners, it did not help my son to learn. He really struggled with his understanding and reasoning of the learning task. In the following year of his schooling and within a different mathematics class, another educator encouraged my son to be actively engaged in the environment in which he was learning. He was able to freely walk up and around the learning space, while articulating his thoughts out loud, and he was able to squeeze a stress ball when learning mathematics. This approach to embodied and sensory learning aided his concentration, cognition and understanding, and he focused much better on the tasks. He grew in confidence as his grasp of the learning intentions and success criteria improved. These two differing approaches to teaching and learning made me question the inclusion of embodied methodologies and the role of sensory affect present within educational environments to address student engagement. I define these notions of bodily awareness within learning spaces as sensory affect.

> *Sensory affect is the influence of experience detected through the body. It is perception through the senses, as a means for participants to analyse and interpret the impact*

DOI: 10.4324/9781003175988-1

of the environment around them. Participants may be sensitive to the sensory affects within their environments, yet the impact of these experiences may go unnoticed or simply be tolerated within the environment in which they are situated.

Marshalsey (2017: 26)

This book arose from many years of my own immersion in and study of sensory affect, learning spaces, and design education. I drew from my own reflective teaching practice, my observations of my colleagues and students, and my continuing research and reading of the senses, affect and design studio learning spaces in design and higher education. My interests in this landscape firmly connected for me when I discovered two seminal influences whose own work directed the fundamentals of this book at its inception. These key texts are from the renowned architect Juhani Pallasmaa *The Eyes of the Skin* (which explores the phenomenological dimensions of human experience) and Eugene Gendlin's notion of embodied knowing through the *Felt Sense* as human experience (Gendlin, 2003; Pallasmaa, 2012). With the work of Pallasmaa and Gendlin as the wind in my sails, I have brought elements of my reflective teaching in design education and higher education, and my research of sensory affect in learning spaces together in this volume. The evidence this book presents also draws from parts of my early doctoral research, which activated my research on sensory affect and studio-based learning spaces, alongside the pedagogical debates on design education teaching and learning being conducted worldwide before, during, and after the pandemic.

This book is, arguably, a call to action to address two differing, yet related matters in my own field of design education today. First, the pressures bearing down on design education in higher education are creating an imbalance between the needs of specialised studio teaching and learning and wider university structures and systems. Second, the need to be aware of what it is to be human today and how to listen to the body for guidance and direction in education is sorely lacking. When we listen to the body through the lens of sensory affect, then we can adjust and empower reflective teaching and student engagement in design education. Sensory affect influences the experiences of many individuals and groups within a diverse array of learning spaces available in design and higher education. Largely due to the pandemic, design educators today have been challenged to convert specialised studio pedagogies into modes of blended, distance, and online learning, moving away from conventional physical, face-to-face design instruction in higher education. To understand these issues, I researched the experiential impact of sensory affect for many years as I sought to bridge the gap between reflective teaching practices, learning spaces (physical and digital) and student engagement in design education. What is it that makes conventional design studio learning spaces 'work' and how might sensory affect be an important consideration in the success of design education today? This book foregrounds an awareness of sensory affect as a navigational guide, to challenge the conditions afforded to design education within higher education today. Through the lens of sensory affect, we (as design educators) can reflect, identify, and address the learning spaces we are provided with (good, bad, or indifferent), to empower our teaching and our students' experiential learning with specialised design education. In this book, three themes are proposed to address the issues within experiential learning and learning spaces, and through the lens of sensory affect, in contemporary design education: *all-surface use, empowerment,* and *flexibility.*

Existing studies

To be clear, it is not my intention to revisit the cultural history and evolution of embodiment in higher education in depth, or to debate the discourse of those who explore the senses in early years education, primary and secondary education. There are many existing texts and studies who do this very capably already (see Probyn, 2004; Zembylas, 2007; Nguyen and Larson, 2015; Garrett and MacGill, 2021; Leigh and Brown, 2021). Numerous educators and researchers have published important research and significantly influenced the trajectories of learning space research (Oblinger, 2006; Woolner, 2010; Boddington and Boys, 2011; Harrison and Hutton, 2014; Scott-Webber et al., 2014; Temple, 2014; Boys, 2015; Salama, 2015; Imms et al., 2016). In more recent years, several key researchers have explored the wide-ranging and ongoing challenges facing the design, and use of, physical and online learning spaces in higher education today (Scott-Webber et al., 2000; Jacobson and Reimann, 2010; Scott-Webber, 2012, 2014; Pates and Sumner, 2016). Key researchers in design education have published further studies investigating the merits of specialised studio learning in architectural and design education (Salama and Wilkinson, 2007; Mewburn, 2012; Boling et al., 2016; Brown, 2016; Farías and Wilkie, 2016; Wallis et al., 2017; Thoring et al., 2018; Corazzo, 2019; Gray et al., 2020; Jones et al., 2021). Despite this plethora of studies, both broader educational and specialist design education research has generally overlooked the experiential impact of sensory affect on educator and student engagement in design-based learning spaces. It is heartening to see a number of emerging studies in the field of study I am exploring, discussing reflective practice, the sensory dimensions of experience and classrooms, embodied inquiry, the efficacy of newer spaces to work and the transition to online pedagogy, mainly as a consequence of the recent pandemic affecting education worldwide (Dreamson, 2020; Marshalsey and Sclater, 2020; Roy and Uekusa, 2020; Slavid, 2020; Chaves and Taylor, 2021; Komarzynska-Swiesciak et al., 2021; Leigh and Brown, 2021; Todd et al., 2021).

The challenges and trends influencing design education

While the pandemic has produced a wealth of published research on the impact of fast-tracking face-to-face education to online modes, prior to the pandemic, the fundamental elements of design education were already being challenged and diluted in the business age of higher education. Rising costs, funding pressures, spiralling tuition fees, student debt, widening participation, and the swift acceleration of technology-enhanced learning (TEL) in mainstream learning spaces have forced higher education institutions to rethink their long-term strategies. Expansion, efficiency, economic, and political accountability has become the focus in education at the detriment of teaching and learning experience (Finlayson and Hayward, 2010). University managements have reshaped educational structures in cost-effective ways, as financial pressures now align with academic accountability on a global scale (Wild, 2013). In recent decades, higher student numbers in tertiary education has transformed the culture and modes of learning, leading to communities of practice that are significantly different from those of the past (Wenger, 2000; Harrison and Hutton, 2014). As wider access and virtual participation in higher education have increased, and as the 2020 pandemic swept through educational institutions, the student population worldwide has embraced flexible forms of curriculum delivery, online learning spaces and distance and blended learning. Large enrolments in design education are also increasing, with traditional small studio group instruction, critiques, and face-to-face discussion becoming rarer in the face of widening, universal participation. Collini (2012) argued we (as educators) must reflect on the different types of challenges and pressures within higher education as these transformations have significantly affected teaching and learning innovation. 'More teaching for less' is expected in formal and informal blended, virtual and online learning spaces designed to encourage flipped learning, self-directed study for large numbers of students, and less face-to-face interaction with educators (Scott-Webber, 2012; Vignoles and Murray, 2016). In this context, educators argue that for deeper learning to occur 'students need to apply information in context for themselves' (Readman et al., 2021: online). This hybridising of space and the accelerated changes to pedagogies and curriculum is not new, yet these have more pertinent value today than ever before, and in terms of blended and online learning. As Harrison and Hutton (2014:1) clearly state, 'the learning environment is . . . in the front line of these volatile developments'.

> *Hybrid education has moved from an esoteric notion to the de-facto norm . . . We share co-working spaces with our families, we bring our classes into our homes and ourselves into our students' homes. Within a week, the term "blended learning" has shifted from referring to a mix of on-site and on-line to signifying the combination of synchronous and a-synchronous online learning.*
>
> Cohen et al. (2020:1039)

The formal learning environment has long been the basis for one 'more knowledgeable other' to plan, control, and transmit information to many students who passively sit and listen in a classroom or lecture theatre in rows (Scott-Webber, 2014). Today, the use of physical lecture theatres as a long-standing method for knowledge transfer continues to be debated and diminished in an age of digital delivery in higher education, particularly in Australia and New Zealand (Readman et al., 2021; Ross, 2021; Williams, 2021). Generally, the conventional lecture format traditionally dictated a one-way delivery of intensive information on a topic to students from a single educator with mixed regular attendance as the academic term progresses, with little consideration of dynamic sensory affect in this format. In design education, the uncertain engagement of dispersed students with recorded lectures has also become an ongoing issue today (Edwards and Clinton, 2019). Boys (2008) suggests that the formal/informal divide hides more than it reveals about the complex relationships between learning and the spaces in which learning takes place. The manner in which a space is organised or transmitted is vitally important to students' learning and community of practice within their educational environments, and the resulting latticework of intricate relationships and actions that supposedly create conducive experiences there (Woolner, 2010).

Now, it is common knowledge that technology has transformed higher education structures and systems at an extraordinary pace and the digital tidal wave shows no sign of slowing down. In design education, 'hot-desking' is common (where students work in whatever free unallocated desk spaces they find on campus) and increasingly 'no-desking' (where students work in whatever free unallocated place they find on campus). Generally, in non-timetabled periods, students in the physical campus students are offered a range of learning spaces and places with the choice and control to select the best environment for their needs and as they study in libraries, unoccupied classrooms, corridors, outdoor settings, and other communal learning environments. Institutional library environments, long been recognised as rich spaces of learning, have moved from silent spaces to a mix of quiet closed spaces and noisy collaborative open working spaces. These libraries now provide an assorted range of aesthetically pleasing and digitally enabled hubs, pods, booths and group study rooms, offering both 'togetherness and separate-ness', and online access (İmamoğlu and Gürel, 2016:66). Therefore, university libraries have now become crowded and noisy in peak times, with libraries accommodating 'large user populations and limited space' (Breen et al., 2018:106). Many university libraries are now removing access to physical books as students access entirely digital texts and e-books, transforming libraries from analogue to digital spaces (Casselden and Pears, 2020). As these policies and arrangements have become widespread in higher education then a reliance on mobile, digital skills, and online communication is necessary – a practice also filtering down to specialist studio learning in design education. The use of social media as a peer learning and collaboration platform is increasingly common, addressing the issue of teaching, and marketing, to larger student populations (Güler, 2015; Filimowicz and Tzankova, 2017). Ongoing debates examine the substantial use of social media and technology in higher education and how this turn has led to a stifling of true creativity with educators arguing for and against the embrace of TEL and networked learning platforms (Beetham, 2013; Bayne, 2015). As Filimowicz and Tzankova (2017:158) suggest 'achieving portfolio quality creative outcomes in large online environments such as MOOCs (Massive Open Online Courses)' can be realised but it is challenging to do so, especially in practice-based design education.

Within higher education, universities prefer that design education focus on "virtual community building where group work, 'crits', and presentations are being carried out online. Moving assessment and engagement to online formats has consequences for practice-based art and design courses: distributed learning changes how we teach and learn" (Marshalsey and Sclater, 2020:abstract). This re-shapes learners' needs, educators' course planning and design, and the use of learning spaces in design education. Aesthetically pleasing, communal classrooms with funky furniture and universal, online communities for large numbers of students do not engage design students who need specialised signature studio learning and resources. Universities are now focusing on,

> . . . *virtual community building, remote distance learning and teaching, moving group work and presentations online and alternative assessment outcomes via digital portals. Distance learning in art and design fundamentally changes how, what, and why we teach and how our students learn* (Marshalsey, 2020). *What, therefore, are the practical implications of art and design studio education in a time of distributed learning? If educators lose control over a practical curriculum, then students may fail to perform, and to the depth and rigour required for creative art and design practice (Giroux and Aronowitz, 1986).*
>
> *(Marshalsey and Sclater, 2020:27)*

Thus, design students are now experiencing learning spaces without consistent exposure to studio values, and access to specialist design teaching and resources in an irregular landscape of TEL, online and social media-based provision. Often, educational designers planning higher education learning spaces rarely consult design educators about their needs for teaching and learning (Boling et al., 2016). And if that wasn't enough design educators are at different junctions in this technologically advanced age. Pre-computer design educators, with valuable technical methods and critical theoretical knowledge of traditional print and product history and culture, are retiring. On the other hand, post-computer design educators and students continually strive to stay up-to-date with a repertoire of digital tools, systems, and responsive devices such as tablets and smartphones that seem to be emerging daily as educational necessities (Maeda, 2020).

Design education in the digital age

Educator and student experiences of design education in the digital age may differ across institutional environments, formal and informal curriculum, learning spaces and time. Today, most teaching practice embraces blended, distance and online iterations of classrooms and channels, while others champion the physical form of a studio environment. Shaping these face-to-face preferences for learning spaces in design education is a nostalgia for slower, sensory, wet-based, hands-on design practice; 'painstaking attention to detail is recognized as a craft approach' (Maeda, 2020:44). These slow practices often do not align with the mass adoption of establishing one-size-fits-all digital campuses in today's global educational climate.

The exploding costs of higher education alongside the rise of digital proficiency and TEL have introduced computer labs as a new central learning spaces for design students (Daniel and Fleischmann, 2014:195; Bowen and Guthrie, 2015). Experiential analogue processes and techniques have been mostly pushed to the side by the complexities of newer, advanced digital practice and production in higher education and this has lasting implications for design education. However, Bayne (2015:11) positions TEL as a field of complexity and importance, which can support human and social needs, learning, teaching and all associated academic practices. Sclater (2016) challenged the assumption children are born with essential technological capabilities and the focus on their digital literacy will be at the expense of critique, and awareness and connectedness to wider social and global issues and interactions. It is a widely held belief students will easily adapt to TEL in design education. Goodyear and Retalis (2010:8) argued future-oriented technology can enhance implicit informal and formal learning, and in combinations of each; 'technology affords a range of opportunities that can transform the learning process, offering enhanced possibilities for knowledge and skills acquisition'. It is true educational technologies can provide access to study materials faster and provide a media for learning through online inquiry. TEL can sustain socially orientated pedagogies, communication, collaboration, assessment, and digital literacy online (Goodyear and Retalis, 2010). However, recent studies have highlighted significant implications of blended, distance and online TEL for practice-based design education (Marshalsey and Sclater, 2020). The emerging picture is one of adaptation, experimentation, and motivation, as we (design educators) learn more about the power and value of integrating blended, distance and online TEL and pedagogies effectively in design education – and as teaching strategies continue to develop from recent world events (Marshalsey and Sclater, 2020:838). However, as Selwyn (2011:175) contends it "could also be said that all 'new' educational practices and activities using technology contain old educational practices and activities".

Consequently, design educators are continually adjusting teaching strategies to embrace new digital futures in teaching and learning and as design students may be geographically and digitally dispersed. Yet, in design education today, there is clearly an absence of understanding and conceptualising the impact of sensory affect on blended, distance, and online TEL – a glaring omission in higher education research. How do we (as design educators) empower reflective teaching practices and reinforce student engagement through the conduit of the body in online pedagogical approaches, curriculum structures, and virtual learning spaces? Consequently, the abundance of data on how learners engage with virtual learning environments has increased significantly in recent years (Sclater, 2007; Sclater and Lally, 2013, 2016; Carvalho et al., 2016). From 2020 to 2021, studies citing these pressures are still emerging and 'blended', 'online' and specifically 'hybrid', have become synonymous with learning space use today (Bennett et al., 2020; Cohen et al., 2020; Cook et al., 2020; Goodyear, 2020; Molloy, 2020; Rhodes and Schmidt, 2021). Elen (2020) cited growing evidence that, in many instances, students do not participate as fully with their learning environments, to engage with and execute learning tasks, as first thought. Indeed, Elen (2020) terms this 'instructional disobedience' as a diverse and widespread phenomenon in education, despite rich educational environments being offered.

Sticky learning spaces in design education

Despite a complex mix of modalities and spaces of learning in design education today, educators attempt to make the student experience 'sticky', relevant and engaging. The notion of the 'sticky campus' emerged in recent years as a place where educators and students are drawn to be and feel they belong even during periods of non-teaching. The 'sticky campus' aimed to encourage educators and students to stay, study, work, create, and socialise actively on safe university-governed grounds, in appealing buildings with a diverse range of formal and informal environments to choose from (Warren and Mahony Architects 2017; Lyon, 2018). The ethos of the 'sticky campus' aimed to reflect students' own personal needs back to them in their educational settings, and to fulfil these needs while promoting student-centred practice, wellbeing, and a sense of belonging. Orr and Shreeve (2018) then presented the idea of the 'sticky curriculum' for contemporary art and design education. They argue a complex 'stickiness' is the posing of uncertain, diverse, and thought-provoking opportunities for learners, which may be found external to formal, assessed curriculum in design education. Therefore, the 'sticky curriculum' can refer to a range of learning experiences. These can be described as enjoyable or endurable, local, or widespread, difficult, or challenging, liberating, explorative, failures or successes, flexible, ambiguous, and reluctant (Orr and Shreeve, 2018; University of the Arts London, 2018). As tensions develop within and between the formal and informal elements of the learning environment, the catalyst of the 'sticky curriculum' is embodied and enacted in multiple ways, including within the university culture, community, and digital practices (University of the Arts London, 2018). The aim of this book is to build upon and develop these 'webs of stickiness' further and to reconcile the gap between broader university learning structures and specialist design education, revealing the critical effects of students' own sensory experiences in learning spaces today.

How might design educators create a 'sticky' learning space for design education (drawing influence from Orr and Shreeve's (2018) notion of the 'sticky curriculum')? In relation to design education and specialised studio learning, we, as reflective educators, who seek to fully engage our students, need to remind ourselves of the modalities encapsulating contemporary learning spaces and create 'sticky' learning spaces. How might design educators through the lens of sensory affect make experiential learning and participation in these spaces more engaging and 'sticky' across physical and digital modes of learning? An awareness of sensory affect can weave a connected narrative between many of these terminologies and modalities to reinforce our formal and informal learning spaces for better student engagement:

- Specialised learning spaces – tailored to specific functions or teaching approaches, formal teaching and often enclosed as a learning space. Contains specialised subject-specific equipment, valued spaces that are managed by the department and institution, regulated by technicians, and controlled by security measures.
- Generic learning spaces – tailored for multiple uses, used for formal teaching, and often comprises open, enclosed, and general population/circulation learning spaces. Access is granted according to a schedule and hours. The flexibility and movement of furniture and space are often limited. Managed by the institution, regulated by estates staff, and controlled by security measures.
- Informal learning spaces – tailored to a wide range of settings, informal and formal, social, open, and enclosed learning spaces. Often visible, unscheduled, and accessible spaces, which are open to the public. Fluid choice of settings and groupings of furniture and users. Food and drink are permitted in these spaces (Harrison and Hutton, 2014:48). Managed less so by the institution and regulated by estates staff if these spaces exist on-campus.

The terminology and modalities of design-based learning spaces

The character of design studio training

The character of studio training and its modes of learning has changed considerably over time, with its heritage stemming from the workshops of 13th-century Europe (Amirsadeghi and Eisler, 2012). Originally, a team of people in a workshop environment produced work according to instructions. The master of the workshop, normally a reputable artist, would supervise, train, and pass on knowledge to groups of students (generally craftsmen), teaching by example as the students copied the hands-on methods. In the mid-16th century, the master/apprentice model evolved into art academy training, which included lecture theatres alongside studios. These academies sought to produce a well-balanced exchange between knowledge, experience, and instruction. This prepared the student to manage the transition out of education and studio-style instruction into his or her own studios within industry (Marshalsey, 2017).

Today, many designers have discarded the conventional artist's studio model in favour of new modes of working facilitated by technological advances. In the late 20th century, artists and designers seized derelict warehouses, factories, and buildings as fashionable workshop spaces, changing the interior and architectural dynamic of studio from the 1960s and 1970s onwards (Blazwick, 2012). Combined working and living studio spaces became fashionable. Now, a studio can now exist not only as a physical large or small room space, but also as a virtual 'studio of the mind', as a computer-based studio desk or via mobile digital devices (Amirsadeghi and Eisler, 2012:6). No matter what the size or platform, every studio should have its own identity, character, and zones to facilitate privacy, freedom, activism, refuge, and expression. The studio should act as an ambiguous, open-ended laboratory of ideas, as a gallery space for display, and 'studio activities are also the assessment tasks, they can be seen to align with the expected learning outcomes of learning to design' (Blazwick, 2012; Crowther, 2013:19). These far-reaching transformations from the original studio context since its inception also reflect a changing print-to-web culture and design practice over time. These changes influence the role that studio, and its signature pedagogies and culture, plays in design education today.

Contemporary terminology and modalities in design education

Contemporary design-based learning spaces are described and identified across a plethora of terminology and modalities, which can be confusing for design educators to plan specialised experiential learning. These include Innovative Learning Environment's (ILE's), studios, workshops, classrooms, makerspaces (where all students are considered as makers and therefore, need spaces to invent, think, work with their hands, and to construct concrete artefacts as products of learning and cognition), lecture halls and fab labs (shared fabrication laboratories), among others (Thornburg, 2014). Many writers, educators, and researchers have devised methods of unpacking the modalities of learning within broader educational learning spaces in different ways. Locke (2007) outlined the six modalities of a social media model for online learning to be participation, watching, performing, group, secret and publishing. McIntosh (2010) examined seven spatial modalities for school environments as participation, watching, performing, group, secret, publishing, and data. Later, Thornburg (2013) defined a model for learning space under the following four definitions:

1 The Campfire. *They watch.* The learning space where students learn from knowledgeable others, the experts. The campfire denotes a storytelling or lecture space, where teaching is supported by the presentation of material for students to learn from.
2 The Watering-hole. *They share group data.* The social learning space where students learn from peers. A place for socially engaged dialogic conversation, collaborative, and co-operative learning.
3 The Cave. *They privately reflect.* A self-directed, reflective learning space for an individual student to consider meaning making.
4 Life. *They perform and participate.* A learning space which reflects the real world to students.

However, one further modality has appeared in education (Rosan Bosch Studio, 2019):

5   The Mountaintop. *They display and discuss.* Serves as a learning space for displaying work and open discussion.

As an active learning spaces researcher in the ILETC (Innovative Learning Environments & Teacher Change) and an Australian Research Council (ARC) funded project, the research of French (2018) focused on designing innovative educational environments based upon the type and use of these room archetypes (The University of Melbourne, 2016; ILETC Innovative Learning Environments and Teacher Change, 2017). Each modality (Campfire, Watering-hole, Cave, Life, Mountaintop) offered several interpretations of each room archetype. For example, Cave could refer to a relaxation and functional ledge, a shared focus and multi-use group cave or a peer-to-peer functional corridor. An additional modality – Lab – was also included.

6   The Lab. *They make.* A technician-led specialist workshop or skilled hands-on resources, which may be digital.

When mapping this landscape of modalities, I also consider the following criteria from Fraser and Achterberg (2014) as important to this narrative of design education today.

7   Places where small groups could meet to work on projects.
8   Places for whole class dialogue.
9   Places where technology can be accessed easily.
10   Places for displaying ideas and working documents.
11   Spaces that can accommodate movement and noise.
12   Spaces that include spill over spaces in corridors.

Building on this, and in recent years, Nair and Doctori (2019:31) proposed 20 consolidated modalities of learning:

1   Independent study
2   Peer-to-peer tutoring
3   One-on-one learning with the teacher
4   Lecture
5   Team collaborative work in small and mid-size groups (2–6 students)
6   Lecture format with the teacher or outside expert at centre stage
7   Distance learning
8   Learning with mobile technology
9   Student presentation

10 Internet-based research
11 Seminar-style instruction
12 Performance-based learning
13 Interdisciplinary study
14 Naturalist learning
15 Art-based learning
16 Social-emotional learning
17 Design-based learning
18 Storytelling
19 Team learning and teaching
20 Play and movement learning

Today, these multi-faceted modalities of learning spaces are interconnected across a plethora of asynchronous and synchronous platforms in design education. Conventionally, it is widely recognised that design education was formed around the single foci of a specialised 'studio', as the central teaching and learning signature space. Yet, design educators today now fight to align these multiple terminologies and modalities of education with specialised design education. As a specialised mode of learning – how can we make design education and its associated contemporary learning spaces 'sticky' in contemporary higher education (Sims and Shreeve, 2012; Crowther, 2013; Motley, 2017; Marshalsey and Sclater, 2020)? In this transient and fast-flowing educational era, how do design educators encourage students to be present in teacher-centred, student-centred, informal, and social online and offline learning spaces, while still receiving the specialist conceptual and practice-based training, they need?

Models of learning in design

Deep, engaged learning differs for design students due to the iterative, open-ended, student-centred nature of design education and the sensory affective conditions present in their learning spaces. Students participate in Project-Based Learning (PBL), engaging the principles of self-directed learning, collaboration, constructive learning, and contextual development. PBL is highly regarded as an effective teaching approach, providing an opening for students to engage deeply with real-life challenges, opportunities, and settings. PBL is an active form of learning and context-specific, and students achieve their results through shared knowledge and social interactions (Kokotsaki et al., 2016). Design students also participate in Studio-Based Learning (SBL), following the original master-apprentice model with project briefs, class critiques, frequent feedback, one-on-one instruction, shared teamwork, peer learning, self-directed learning, portfolio production, and the display of exhibition outcomes as standard practice (Mitchell, 2017). SBL is a dynamic approach to solving design problems through experimentation, development, and collaborative teamwork. The SBL method is defined as 'Instructor's support students as they grapple with complexity of design problem-solving through pedagogical practices that include assignments, associated meta-discussions, explicit prompts, reminders, modelling, and coaching' (Cennamo et al., 2011:12). SBL is often compared with PBL, an approach where students are presented with an open-ended, authentic question to address or explore and due to the nature of the complex linear, diagnostic, inductive, and ambiguous problem-solving occurring in the studio environment (Cennamo et al., 2011). Recently, PBL and SBL are gaining traction in educational and engineering disciplines (Trede et al., 2020). This combination of PBL and SBL student-centred approaches to teaching and learning provides the basis of design education; to absorb conceptual and experiential knowledge and to process and produce refined design solutions or products through exploratory discovery. Similar approaches are embraced in experiential or collaborative learning strategies in education, more generally.

The learning modes and the specific ways in which learning occurs in design education should be based on experience. Ma (2021:10) thematic findings identified four main models of learning as social, personal, information processing, and behavioural, providing direction and guidance to teaching practitioners towards designing activities and environments for thoughtful learning. Their table (Table 1.1) summarises the emerging keywords and concepts for each model of learning, derived from a study of 339 articles. Consequently, the content analysis of 'social' evidenced 'peer learning and teaching, group projects, collaborative group work, and online learning communities were frequently identified as activities that contribute to deep learning and that result in more engaging and effective learning'. The mode 'personal' supported personal growth, clear goals, self-awareness, and self-confidence to accomplish deep learning. 'Information processing' reinforced the need for scientific inquiry and systematic thinking to solve problems, and 'behavioural' fostered a need for structured systems or environments to facilitate feedback to students for deeper learning (Ma, 2021:11–12).

The multi-faceted modalities and the four models of learning in design education are enacted and embedded in the conventional design studio environment in a complex web of experiential 'comings and goings'. Today, design educators are expected to continue this approach across diverse asynchronous and synchronous platforms, while instilling robust and rigorous hands-on learning for students to cognitively accelerate their knowledge, understanding, processes, and production of design practice.

Experiential learning

Generally, design education, as an overarching structure, relates to two streams – the *knowledge and understanding stream*, which includes conceptual and theoretical investigation, and research-based practice and second, the *process and production* (the technical context) stream. The signature pedagogies of studio learning and design education are modes of strategic, experiential learning, embedded within these two streams and realised in formal and informal learning spaces occupied with objects, visuals, materials, sketchbooks, and artefacts (Sims and Shreeve, 2012). To

TABLE 1.1 Emerging keywords and concepts for four main models of learning, derived from a study of 339 articles.

Social	Personal	Information processing	Behavioural
Group (151)	Development (214)	Questioning (85)	Assessment (314)
Discussions (111)	Reflects (161)	Critical (77)	Practices (140)
Project (106)	Self (157)	Cognitive (73)	Scores/grades/marks
Support (106)	Experience (173)	Thinking (63)	(123)
Community (82)	Goals (96)	Solving (48)	Text/exam (121)
Social (81)	Motivation (89)	Construct (47)	Evaluation (104)
Collaboration (71)	Needs (88)	Conceptual (31)	Online (117)
Peer (68)	Values (87)	Competence (23)	Technology (105)
Help (52)	Cultures (71)	Inquiry (23)	Feedback (102)
Team (29)	Styles (68)	Scientific (12)	Environment (95)
Sharing (24)	Professional (65)		Systems (90)
Dialogue (33)	Personally (60)		Interactive (85)
Connection (19)	Perceptions (59)		Responses (62)
Cooperative (14)	Attitudes (48)		Tutoring (44)
Constructivist (11)	Beliefs (28)		Game (40)
Guidance (22)	Efficacy (28)		Behaviour (35)
Partners (10)	Placement (27)		Memory/recall/
	Confidence (15)		retention (34)
	Enjoyment (13)		Adaptive (30)
	Growth (22)		Simulations (28)
	Identity (10)		Stimulate (21)
	Emotions (10)		Assignments (19)
			Intervention (18)
			Flexible (16)
			Tutorial (16)
			Multimedia (11)
Concept phrases			
	Self-regulated	Problem-solving (40)	E-learning (30)
	learning (10)	Problem-based	Online learning (13)
		Learning (30)	
		Reasoning (32)	
		Critical thinking (28)	

Source: © Ma, 2021.

understand how design education operates today, we must draw from Kolb's experiential learning model (Kolb, 1983; Kolb and Kolb, 2005). Drawing on the fundamental theories of John Dewey (1859–1952) and Kurt Lewin (1890–1947), Kolb and Kolb (2005:193) examined the theories of experiential learning to 'explore how this knowledge can be used to enhance learning in higher education'. They denote the characteristics of experiential learning as:

1   Engaging learning as a process, where the student receives feedback on the continual progress and growth of their learning efforts.

2   Learning and re-learning, which draws out the students' beliefs and ideas, to produce and question more refined ideas and notions.
3   A continual cycle of reflective thinking-by-doing to resolve issues and challenges to drive the project-based learning.
4   Learning involves the complete person and how they think, feel, perceive, behave, and sense supports cognition.
5   Learning results from the active interactions between the student and their environment. Therefore, learning occurs through the exchange of new and existing exchanges and experiences to form judgements.
6   Learning is the process of a student creating their individual knowledge via an active constructivist approach and the co-creation of social knowledge in real-life studio-based projects and settings (Kolb and Kolb, 2005:194).

Kolb and Kolb (2005:194) argued it is critical for experiential learners to grasp the two modes of experience (Concrete Experience (CE) and Abstract Conceptualisation (AC)) and to then transform them (Reflective Observation (RO) and Active Experimentation (AE)). CE necessitates feeling or sensing when learning from experience. AC involves analysing, interpreting, and making sense of experience to make comparisons and judgements of their learning. Then, the design student can reflect, consider, and modify their actions to re-direct, test, and transform their design process (RO and AE). The student can construct knowledge through the 'creative tension' occurring at the intersections of these four learning modes: 'experiencing, reflecting, thinking, and acting' (Kolb and Kolb, 2005:194). These actions frame the Experiential Learning Cycle and 'the enhancement of experiential learning in higher education can be achieved through the creation of learning spaces that promote growth-producing experiences for learners' (Kolb and Kolb, 2005:205). Design education (and its learning spaces) fosters this feeling, thinking, and sensing cycle through creative projects, resources, social interactions, curriculum, pedagogy, and its learning spaces.

Students engaging in design education appear to experience the design process as much 'felt' as it is 'thought', triggered by instinct, intuition, perception, and sensation. Design studio learning is a process that happens best when the student is engaged and stimulated; 'open to and affected by different environments and issues' (Lyon, 2011:7). As reflective educators regain control, then student engagement may be improved in design education that has become obsessively technological in physical and online environments. And with the increasingly complexity of TEL in relation to the number of platforms and tools available to teach design education in this post-digital age, this is no easy feat. The research of Carvalho and Yeoman (2019:1104) attempts to disentangle this complexity and 'distinguish between the elements that are open to alteration through design and those that are not, educational designers gain deeper insights into the flows of matter, information and humans characteristic of productive networked learning environments'.

Student engagement is personalised, individual, and iterative. This engagement ebbs and flows in cycles and continually changes in preferred conditions. For example, one day a collaborative seminar room may serve for a student's socially engaged learning, yet the next day that student may require a quiet home environment for engagement. These changing conditions are influenced by sensory affect and the students' own perception of sensations beneficial to them in any given day; 'Examining and foregrounding the specific experiential characteristics of sensory affect in studio education can allow students and educators to facilitate better engagement with their daily studio environment' (Marshalsey, 2017:45). The free will of the student and their unique, individual learning preferences should be prioritised, particularly as online classes have changed the dynamic of teaching and learning in contemporary design education (Marshalsey and Sclater, 2020). Therefore, experiential learning, as a mode of learning, is critical to a student's journey through design education.

Engaging with experiential learning and learning spaces via three themes: all-surface use, empowerment, and flexibility

This book first seeks to illuminate the issues facing design education today, and as the future of design teaching and learning has been largely directed to mass, high-participation online platforms. Consequently, teaching strategies and learning spaces in design education continue to evolve rapidly in higher education. The importance of design education and its signature studio pedagogies and learning spaces must be acknowledged as a hands-on, dynamic, experiential, and playful curriculum with specialised resources and facilities. It is imperative to foreground the critical values of studio learning and design education in higher education, recognising and acclimatising a subjective 'designerly way of knowing' for students as a vital education for our future designers (Cross, 2011). This book is aimed at those interested in specialised design education and studio learning, whether educators or researchers, and those interested in the development of campus learning spaces in higher education, more broadly. Once sensory affect, as a critical consciousness, is embedded in reflective teaching practices, spaces for learning and in approaches to student engagement then motivation for participation, learning, and cognition can improve. In these challenging times – when physical design studio learning is under threat, and online learning platforms bring their own complexities and challenges to teaching and learning – this book seeks to propose that an awareness of sensory affect is critical to stabilising design education today.

> Some of the oldest, most deeply-rooted and most powerful methods of human learning – through observation, imitation, and participation – work best when what must be learned is directly available to the senses.
>
> (Goodyear and Retalis, 2010:2)

The experiential impact of sensory affect on educators and students begins with understanding the sensory characteristics of their learning spaces. The quality of

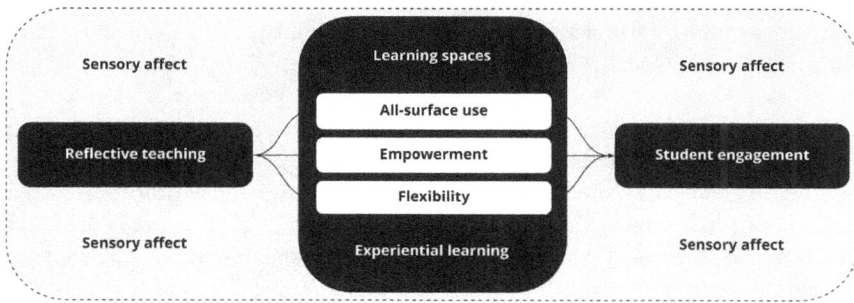

FIGURE 1.1   The framework of three distinct themes – *all-surface use, empowerment, and flexibility*.

Source: © L Marshalsey 2022.

the learning space has repercussions for teaching and learning across social, cultural, and relational interactions, inculcation of the curriculum, implantation of pedagogy, and experiential practice. A key aspect of reflective teaching and student engagement is the approach adopted within learning spaces across three key areas of consideration: *all-surface use, flexibility*, and *empowerment*. If educators and students reflect upon their own bodily experiences and their teaching and learning spaces in their daily educational environments through the lens of sensory affect, they may be empowered to engage more effectively in design education. The visual diagram outlines the importance of sensory affect and the *felt sense* as a lens to which reflective educators address these three key areas in design education (Figure 1.1). By implementing *all-surface use, empowerment*, and *flexibility* strategies to improve experiential learning and learning spaces means educator reflection and student engagement can be supported in design education today.

Summary

The wide-ranging definitions and provisions of teaching approaches, experiential learning and learning spaces between specialist design education and the broader, modern university structures have led to ongoing unstable longitudinal partnerships (Boddington and Boys, 2011). Accordingly, specialised art and design schools, colleges of art, and creative departments located within mainstream universities have assumed varied and uneven guises in the current commercialisation of higher education. Design courses today can rarely afford separate dedicated studios, specialist workshop technicians, or resources that embrace both traditionally wet and digitally dry creative practice (Boling et al., 2016:161). In tandem, there has been a shift from formal craft and skill-related workshop instruction, where students occupy their own personal studio desk space within the studio, to informal, blended and classroom-based teaching approaches common in modular and online delivery (Scott-Webber, 2012). Today, tension exists between the need to deliver both craft-orientated and technological forms of experiential learning by doing while maintaining creativity and innovation in design, bringing 'the 'design track' (largely principles and theory-based) and 'media track' (direct practice and craft-based) closer together' (Boling, 2016:89). Despite current challenges to provision and space, it is still possible for students within some higher education institutions to engage with established traditional practices of production, such as letterpress – offering ink and paint-based techniques – alongside faster digital processes, such as laser cutting (Alexenberg, 2009; Sassoon, 2009; Facer, 2011; Cooper et al., 2013; Turcotte, 2015). However, students' experiential learning of design (and its unique modes of learning) as a specialised discipline, and its range of production methods, would seem to be lessening as traditional resources and space become less common (Dugdale, 2009:52; Scott-Webber, 2012).

Furthermore, there has been an increasingly urgent need to defend the provision of open-ended time to create in design education (the meandering twists and turns of an imaginative journey), to access specialist practice-based resources and processes, to allocate individualised and personalised workspaces to reinforce the community of practice, and no time to nurture failure as learning via 'thinking and doing as learning', among others (Wenger, 2000). Financial pressure has forced change on creative education courses, resources, and educational environments, with the loss of critical art and design teaching staff as evidenced in recent literature and in the reporting of student and staff protests in the media (ArtsHub Australia, 2021; Bond, 2021; Stephen, 2021). The characteristic principles of conventional studio learning and design education are being subjugated in contemporary higher education.

In this digital age of education, the future of curriculum delivery and educational environments has been largely directed to mass, high-participation online platforms and less towards physical SBL spaces. Marginson's (2017) examination of Martin Trow's three phases of higher education – elite, mass, and high-participation – cites the 'shift from a privilege (elite) to a right (mass) and to an "obligation" (universal) for at least middle-class families and ultimately for everyone'. This 'massification has ambiguous implications for institutional diversity', and particularly the creative disciplines (Marginson, 2017:370). Similarly, Baines (2021) argues higher education must 'adapt to the new circumstances or face long-term extinction'. He continues, 'costly bricks-and-mortar estate should be rethought in terms of a digital infrastructure' (Baines, 2021). Indeed, 'rising costs, funding challenges, spiralling tuition fees, student debt and other factors' have also forced higher education institutions to rethink their long-term strategies (KPMG Global, 2021).

This book is, arguably, a call to action to keep SBL and design education at the forefront of higher education. Today, in this fast-paced digital and online world, there is a marked need to be aware of the day-to-day impact of learning spaces (on our bodies and minds). We must remind ourselves of what it is to be human and how to listen to the body for direction in design education. When we listen to the body via sensory affect, then we can adjust and empower reflective teaching and student engagement. This book suggests a series of methodologies, methods, and practical strategies to encourage design educators and researchers, educational designers, and planners to address and adapt to the issues evident in learning spaces, curriculum, and pedagogy today. In these challenging times, the suggested series of *all-surface use, empowerment*, and *flexibility* strategies will encourage design educators to (1) adapt learning spaces to embrace the values and properties of a studio-based design education, (2) to foster social engagement, collegiality, and the Community of [Design] Practice (Co[D]P), (3) to reinforce a distinct design curriculum and signature studio pedagogies (critical, informal, ambiguous, and feedback mechanisms such as the 'crit'), and (4) to foster experiential, material, practice-based, and hands-on learning-by-doing. Therefore, this book provides the tools and techniques to personalise and invest in teaching and learning experiences in design education through a bodily awareness in higher education today.

This book aims to guide the reader through a specific journey; from understanding the key aspects of sensory affect and its theories towards sensory affect in practice, and to revisit what is known about the senses in design and design education. The following chapters will provide the knowledge, understanding, and strategies for design educators to personalise and invest in teaching and learning experiences through a subjective bodily awareness. Then, sensory affect in design education is unpacked, mainly via learning spaces and experiential learning, through three distinct themes – *all-surface use, empowerment, and flexibility* (Figure 1.1). Three chapters survey these themes across Chapter 4: All-surface use in design-based learning spaces, Chapter 5: Environmental empowerment in design education, and Chapter 6: Flexibility and capacities to adjust experiential learning, learning spaces, and design education. It is my hope that educators and researchers may find the answers they need in this book and employ the suggested sensory-led strategies as a part-solution to the challenges pressing down on design education today – without forgetting what it is to be human.

References

Ackerman, D. (1992) *A Natural History of the Senses*. New York: Vintage Books.

Alexenberg, M. (2009) *Educating Artists for the Future: Learning at the Intersections of Art, Science, Technology and Culture*. Bristol: Intellect.

Amirsadeghi, H. and Eisler, M. (2012) *Sanctuary: Britain's Artists and Their Studios*. London: Thames and Hudson Ltd.

ArtsHub Australia (2021) *Art schools: Legacy in crisis, ArtsHub*. Available at: www.artshub.com.au/news/features/art-schools-legacy-in-crisis-261614-2369435/.

Baines, P. (2021) Universities must swap physical for digital estates – At warp speed, *Times Higher Education (THE)*. Available at: www.timeshighereducation.com/opinion/universities-must-swap-physical-digital-estates-warp-speed?fbclid=IwAR0JEh7DjdUs3VU-15r1d3pIlTEzvPOS-boTlRgmcEuSDY1K47I1sWSGIX0.

Bayne, S. (2015) 'What's the matter with "technology-enhanced learning"?', *Learning, Media and Technology*, 40(1), 5–20. doi: 10.1080/17439884.2014.915851.

Beetham, H. (2013) *Rethinking Pedagogy for a Digital Age: Designing for 21st Century Learning*. New York: Routledge. doi: 10.4324/9780203078952.

Bennett, D., Knight, E. and Rowley, J. (2020) 'The role of hybrid learning spaces in enhancing higher education students' employability', *British Journal of Educational Technology*, 51(4), 1188–1202. doi: 10.1111/bjet.12931.

Blazwick, I. (2012) 'The Studio – An A to Z', In *Sanctuary: Britain's Artists and Their Studios*. London: Thames & Hudson, pp. 19–25.

Boddington, A. and Boys, J. (2011) *Re-Shaping Learning: A Critical Reader – The Future of Learning Spaces in Post-Compulsory Education*. Rotterdam: Sense Publishers.

Boling, E. (2016) 'How I Learned, Unlearned, and Learned Studio Again', In Boling, E. et al (eds), *Studio Teaching in Higher Education*. New York: Routledge.

Boling, E., Schwier, R.A., Gray, C.A., Smith, K.M. and Campbell, K. (2016) *Studio Teaching in Higher Education*. New York: Routledge.

Bond, P. (2021) Anger mounts at UK government proposal to halve arts education subsidy, *World Socialist Web Site*. Available at: www.wsws.org/en/articles/2021/05/20/aruk-m20.html.

Bowen, W.G. and Guthrie, K.M. (2015) *Higher Education in the Digital Age*. Oxford: Princeton University Press.

Boys, J. (2008) Beyond the beanbag? Towards new ways of thinking about learning spaces, *Centre for Excellence in Teaching and Learning Through Design* (CETLD) (Brighton). Available at: http://arts.brighton.ac.uk/__data/assets/pdf_file/0019/64180/Jos-Boys-article-Networks08-pages-16–19.pdf.

Boys, J. (2015) *Building Better Universities. Strategies, Spaces, Technologies*. New York: Routledge.

Breen, M., Dundon, M. and McCaffrey, C. (2018) 'Making every seat count: Space management at peak times in a university library', *New Review of Academic Librarianship*, 24(1), 105–118. doi: 10.1080/13614533.2017.1414066.

Brown, J.B. (2016) 'Making the studio smaller', *Design and Technology Education: An International Journal*, 26(4), 256–268.

Carvalho, L., Goodyear, P. and Laat, M.de (2016) *Place-Based Spaces for Networked Learning*. New York: Routledge.

Carvalho, L. and Yeoman, P. (2019) 'Connecting the dots: Theorizing and mapping learning entanglement through archaeology and design', *British Journal of Educational Technology*, 50(3), 1104–1117. doi: 10.1111/bjet.12761.

Casselden, B. and Pears, R. (2020) 'Higher education student pathways to ebook usage and engagement, and understanding: Highways and cul de sacs', *Journal of Librarianship and Information Science*, 52(2), 601–619. doi: 10.1177/0961000619841429.

Cennamo, K., Brandt, C., Scott, B., Douglas, S., McGrath, M., Reimer, Y. and Vernon, M. (2011) 'Managing the complexity of design problems through studio-based learning', *Interdisciplinary Journal of Problem-Based Learning*, 5(2), 12–36. doi: 10.7771/1541-5015.1253.

Chaves, J. and Taylor, A. (2021) *Creating Sensory Smart Classrooms. A Practical Guide for Educators*. Abingdon: Routledge. doi: 10.4324/9781003050797.

Cohen, A., Nørgård, R.T. and Mor, Y. (2020) 'Hybrid learning spaces – Design, data, didactics', *British Journal of Educational Technology*, 51(4), 1039–1044. doi: 10.1111/bjet.12964.

Collini, S. (2012) *What are Universities for?* London: Penguin.

Cook, J., Mor, Y. and Santos, P. (2020) 'Three cases of hybridity in learning spaces: Towards a design for a zone of possibility', *British Journal of Educational Technology*, 51(4), 1155–1167. doi: 10.1111/bjet.12945.

Cooper, A., Gridneff, R., & Haslam, A. (2013) Letterpress: looking backward to look forward. In *AIGA Blunt: Explicit & Graphic Design Criticism Now*. Norfolk, VA, USA : AIGA Design Educator's Committee. pp. 1–11.

Corazzo, J. (2019) 'Materialising the Studio. A systematic review of the role of the material space of the studio in art, design and architecture education', *The Design Journal*, 22(1), 1249–1265. doi: 10.1080/14606925.2019.1594953.

Cross, N. (2011) *Design Thinking : Understanding How Designers Think and Work*. Oxford: Berg/Bloomsbury.

Crowther, P. (2013) 'Understanding the signature pedagogy of the design studio and the opportunities for its technological enhancement', *Journal of Learning Design*, 6, 18–28. doi: 10.5204/jld.v6i3.155.

Daniel, R. and Fleischmann, K. (2014) 'Designing a Learning Space for Creativity and Collaboration: From Studio to Computer Lab in Design Education', In Scott-Webber, L. et al (eds), *Learning Space Design in Higher Education*. Faringdon: Libri Publishing, pp. 191–208.

Dreamson, N. (2020) 'Online design education: Meta-connective pedagogy', *International Journal of Art & Design Education*, 39(3), 483–497. doi: 10.1111/jade.12314.

Dugdale, S. (2009) 'Space strategies for the new learning landscape', *Educause*, 50–63.

Edwards, M.R. and Clinton, M.E. (2019) 'A study exploring the impact of lecture capture availability and lecture capture usage on student attendance and attainment', *Higher Education*, 77(3), 403–421. doi: 10.1007/s10734-018-0275-9.

Elen, J. (2020) ' "Instructional disobedience": A largely neglected phenomenon deserving more systematic research attention', *Educational Technology Research and Development*, 68(5), 2021–2032. doi: 10.1007/s11423-020-09776-3.

Facer, K. (2011) *Learning Futures: Education, Technology and Social Change*. Abingdon: Routledge.

Farías, I. and Wilkie, A. (2016) *Studio Studies: Operations, Topologies & Displacements*, *Studio Studies: Operations, Topologies and Displacements*. London: Routledge. doi: 10.4324/9781315756523.

Filimowicz, M.A. and Tzankova, V.K. (2017) 'Creative making, large lectures, and social media: Breaking with tradition in art and design education', *Arts and Humanities in Higher Education*, 16(2), 156–172. doi: 10.1177/1474022214552197.

Finlayson, G. and Hayward, D. (2010) 'Education towards heteronomy: A critical analysis of the reform of UK universities since 1978', *Labour*, 1–25.

Fraser, K. and Achterberg, A. (2014) *Future of Learning and Teaching in Next Generation Learning Spaces*. Bingley: Emerald.

French, R. (2018) *Innovative Learning Environments and Our 'Heschong Mahone Moment, Building Design & Construction*. Arlington Heights: SGC Horizon Building & Construction Group.

Garrett, R. and MacGill, B. (2021) 'Fostering inclusion in school through creative and body-based learning', *International Journal of Inclusive Education*, 25(11), 1221–1235. doi: 10.1080/13603116.2019.1606349.

Gendlin, E.T. (2003) *Focusing*. London: Rider.

Giroux, H.A. and Aronowitz, S. (1986) *Education Under Siege: The Conservative, Liberal and Radical Debate over Schooling*. London: Routledge & Kegan Paul Ltd.

Goodyear, P. (2020) 'Design and co-configuration for hybrid learning: Theorising the practices of learning space design', *British Journal of Educational Technology*, 51(4), 1045–1060. doi: 10.1111/bjet.12925.

Goodyear, P. and Retalis, S. (2010) 'Learning, Technology and Design', In *Technology-Enhanced Learning: Design Patterns and Pattern Languages*. Rotterdam: Sense Publishers, pp. 1–27. doi: 10.1080/14759390802383827.

Gray, C.M., Parsons, P. and Toombs, A.L. (2020) 'Building a Holistic Design Identity Through Integrated Studio Education', In *Nature*. Cham: Springer, pp. 43–55. doi: 10.1007/978-3-030-37254-5_4.

Güler, K. (2015) 'Social media-based learning in the design studio: A comparative study', *Computers & Education*, 87, 192–203. doi: 10.1016/j.compedu.2015.06.004.

Harrison, A. and Hutton, L. (2014) *Design for the Changing Educational Landscape: Space, Place and the Future of Learning.* Abingdon: Routledge.

ILETC Innovative Learning Environments & Teacher Change (2017) *Type and Use of Innovative Learning Environments in Australasian Schools.* Melbourne: University of Melbourne.

İmamoğlu, Ç. and Gürel, M.Ö. (2016) ' "Good fences make good neighbors": Territorial dividers increase user satisfaction and efficiency in library study spaces', *The Journal of Academic Librarianship*, 42(1), 65–73. doi: 10.1016/j.acalib.2015.10.009.

Imms, W., Cleveland, B. and Fisher, K. (2016) *Evaluating Learning Environments. Snapshots of Emerging Issues, Methods and Knowledge.* Rotterdam: Sense Publishers.

Jacobson, M.J. and Reimann, P. (2010) *Designs for Learning Environments of the Future : International Perspectives From the Learning Sciences.* New York: Springer.

Jones, D., Lotz, N. and Holden, G. (2021) 'A longitudinal study of virtual design studio (VDS) use in STEM distance design education', *International Journal of Technology and Design Education*, 31(4), 839–865. doi: 10.1007/s10798-020-09576-z.

Kokotsaki, D., Menzies, V. and Wiggins, A. (2016) 'Project-based learning: A review of the literature', *Improving Schools*, 19(3), 267–277. doi: 10.1177/1365480216659733.

Kolb, A.Y. and Kolb, D.A. (2005) 'Learning styles and learning spaces: Enhancing Experiential learning in higher education', *Academy of Management Learning & Education*, 4, 193–212. doi: 10.5465/AMLE.2005.17268566.

Kolb, D.A. (1983) *Experiential Learning: Experience as the Source of Learning and Development.* Upper Saddle River: Financial Times/Prentice Hall.

Komarzynska-Swiesciak, E., Adams, B. and Thomas, L. (2021) 'Transition from physical design studio to emergency virtual design studio. Available teaching and learning methods and tools – A case study', *Buildings*, 11(312), 1–20.

KPMG Global (2021) *End of a golden age for universities*, KPMG. Available at: https://home.kpmg/xx/en/home/industries/government-public-sector/education/the-future-of-higher-education-in-a-disruptive-world/end-of-a-golden-age-for-universities.html.

Leigh, J. and Brown, N. (2021) 'Embodied Inquiry', In *Embodied Inquiry*. London: Bloomsbury Academic. doi: 10.5040/9781350118805.

Locke, M. (2007) *Six spaces of social media*. Available at: https://test.org.uk/2007/08/10/six-spaces-of-social-media/.

Lyon, C. (2018) Getting sticky with it: Digital revolution driving new-look campuses, *Campus Review*. Available at: www.campusreview.com.au/2018/12/getting-sticky-with-it-digital-revolution-driving-new-look-campuses/.

Lyon, P. (2011) *Design Education: Learning, Teaching and Researching Through Design.* Farnham: Taylor & Francis Group.

Ma, W.W.K. (2021) 'Effective Learning Through Deep Learning, What Matters: Self, Others, Way of Thinking, and/or Design of Learning Environment?', In Ma, W.W.K., Tong, K., and Tso, W.B.A. (eds), *Learning Environment and Design: Current and Future Impacts.* Singapore: Springer, pp. 3–17.

Maeda, J. (2020) 'Design education in the post-digital age', *Design Management Review*, 31(1), 41–48. doi: 10.1111/drev.12201.

Marginson, S. (2017) 'Elite, Mass, and High-Participation Higher Education', In *Encyclopedia of International Higher Education Systems and Institutions.* Dordrecht: Springer Netherlands, pp. 1–9. doi: 10.1007/978-94-017-9553-1_50-1.

Marshalsey, L. (2017) *An investigation into the experiential impact of sensory affect in contemporary communication design studio education* (Thesis). The Glasgow School of Art. Available at: http://radar.gsa.ac.uk/5894/.

Marshalsey, L. and Sclater, M. (2020) 'Together but apart: Creating and supporting online learning communities in an era of distributed studio education', *International Journal of Art & Design Education*, 39(4), 826–840. doi: 10.1111/jade.12331.

McIntosh, E. (2010) *The seven spaces of technology in school environments*. Available at: https://vimeo.com/15945912.

Mewburn, I. (2012) 'Lost in translation: Reconsidering reflective practice and design studio pedagogy', *Arts and Humanities in Higher Education*, 11(4), 363–379. doi: 10.1177/1474022210393912.

Mitchell, P. (2017) 'A Case Study of the Application of Studio-Based Learning Pedagogy in Ngee Ann Polytechnic's Animation and 3D Arts (A3DA) Diploma', In *Redesigning Pedagogy International Conference*. Singapore: National Institute of Education.

Molloy, C.B. (2020) 'O'Donnell and Tuomey's university architecture: Informal learning spaces that enhance user engagement', *Architecture and Culture*, 9(1), 98–120. doi: 10.1080/20507828.2020.1794711.

Motley, P. (2017) 'Critique and process: Signature pedagogies in the graphic design classroom', *Arts and Humanities in Higher Education*, 16(3), 229–240. doi: 10.1177/1474022216652765.

Nair, P. and Doctori, R.Z. (2019) *Learning by Design : Live Play Engage Create*. Bangalore: Education Design Architects.

Nguyen, D.J. and Larson, J.B. (2015) 'Don't forget about the body: Exploring the curricular possibilities of embodied pedagogy', *Innovative Higher Education*, 40(4), 331–344. doi: 10.1007/s10755-015-9319-6.

Oblinger, D.G. (2006) 'Learning spaces', *British Journal of Educational Technology*. doi: 10.1111/j.1467-8535.2009.00974.x.

Orr, S. and Shreeve, A. (2018) 'The Sticky Curriculum in Art and Design', In Orr, S. and Shreeve, A. (eds), *Art and Design Pedagogy in Higher Education*. Abingdon: Routledge, pp. 71–87. doi: 10.4324/9781315415130-5.

Pallasmaa, J. (2012) *The Eyes of the Skin: Architecture and the Senses*. Chichester: John Wiley & Sons.

Pates, D. and Sumner, N. (2016) 'E-learning spaces and the digital university', *The International Journal of Information and Learning Technology*, 33(3), 159–171. doi: 10.1108/IJILT-10-2015-0028.

Probyn, E. (2004) 'Teaching bodies: Affects in the classroom', *Body & Society*, 10(4), 21–43. doi: 10.1177/1357034X04047854.

Readman, K., Maker, G. and Davine, A. (2021) The lecture is dead, long live the lecture: Redefining higher education in a digital age, *Times Higher Education (THE)*. Available at: www.timeshighereducation.com/campus/lecture-dead-long-live-lecture-redefining-higher-education-digital-age.

Rhodes, C.M. and Schmidt, S.W. (2021) 'Being "present" in the online learning space', *New Directions for Adult and Continuing Education*, 2021(169), 81–88. doi: 10.1002/ACE.20416.

Rosan Bosch Studio (2019) *Learning spaces need to enable and motivate every learner*. Available at: https://rosanbosch.com/en/approach/learning-spaces-need-enable-and-motivate-every-learner.

Ross, J. (2021) Lectures on the way out in Australia and New Zealand, says survey, *Times Higher Education (THE)*. Available at: www.timeshighereducation.com/news/lectures-way-out-australia-and-new-zealand-says-survey.

Roy, R. and Uekusa, S. (2020) 'Collaborative autoethnography: "Self-reflection" as a timely alternative research approach during the global pandemic', *Qualitative Research Journal*, 20(4), 383–392. doi: 10.1108/QRJ-06-2020-0054.

Salama, A.M. (2015) *Spatial Design Education: New Directions for Pedagogy in Architecture and Beyond*. Farnham: Ashgate Publishing Limited.

Salama, A.M. and Wilkinson, N. (2007) *Design Studio Pedagogy: Horizons for the Future*. Gateshead: The Urban International Press.

Sassoon, R. (2009) *The Designer: Half a Century of Change in Image, Training, and Techniques*. Bristol: Intellect.

Sclater, M. (2007) *Freedom to create? Computer supported co-operative and collaborative learning in art and design education, art therapy* (Thesis). Glasgow School Of Art. Available at: http://ethos.bl.uk/OrderDetails.do?uin=uk.bl.ethos.484877.

Sclater, M. (2016) 'Beneath our eyes: An exploration of the relationship between technology enhanced learning and socio-ecological sustainability in art and design higher education', *International Journal of Art & Design Education*, 35(3), 296–306. doi: 10.1111/jade.12125.

Sclater, M. and Lally, V. (2013) 'Virtual voices: Exploring creative practices to support life skills development among young people working in a virtual world community', *International Journal of Art & Design Education*, 32(3), 331–344. doi: 10.1111/j.1476-8070.2013.12024.x.

Sclater, M. and Lally, V. (2016) 'Critical perspectives on TEL: Art and design education, theory, communities and space', *Interactive Learning Environments*, 24(5), 968–978. doi: 10.1080/10494820.2015.1128210.

Scott-Webber, L. (2012) 'Institutions, educators, and designers: Wake up!: Current teaching and learning places along with teaching strategies are obsolete-teaching styles and learning spaces must change for 21st-century needs – ProQuest', *Planning for Higher Education*, 41(1).

Scott-Webber, L. (2014) 'The Perfect Storm: Educations Immediate Challenges', In Scott-Webber, L. et al. (eds), *Learning Space Design in Higher Education*. Faringdon: Libri Publishing, pp. 151–167.

Scott-Webber, L., Abraham, J. and Marini, M. (2000) 'Higher education classrooms fail to meet needs of faculty and students', *Journal of Interior Design*, 26(2), 16–34.

Scott-Webber, L., Branch, J., Bartholomew, P. and Nygaard, C. (2014) *Learning Space Design in Higher Education*. Faringdon: Libri Publishing.

Selwyn, N. (2011) *Education and Technology: Key Issues and Debates*. New York: Continuum International Pub. Group.

Sims, E. and Shreeve, A. (2012) 'Signature Pedagogies in Art and Design', In Chick, N.L. et al. (eds), *Exploring More Signature Pedagogies*. Sterling, VA: Stylus Publishing, pp. 55–67.

Slavid, R. (2020) *New Work New WorkSpace : Innovative design in a Connected World*, New Work New WorkSpace. London: RIBA Publishing. doi: 10.4324/9781003106432.

Stephen, A. (2021) 'Art education in crisis under COVID', *Art Monthly Australasia*, 37, 100–105.

Temple, P. (2014) *The Physical University: Contours of Space and Place in Higher Education*. Abingdon: Routledge.

The University of Melbourne (2016) *ILETC innovative learning environments & teacher change*. Available at: www.iletc.com.au/.

Thoring, K., Desmet, P. and Badke-Schaub, P. (2018) 'Creative environments for design education and practice: A typology of creative spaces', *Design Studies*, 56, 54–83. doi: 10.1016/j.destud.2018.02.001.

Thornburg, D. (2013) *From the Campfire to the Holodeck: Creating Engaging and Powerful 21st Century Learning Environments*. San Francisco: Jossey-Bass.

Todd, S., Hoveid, M.H. and Langmann, E. (2021) 'Educating the senses: Explorations', *Aesthetics, Embodiment and Sensory Pedagogy*, 40, 243–248. doi: 10.1007/s11217-021-09776-7.

Trede, F., Braun, R. and Brookes, W. (2020) 'Engineering students' expectations and perceptions of studio-based learning', *European Journal of Engineering Education*, 46(3), 402–415. doi: 10.1080/03043797.2020.1758630.

Turcotte, C.L. (2015) 'University trends: Contemporary campus design', *Planning for Higher Education*, 43(3), 80–84.

University of the Arts London (2018) The sticky curriculum in the art school, *UAL Teaching and Learning Exchange*. Available at: https://vimeo.com/287081420?fbclid=IwAR0Qr0wzMPIYWUwS7MZUdGioqOwq79W-XOwcsiA7z_cH39OVmqbA8jsiZlg.

Vignoles, A. and Murray, N. (2016) 'Widening participation in higher education', *Education Sciences*, 6(13), 1–4.

Wallis, L., Williams, A. and Ostwald, M.J. (2017) 'Studio models in a changing higher education landscape', *Australian Art Education*, 38(1), 122–140.

Warren and Mahony Architects (2017) *Sticky campus, Warren and Mahony*. Available at: https://warrenandmahoney.com/articles/sticky-campus.

Wenger, E. (2000) *Communities of Practice: Learning, Meaning, and Identity*. New York: Cambridge University Press.

Wild, C. (2013) 'Who owns the classroom? Profit, pedagogy, belonging, power', *International Journal of Art & Design Education*, 3(32), 288–299.

Williams, S. (2021) Don't lecture me about the future of the lecture, *Times Higher Education (THE)*. Available at: www.timeshighereducation.com/opinion/dont-lecture-me-about-future-lecture.

Woolner, P. (2010) *The Design of Learning Spaces*. London: Continuum.

Zembylas, M. (2007) 'The specters of bodies and affects in the classroom: A rhizo-ethological approach', *Pedagogy, Culture and Society*, 15(1), 19–35. doi: 10.1080/14681360601162030.

2
WHAT IS SENSORY AFFECT?

Introduction

Chapter 2 presents this book's critical questions: What is sensory affect? And why is sensory affect relevant to teaching and student engagement within experiential learning and learning spaces in design education? It is critical to bring together and to understand our multiple perspectives of sensory experience through the lens of existing theories, theorists, scientists, educators, artists, and designers. Sensory affect can be considered as a contemporary term for the connective 'melting pot' of theories and influences which refer to the senses; a place where we can gather and assimilate much of what has been published and explored in the realm of human experience from those who have gone before this text. It should be noted that this network of influences forming the narrative of sensory affect in this book is assembled from the authors' subjective ideology. The author does intentionally overlook additional key contributors and figures in favour of others in this book's subjective narrative.

Although this chapter explains in depth how the senses are tools to receive affective bodily experience, it does not seek to illuminate or discuss the vast history of physiological, psychological, and scientific research evident in this field. Instead, the ideas underpinning sensory affect are explored to connect the notion of bodily experience (and not the linguistical forces of experience) with the context of practice-based design education. Separate from cognition (the mental processing of thought, reasoning, and understanding), sensory affective experience can influence behaviours, such as direction, intensity, and persistence, affecting individual, relational and collective goals, and an individual's commitment to teaching and learning (Russ, 1998; Seo et al., 2004; Marshalsey, 2017). Therefore, design educators and students' motivation to participate, engagement and creativity, can be affected by the sensory conditions present in their learning spaces.

DOI: 10.4324/9781003175988-2

Consequently, to unpack sensory affect for the reader, this chapter begins by offering interpretations of the senses and sensory affect. Briefly, the scientific character and structure of the senses, sensation, and perception are explored to shape the broader meaning of sensory affect. Then, the critical intricacies of Eugene Gendlins' *Felt Sense* and embodied knowing reinforce the contribution sensory affect can make when engaging with experiential learning and learning spaces in design education. Furthermore, a consideration of theoretical, educational, and creative perspectives aligning with sensory experience is unpacked to provide a diverse framework of bodily experience.

What is sensory affect?

> *Depravation . . . could jeopardise a person's ability to learn. That deficit impacts those in higher education. Brain science also tells us that all of our information comes to use through sensory input* (Erlauer, 2003; Lengel and Kuczala, 2010; Wolfe, 2010); *meaning all of our senses are engaged. Stimulus comes from our immediate environment. However, all sensory input is just noise until the brain figures out how to make sense of all of the stimuli it receives* (Wolfe, 2010).
>
> —(cited in Scott-Webber, 2014:159)

Affect broadly measures and influences feelings, emotions, moods, creativity, well-being, and engagement. Affect can also yield multiple interpreted meanings, as evidenced by the work of many prominent philosophers. In the context of education, affect is an understanding of perceptive and conscious sensations within contemporary learning spaces (Marshalsey, 2017:24). Sensory evaluation is often used to evoke, measure, analyse, and interpret experience. Together, sensory affect is the influence of experience detected through the body. It is perception through the senses, as a means for educators and students to analyse and interpret the impact of teaching, learning and the environment around them. To make sense of sensory affect and its complexities the term should, at this point, be clarified to consolidate the multifaceted and broad connotations of sensory affect as a branch of knowledge. The table below attempts to encapsulate the intricacies of sensory affect using a complete set of appropriate vocabulary (Table 2.1). Sensory effect, and its navigational lexicon, can be used to illuminate a range of physical and internal issues, and can be used to identify and describe body shifts in the process of foregrounding an experiential awareness of the conditions affecting teaching, learning, and learning spaces today.

The characteristics of the five senses

> *The very essence of the lived experience is moulded by hapticity and peripheral unfocused vision. Focused vision confronts us with the world whereas peripheral vision envelops us in the flesh of the world.*
>
> (Pallasmaa, 2012:14)

TABLE 2.1 The appropriate vocabulary of sensory affect.

Sensory Affect

Receptivity	Tangible	Feelings
Empathic	Affective	Bodily
Reflective	Instinctive	Felt
Consciousness	Knowing	Reactions
Embodied	Awareness	Experiential
Sensing	Understanding	Sensation
Realisation	Opinions	Influences
Intuitive	Sensitivity	Perception
Stimulation	Subjective	Emotions

Source: © L Marshalsey.

To begin, the organs responsible for the five senses are the conduit tools to absorb the impact of sensory affect through the body. The eyes, skin, ears, tongue, and nose are the critical points of reception for our bodies to register a new detection or change of sensation stimulus. The identification of five senses can be traced back to the time of the Greek philosopher Aristotle (384–322 BC), who sought to observe and conceptualise this field of study. In the 19th century, tangible efforts to measure and enumerate the sensations of the mind led to the emergence of psychophysics – a quantitative examination of the relationship between physical stimuli and the sensations and perceptions they create – led by the German psychologist Gustav Fechner (1801–1887). In the past 20 years, there has been a veritable explosion in the multidisciplinary study of sensory experiences, artwork and interfaces by psychologists, engineers, designers, artists, and computer scientists. To add to this momentum, understanding the role of the five senses and how they can be used to engage with experiential learning and learning spaces is important to comprehend why design educators and students need to be empowered to foreground their day-to-day experiences.

Touch

Skin is the largest sensory system of the human body and has a long history of being the most responsive sense. Skin can detect pain signals, changes in temperature and drafts, active deliberate and passive unintentional touch through a wide range of receptors sending this information to the brain. The systematic scrutiny of the human sense of touch began with Ernst Heinrich Weber (1795–1878), an anatomist and physiologist from Leipzig, Germany. Weber conducted early experimental testing of the sensory thresholds of touch and is regarded as a leading influence in our development of understanding haptic capabilities (Grunwald, 2008). Austrian-German physiologist Maximilian von Frey (1852–1932) also proposed a variety of receptors are essential for touch (through the deformation of the skin), and feeling warmth, cold, and pain. Temperature is sensed as the body perceives stimuli that is warmer or colder than its surface (Levine, 2000). Then, Max Dessoir (1867–1947) presented numerous experimental and phenomenological studies about the psychology of the sense of touch. Dessoir also termed the notion of the 'Skin Sense' and defined the designation of haptic as relating to touch and skin (Grunwald, 2008:21–22). The Scot, Sir Charles Bell (1774–1842) also contributed a rigorous understanding of haptic engagement with his book *The Hand; Its Mechanism and Vital Endowments as Evincing Design* (Bell, 1833).

Furthermore, the somatosensory system entrenched within our bodies (a whole-body physical map of touch-related sensory receptors) has three perceptive states: an internal state, an interpretation state, and an informative state. These perceptive states locate and know where all our body parts are at any one time. The somatosensory system has four distinct qualities: proprioception, tactile sensation, nociception, and temperature. Proprioception is the sense of always knowing where the body and its limbs are. Tactile sensation relates to sensing touch when stimuli are placed or brush against your body's surface. Nociception senses painful and unpleasant stimuli affecting the body and temperature senses degrees of heat and cold (Foley and Matlin, 2010). A two-point discrimination threshold also dictates the ability to detect two or more stimuli touching the body and any adaptation of contact on the skin (Foley and Matlin, 2010). Scientific, designer and artist explorations of touch can focus on understanding the affective aspects of these sensory modalities, such as enjoyment, physical and mental engagement, and emotional expression (Lederman and Klatzky, 2009). Additionally, kinaesthesia is the perception of active and passive movement and the placement of the body and its parts, as components of the somatosensory system. Kinaesthesia is the ability to perceive the dimensions of architecture via muscles that cannot be instantly linked to one of the five sense organs (Otero-Pailos, 2010). The acute awareness of kinaesthetic perception can deteriorate with ageing or disability (Foley and Matlin, 2010).

The sensory modality of touch affects the whole body. Architect Juhani Pallasmaa (1936–2012) signalled all our senses originate from touch. Touch as degrees of roughness can reflect the properties of the surface, object, material, and environment each educator or student meets, in a learning space, often by the hands. The compliance of a touched object provides an account of its deformability under manual static contact, unsupported holding, lateral movement, contours, pressure or weight, and based on the touched objects' density and structure (Lederman and Klatzky, 2009). The German philosopher Edmund Husserl (1859–1938) stressed the importance of *double-touch* and how the body both touches things and is touched in return. For example, *double-touch* is when a hand might push a door open, and the door synchronously pushes back on the hand in return, or when clay is manipulated by the fingers, the clay traces the fingers simultaneously (Cerbone, 2006). The French phenomenological philosopher Maurice Merleau-Ponty (1908–1961) placed significance on the ability to 'touch ourselves, to touch and to be touched' (Merleau-Ponty cited in Moran, 1999:423). He argued touch and being touched cannot happen concurrently as they are exclusive to each other (Gumtau, 2011).

If hands are perceived as our direct tools of practical engagement and the conduits by which knowledge enters the body, then how does the sensory engagement of touching a flat, digital screen affect the transfer of knowledge through the skin (Kensinger, 1991:40)? In the past 20 years, the boom in digital practice within society and its influence on higher education has meant information about the world is mainly relayed through touching screens, smartphones, and computers on a daily basis (Howes, 2005:30; Facer, 2011; Marshalsey, 2017). Although Holl et al. (2006:29) argued the senses form a hierarchical system from the highest sense of vision down to the lowest sense, touch, Marinetti (2005:331) stated a visual sense is born in the fingertips. Marinetti (2005) specified sight, smell, hearing, touch, and taste are modifications of touch, divided in different ways and localised at different points. Similarly, Massumi (2002:158) insisted the senses co-function, for example, vision anticipates texture and touch. Using vision alone without touch fosters assumptions of a new texture rather than to truly experience it. Touch sensors can also be activated by stimulation or tedium, in line with constant or irregular pressure over time – short and sharp or steady and consistent. Touch also stops responding to regular stimuli over time as it adapts to and recognises familiar, repetitive everyday sensations (Gumtau, 2011; Marshalsey, 2017:90). Pallasmaa describes his observation of this experience:

> Computer imaging tends to flatten our magnificent, multi-sensory, simultaneous, and synchronic capacities of imagination by turning the design process into a passive visual manipulation, a retinal journey. The computer creates a distance between the maker and the object, whereas drawing by hand as well as working with models put the designer in a haptic contact with the object, or space.
>
> *(Pallasmaa, 2012:14)*

Touch signalling and its sensory responses, haptic perception (a form of tactile awareness) is not only the consciousness of nearby objects, surfaces, materials, and environments, but also a mindfulness of the social interactions we have with other people. The most sensitive area of the body is the human face, and this is a significant stimulus; the feet are the least responsive. Interestingly, females are more sensitive to touch than males as their specific patterns of sensitivity vary with gender biology. Haptic engagement transcends sensation or perception as touch is a vital component of our human-to-human relationships and in the lifeworld of the design studio (Andersen and Guerrero, 2008).

> Human haptic behaviour extends far beyond the sensory world to every aspect of the social world. Interpersonal touch expresses warmth, affection, intimacy, immediacy, and love but can also threaten and even injure. Haptic behaviour also plays a central role in promoting health and happiness throughout the lifespan. Within social relationships, touch differs based on sex differences and relational stage. Cultural differences in touch also exist. Finally, sometimes touch is avoided, either because people

have a predisposition that causes them to be touch avoidant, or because there is a taboo against touch.

(Andersen and Guerrero, 2008:155)

This haptic social nearness of, and engagement with, others (giving and receiving touch) is relevant to design education in terms of the relational exchanges, collaborations, and co-designing activities occurring within the teaching and learning population.

Vision

Vision allows the body to know if an object or a person is near or beyond reach as visual sensing helps us to create a perceived lifeworld. Our visual sensing system relies on the image-retina and eye-head movement systems to feed this information to the body (Levine, 2000). Vision perceives the structural features of stimuli such as spatial location, shape, colour, texture, and size (Foley and Matlin, 2010). Colour perception is encoded at the retina level and people can experience diverse experiences of colour, as colour vision is linked to genetic factors and, of course, colour vision deficiencies (Foley and Matlin, 2010). Peripheral vision is particularly adept at capturing motion and allows you to classify the objects and images you see. People are highly perceptive to motion and movement produced by objects, people, and animals (Hiris, 2007). However, several factors can influence our visual perception of real movement including 'the luminance of the stimuli, the presence of a stationary background, and the region of the retina on which the movement occurs' (Foley and Matlin, 2010:225). We view the world as mostly stable, except when distracted by changes in movement around us, and this occurs in learning spaces – distraction and interruption caused by others. We perceive socially important information when detecting movement such as an unfamiliar visitors' gender and the presence of familiar people known to us (Foley and Matlin, 2010).

Vision can be inseparable from the other senses when we experience our lifeworld. For example, Lauwrens (2019:307) argues for the activation of sensory modalities beyond vision to embody the traditionally visual experience of artwork, and as 'vision opens onto and opens up the tactile world'. However, Pallasmaa (2012) became increasingly concerned of the dominance of vision and the suppression of the other senses in architecture. He argued although vision is the overriding sense among all the senses, our lifeworld must include a blend of our five senses to fully understand it. It may be argued our vital sensory needs and qualities are being discounted as ocular-centrism and the hegemony of vision dominate today, especially in this technologically driven age (Levin, 1993).

Sound

We hear sounds before we see them, and therefore, hearing is principal to vision in our senses when providing us information related to our immediate environment

(Foley and Matlin, 2010). Hearing can also be social as social knowledge is gained through and resides in the ears; this is audio-social (Kensinger, 1991:42; Ingold, 2002:252). Detecting the presence of people and movement through sound, auditory stimuli can provide many indications to the location of others and ourselves, and the spaces around the body, within an array of acoustic experiences (Levine, 2000). German philosopher Martin Heidegger (1889–1976) positioned the notion that we do not hear bare sound. Instead, we hear everyday things and activities as the ear favours sound from any direction (Ingold, 2002:244). Sound created by people, animals, objects, and their vibrations can rebound against other objects in the environment and can be distorted by the location itself. We experience audio sensitivity in our immediate environment, which can be affected by tinnitus, hearing loss, pitch, intensity, frequency, amplified noise, pressure changes and exposure to loud surroundings. Sensory fatigue may also be present when disruptive sound is endured over periods of time, and this is true of heavily populated educational environments and learning spaces (Foley and Matlin, 2010). Noise pollution may vary across formal and informal, communal, and physical learning spaces, both off and on campus (particularly in an era of greater student numbers in education). Even in designated quiet or silent spaces (e.g. at home or online), unwelcome sound originating from people demands unintentional participation. We cannot exclude unwanted sound without action on our part (Seamon and Mugerauer, 2000:87).

Desired sound, such as background music, participating in conversation or hearing low-level ambience in learning spaces can originate from many sources. Welcome sound originating from music, people, white noise or silence may influence our processing of visual information, enhancing our cognitive abilities and stabilising engagement in personalised learning spaces (Carvalho et al., 2016:97). Music rhythmically impresses on the senses; the beauty of its sound is of greater value than the meaning and the more alive the impression on the ear becomes (Steiner, 1996:23). Only when the eyes are closed and vision excluded can unadorned sounds, such as music or silence be heard, as the auditory world is vibrant and the visual world still (Ingold, 2002:244, 251). External noise tends to recede and lessen within home study and private learning environments, and when learning via online platforms sound often emerges as interruptions – interruptions from house mates, dogs barking, doorbells ringing, and unexpected phone calls. Generally, people deviate to the sensory system that provides the most direct information to them at that moment in time (Foley and Matlin, 2010).

Smell and taste

It may be argued smell and taste might not prevail as often as touch, sound, and vision in the creative and learning processes that take place in learning spaces today. Smell and taste are passive senses and often inseparable (Tuan, 1978). Olfaction; recognising, identifying, and considering odours is considered a chemical sense (Foley and Matlin, 2010). Every environment has its own olfactory presence, which is unique and embedded (Bachelard, 1994). Smell is a lingering sense provoking short- and long-term memories more than any other sense. Visual memories erode with time, yet scent memories have a long recall (Malnar and Vodvarka, 2004). In the traditional physical design studio, the smell of wet-based production processes (such as the odours emanating from letterpress inks, paints, and solvents) might linger for years and evoke memories of previous eras of creative learning to students (Jury, 2011).

Taste is referred to as a social sense, as students may congregate together on campus over communal and shared food and drink, and to informally discuss projects and assignments in their social structures at sustenance breaks. However, visual impact in the environment can influence taste and when used for eating, spaces should be clean and comfortable (Foley and Matlin, 2010).

Sensation and perception

Today, and in the realm of psychology, the study of sensation and perception relates to how the nervous system is connected to human behaviour (Levine, 2000; Schwartz and Krantz, 2016). The mind circumnavigates the entire body as it makes sense of touch, taste, smell, sound, and vision information to know bodily sensation, perception, and experience (Ackerman, 1992). The properties and meanings associated with sensory affect can refer to intuition, wellbeing, sensing, feelings, embodiment: conscious and unconscious sensation and subjective perception. Sensation and perception can be linked to active processes such as when fingers touch an object, eyes view a scene or an object, or when the nose picks up pleasant or noxious odours, ears detect the vibration of sounds, and as tongue tastes (Levine, 2000).

Perception follows sensation detection and translates sensory input into sensory affect as a form of meaning making – understanding and making sense of conscious bodily experiences. Sensation is the process of detecting a stimulus in the immediate or broader environment. Perception is the known physiological response of the bodies' sensory systems to the sensations produced by these stimuli. Sensory affect refers to those experiences detected by the body, which may influence a change on an individual's behaviour, concentration, motivation, or engagement. Sensory affect is the guide emerging from the process of sensation detection and subjective perception. Sensory affect senses and externalises our internal sensory reactions to our immediate environments. Physical stimuli can influence perception – a type of 'bottom-up' processing – whereas 'top-down' processing involves elements of pre-existing knowledge and the assumptions of objects, people, and environments (Schwartz and Krantz, 2016).

Our bodies gather, interpret, and process sensory information in a continual cycle of individualised sense and perceive, and our perception is only as accurate as the information our senses detect. For example, sound and light information emitted by objects and events can travel substantial distances before they are sensed by the human body in different ways. Personal and subjective biases can impact perception. Sensing sound and light is subject to the way an individual might sense them. Light and sound can also be shaped, changed, and formed by objects encountered on the journey towards the physical body, such as reflecting light from other sources and the bouncing of sound waves off obstacles in the path to the body. This is also dependent on the body's physical position, the intensity of the light or sound source, and how much you're paying attention to these stimuli. In addition, masking can interfere with the experience of the stimuli when one stimulus conceals another (Levine, 2000; Schwartz and Krantz, 2016). In a world abundant with rich stimuli, our physiological senses have naturally adapted, developed similarities, and interacted with each other over time to assist us in appropriately perceiving and responding to the information contained in our environments. Perception, cognitive processes, and memory are inextricably linked processes enabling us, as humans, to sense and construct our own subjective perceptions (derived from our prior experiences and expectations) and as we interpret meaning, identify, organise, and navigate our lifeworld effectively. Often the theoretical boundaries between perception and cognition are blurred as both involve 'the acquisition, storage, transformation and use of information' (Foley and Matlin, 2010:2).

There are several theoretical approaches to sensation and perception. These include the Empiricist method, formed by George Berkley (1685–1753), who reasoned sensory information alone was unable to recognise awareness. Instead, Berkley argued sensory information combined with pre-loaded kinaesthetic information in the brain constructs perception and as visual stimulus alone is insufficient to define what we perceive. The Constructivist approach to learning (when we actively use our previous personal, social, and shared knowledge as a foundation to build on), sought to establish that perception is constructed using information from the senses in relation to the mental action of cognitive processes. This notion permits us to acquire intellectual knowledge and understanding through bodily experience and the senses. However, German researcher Hermann von Helmholtz (1821–1894) proposed unconscious inference theory, when perception involves an 'educated guess' as part of a non-conscious cognition process (Schwartz and Krantz, 2016). American psychologist James J. Gibson (1904–1979), known for the direct Gibsonian approach, argued for the opposite to be true. Gibson claimed sensory information alone was sufficient to form awareness and reasoning processes were not crucial to forming perception. Gibson reasoned real world direct perception, and the information needed to perceive, is provided entirely by complex and abundant stimulus. Gibson also distinguished the variance between passive and active feelings, and noted visual stimulus, texture gradients, and motion perspective are especially significant to sensation and perception: an experiential understanding of our immediate environment is critical (Levine, 2000; Foley and Matlin, 2010; Schwartz and Krantz, 2016). The sphere of activity that is human experience is complex and vast. Becoming aware of sensation and perception – as the 'signposting' of embodied knowing and enactive cognition – is fundamental to understanding how sensory affect might impact educators and students in design education today.

Existing studies on sensory and affective experience

> *The messiness of the experiential, the unfolding of bodies into worlds, and the drama of contingency, how we are touched by what we are near.*
>
> (Ahmed, 2020:30)

Sensory and affective experiences are inseparable, yet complex, difficult to establish and are studied from a range of philosophical, psychological, historical, and biological viewpoints. Existing studies on sensory and affective experience are comprehensive and no single author can claim to identify all the necessary components in any one field of study (Highmore, 2020:119–120). In essence, sensory affect acts as an umbrella term from which sensation, perception, awareness, emotions, experiential, and all body-focused research in learning spaces can emerge. In the mid-2010s, the majority of studies researching sensory and affective experiences are based on interdisciplinary, perceptual, and learning experiences as seen in the research studies of Fors et al. (2013), Stein (2013), Simm and Marvell (2015), Bolkan (2015), and Satpute et al. (2015). In addition, the *Senses and Society Journal* (first published in 2006) publishes current sensory research trends, themes, and experiences in wide-ranging variable contexts, including sensory museology (the history of sense-related display in contemporary curatorial practice). Articles in this journal also explore heightened sensory experiences in design exhibitions, galleries (Classen, 2020; Deal, 2020), museums (Howes, 2014), the anthropology of sound, touch, olfactory and gustatory experiences, and creativity (Braithwaite, 2017; Harris et al., 2019).

In practical approaches to published sensory research in education, Harris et al. (2019) designed an instructional sensory tool, the *Puzzling Pieces* card activity, for design education. This learning tool mapped sensory qualities (in unlimited combinations) that may be employed by students when designing products, environments, and services. Then, Harris (2020) collated instructions, techniques, and materials to impart sensory awareness in real-life learning using guided lessons, media, and equipment. The lessons include experimenting with food to demonstrate aspects of illness and hosting a sensory dinner party. Harris (2020:119) argued 'despite theoretically attending to the body through theories of embodiment and enskillment, there is little explicit attention given to sensory ways of learning'. It is true that students are often not provided enough space within a restrictive timetable to engage with playful, hands-on, practical workshops, and sensory forms of learning beyond the parameters of their tight curriculum. Furthermore, sensory play is regularly published within texts aimed at researching early years and primary school years rather than secondary or higher education (Gascoyne, 2011; Patch, 2020). Of the few studies that do publish sensory affective experience, Park and Alderman (2018:preface) produced *Designing Across Senses*. This text aimed to provide teams of product design students with new approaches to designing multimodal interactions, as they consider new modalities across the growing number of technological devices in daily existence today. In relation to learning spaces, Chaves and Taylor

(2021) published *Creating Sensory Smart Classrooms*, which suggests how educators can assimilate diverse sensory inputs into the school environment to address and influence student engagement.

However, there is a wealth of research exploring TEL Smart Schools in educational institutions, often revelled as state-of-the-art teaching and learning presentation spaces. Bull (2019) provided an interesting chronological account of the development of sensory environments through media, from engaging the senses of sight and hearing in radio, film, and television to current forms of virtual reality and integration of the body and technology in virtual communities. The adoption of iPads and digital tablets in these 'smart' learning spaces is common in educational research studies (Reychav et al., 2016). However, De Freitas et al. (2020:abstract) describe these learning spaces as incessantly sensing, regulating, and controlling through complex sensory ecosystems and data infrastructures.

> *Growing up in this altered "mixed reality" makes for new challenges in developing sensibilities about place, environment, and belonging. Although sensing technologies are increasingly embedded in UK schools and worn by students and teachers, the social and political implications of these technologies for school communities have yet to be substantively explored.*
>
> *(de Freitas et al., 2020:11)*

In many of these existing studies of sensory and affective experience in education, there are two distinct themes: (1) the support of the latest static and mobile digital platforms, tools, and systems in education via 2D, 3D, and 4D (in the use of augmented, mixed, and virtual reality as a training mechanism), mainly using touch and vision, and (2) examining sensory pedagogy and engagement for those students with learning challenges, and physical and intellectual disabilities. However, studies are beginning to emerge which embrace practical, sensory exploration in mainstream learning such as those from Harris et al. (2019), Harris (2020), Park and Alderman (2018) and Chaves and Taylor (2021). Many more studies are needed to investigate the critical integration of sensory affect in learning spaces today, and the impact this may have on teaching practice and student engagement.

Educational theorists who support bodily experience

Kant, Dewey, Vygotsky, and Social Constructivism

To expand this discussion of sensory affect and educational research, it is necessary to highlight the educational theories, past and present, which support bodily experience in this field. German philosopher Immanuel Kant (1724–1804) was the major influence on the creation of Social Constructivism and presented the notion the mind orders and structures the sense data of experiences (Given, 2008; Webb, 2020). Kant also proposed experience leads to the formation of broad conceptions or constructs that are models of reality. He focused on how meaning is made and argued that all knowledge begins with experience (Varbelow, 2015). In Kant's view, the human mind does not passively receive sense data. Instead, it actively digests and organises sense data cognitively to make meaning, interpreting perceptions and experiences (Kant, 1781).

Later, the renowned American philosopher and educator John Dewey (1859–1952) advocated for a progressive, student-centred democratic approach to education and of shaping experiences through well-planned environments (Mooney, 2000).

> *An experience is always what it is because of a transaction taking place between an individual and what, at the time, constitutes his environment, . . . The environment, in other words, is whatever conditions interact with personal needs, desires purposes, and capacities to create the experience which is had.*
>
> *(Dewey, 1936:43)*

Dewey also insisted that education and experience are related but not equal; an experience can only be educational when it adds to the understanding of the lifeworld (Dewey, 1936; Goldblatt, 2006). According to Dewey, real-life active and interactive experiences in education should encourage experimentation, social community, and independent thinking. In addition to advocating progressive educational experiences within a flexible curriculum delivery to develop students' interests, Dewey noted the importance of shaping sensory forms of experience and he explicated sense qualities as the carriers of meaning (Dewey, 2009:118). Through interactions with the environment, individuals receptively accumulate experiences; they are constantly reflecting, reorganising, and reinterpreting the confusing sense information present in their day-to-day environments. He thought educators should understand students' 'instincts and impulses' and subsequently guide them into productive activities leading to the development of judgement (Goldblatt, 2006:22). Dewey's philosophy of interconnecting experience and education can elicit educators and students to articulate their responses to the phenomena of sensory affect as they consider their past, present, and future sensory experiences to shape their 'continuity of experience' (Moszkowicz, 2009:199). An awareness of bodily experience in the real-life interactions present within experiential learning and learning spaces in design education can foster necessary educational experiences to support student learning (Marton, 2014).

In Constructivist learning spaces, the educator guides the class discussion by presenting concepts, problems, scenarios, and information in social settings. Peer groups construct knowledge from one another, and as learning cannot be separated from action (Kurt, 2009). Following this, concepts are interrogated to provide students with opportunities to test their understanding and to develop an awareness of their experiences of learning. The student continuously builds and adjusts their earlier structures of experiences, as new and evolving experiences, actions, and knowledge. Social Constructivism infers that systems of meaning and a shared reality are formed between student, educator, and their peers who directly explore learning (with time and encouragement to reflect on what they are learning)

(Vygotsky, 1978; Woolner et al., 2012). Socially constructed meaning emerges from three fundamental principles; the first denoting learning is constructed as a response to each individual's experiences, with values placed on cultural experience and previous knowledge; the second positions learning as occurring through active exploration; and the third principle states learning emerges through social interaction and the processes of collaborative peer learning (Gray and Malins, 2004).

It is widely known that Lev Vygotsky (1896–1934) was considered to be Social Constructivism's first major theorist, while Jean Piaget (1886–1980) was one of the first to articulate its principles (Piaget, 1952; Vygotsky, 1978; Daniels, 2001; Kozulin et al., 2003). Educational psychologist Piaget was one of the most prominent theorists in cognitive Constructivism to emerge from the 20th century. Piaget's seminal works from the 1950s focused on internal and individual cognitive growth rather than interactive abilities, albeit for very young children. He encouraged active learning through the senses and reflexes to form new knowledge constructions. According to Piaget, haptic exploration and learning by doing enable a student to gather information about their learning environment, and therefore, understand it better. Encouraging a sensorimotor response to the manipulation of materials and real-world stimuli, students construct their own knowledge by giving new meaning to people, places, and things in their world. Piaget believed there is no knowledge without sensory experiential learning when both participant and object are active and involved in their dynamic interactions between themselves and their immediate environment, activating 'learning through reflection by doing' (Piaget, 1955; Minogue and Jones, 2006; Felicia, 2011).

Montessori

Maria Montessori (1870–1952) was one of the earliest educators to impart the value of sensory materials and embodied practice in teaching and learning as she devised theories of sensory play and learning for early years education (The Montessori Foundation, 2021). Montessori was one of the most important teaching practitioners of the 20th century. Her methods and ideas included a range of resources specifically for sensory play and experiential learning, and these were originally developed within a nursery and primary school context. She consistently integrated the senses and the real world into learning and disregarded imaginary tasks, which she considered of no real purpose (Mooney, 2000; Lillard, 2008; The Montessori Foundation, 2021). As Lillard (2008:57) stated, 'Traditional schooling does not . . . have a curriculum to educate the senses', and Montessori's 'materials have been . . . designed to . . . introduce increasingly complex concepts' through the use of eyes and ears but primarily hands'. Montessori's methods use the body as a learning tool, utilising movement to grasp geometric forms and serve a primary purpose in sequential learning steps via a tightly structured curriculum, which the students were free to approach in any way they chose to. These selected steps formed a scaffolded approach, accumulating into one summative learning intention for the student. The student would be asked to classify various pre-designed objects, which, in turn would help them to shape their own experiences within their environment. Students can work within a managed sensory experience accompanied by freedom and self-directed learning, reinforcing a sensorial approach to teaching practice in student-centred learning spaces.

Montessori created Sensorial Materials, a series of objects designed to educate a student's senses as they observe and begin to understand their environment. Montessori introduced bright and cheerful colour palettes as an integral part of educational environments for early years education, with student-sized tactile furnishings, real tools, and utensils. Consequently, a series of Sensorial Materials was designed to stimulate vision, touch, baric pressure, or weight, thermic or temperature, auditory sound, olfactory smell, gustatory taste, and stereo gnostic forms (Montessori Primary Guide, 2013). These objects incorporate sound cylinders, colour tablets and tactile rough or smooth boards to stimulate perceptual judgements by utilising the action or movement of the body while engaging in conscious thought. Sensorial Materials introduced increasingly complex concepts through the hands, eyes, and ears to stimulate perceptual judgements by utilising the action or movement of the body while engaging in conscious thought (Lillard, 2008:57). Montessori advocated that these materials assisted students' concentration and ability to make judgements and allow them to move with purpose in contrast to a conventional curriculum. Montessori's teaching practices articulated the importance of movement, colour and materials, as she sought to encapsulate the whole curriculum through her pre-designed tools, and as students were encouraged to work without conscious effort or permission (Lillard, 2008). For example, Montessori's 'Metal Insets' was used for teaching students how to write, grip, and control drawing materials such as pencils, using the student's experience of the weight and structure of drawn outlines. The student traces, with coloured or graded art pencils, the perimeter of each 'Metal Inset' using a positive or negative frame or shape to create single or double outlines, which may be further apart, closer together or progressively shaded. The students can master dark and light tonal values using pressure on the pencil or overlay contrasting shapes to form new patterns. By using 'Metal Insets' in lessons, the student experiences the effects of pressure on the pencil, and the variety of bodily and haptic movements and control involved when changing directions. The range of movements – keeping the point of the pencil on the edge of the frame or the inset, using continuous or steadying strokes – creates a physical experience. Another method introduced abstract concepts via three-dimensional concrete objects. 'The Pink Tower' consists of ten pink wooden cubes increasing in size progressively. The direct visual discrimination between the dimensions is reinforced with a hands-on approach to the materials and their organisation as different forms. Sensorial Materials, such as these, reinforce the student's ability to perceive, build and organise structures, and make judgements on size and layout using three-dimensional forms, like the construction of maquettes and prototyping in design education. Montessori students were also free to engage with a sensorial curriculum and with these Sensorial Materials without assistance and without permission. Although Montessori's teaching practices were developed for young students there may be a case for suggesting that these methods can be cultivated and employed in higher education as a form of sensory experiential learning, adaptable for all learning styles. This sensorial teaching approach could convey the mindset of constructivist designer to design students as they develop concepts by feeling objects and making recognition based on hand-driven manipulation (The Montessori Foundation, 2021).

The prepared environment was also important in Montessori's approach to education to attract, engage, and stimulate the student in critical play. However, there are also collective responsibilities in a Montessori classroom. Similarly, these notions can be applied in the management of a design studio setting, such as taking responsibility for the learning space, taking ownership of creative mess, and organising resources. Place-making is also key in Montessori education through the display of students' playful experimentation, work-in-progress, and prototype/ artefacts. The students' own and collective works are openly reflected back into the community of practice who made them, in and around the proximity of the learning space for others to view. As a form of belonging (and not just decoration) in learning space, the student 'does more than working with the material. He also looks around him' (Montessori, 1964:8).

Contemporary sensory-based teaching practices

Today, higher education pedagogies that support bodily or sensory experience in teaching and learning are rare to locate. Sensory pedagogies are ways in which the bodily sense can be integrated into teaching approaches and learning intentions, with diverse precedents emerging in this field of study. For too long, the body has been ignored in education and pedagogy, dominated by knowledge-based transfer and practice. Our bodies are our navigational guides in the world and are, therefore, also critical to teaching and learning. Sensory affect is integral as an experiential intervention to allow educators and students to make sense of the taxonomy of learning spaces available to contemporary design education. A learning space can be defined by its audience, activities, attributes (such as group size), technology, and components (such as seating and production surfaces). Generally, e-learning, and online pedagogies are widely embedded in higher education yet play-based, sensory, and embodied pedagogies and practices are infrequent in learning spaces.

To date, there are few sensory pedagogies, embodied pedagogies, and body-based learning (BBL) approaches invoking sensory-formed learning experiences in higher education today. In architectural education, visual practices have traditionally dominated over bodily or spatial experiences. To counter-act this notion, Papadopoulou (2019:abstract) proposed the use of wearable, computational tool (known as a 'sensing creature') for 'body-centred situated learning of space'. Papadopoulou's study established how tools can become extensions of our bodies and minds in learning spaces, initiating enactive cognition in the dynamic interaction between body and space. Another example comes from Dr Cecilia Bischeri, who designed and taught the course, *Architecture Studio 1 – Cutting through Public Space* at Griffith

University in Queensland, Australia. This hands-on, project-focused course within the Bachelor of Architectural Design program aimed to develop critical architectural design skills and communication strategies with first-year students. The key learning intention was the emphasis placed upon the development of producing and clearly representing the plan and sections of a structure accordingly to architectural conventions. In the first stage of this course, a clay exercise introduced students to the design and experiences of architectural space through the embodied use of clay (Figure 2.1). The students used clay as a tool to construct the first iteration of architectural modelling with no digital input into the design. Clay was chosen for its intrinsic material properties, as it is easy to mould and allows flexible testing and alterations. Functioning differently from cardboard or balsa construction, clay supports a process of subtraction rather than assembling to define and map internal space. As Heidegger stated, the idea of handling, as sensory engagement with the world, is what leads to comprehension (Bolt, 2006). The aim of this model making exercise was for the students to produce a dramatic space via handling. Neither brief nor scale was provided. The scope of the exercise was to push the students to experiment with the architectural qualities of space and, at the same time, to encourage an original exploration in the process of space-making – deterring them away from making what first-year students generally assume to be architectural space when using technology. The students then submitted photos of their clay model for assessment, showing both whole and sectioned components, with sketches or photos that emphasised the spatial quality of their creations.

During my own doctoral research, I provided an open-ended design brief to design student participants of my study at Glasgow School of Art during a research

FIGURE 2.1   Clay exercises introduced students to architectural design and experiences of space.

Source: © Cecilia Bischeri, Griffith University, 2022.

FIGURE 2.2 A student's clay cube as an expression of sound within their studio learning space.

Source: © Lorraine Marshalsey.

methodology exercise. I asked the students to create an expression of sound representing their impressions of their own studio learning environment and the sensory impact this has on them as students. The outcome would be entirely open to their own interpretation. While some students used the conventional tools of design such as computers and pencils, one student produced a clay cube, which was hollowed in the centre (Figure 2.2). When I asked him why he had produced this artefact as a response to the sensory affect impacting on him in his learning space, the student said: 'If you hold the cube up to your ear, like a shell, then you can hear the sounds of the studio'. I was surprised at this student's natural sensory selection of clay as a material solution to the brief, rather than traditional design materials within his specialism, such as paper or technology.

In 2009, an article appeared in *Ceramics Monthly* on the possibility of 3D printing with clay. This idea originated at the University of Washington and was led by Mark Ganter (Rael and San Fratello, 2018). Ganter had begun to publish a series of open-source recipes for 3D printable materials. Through the lens of 3D-printing technology and coupled with an interest in traditional craft processes and techniques, new materials were being explored and developed for architecture and design, including clay, steel, and concrete printing. Today, the conventional hand-driven properties of clay have merged with digital methods of production to bring new and evolving possibilities for creative practice in design education. Due to the revival in demand for ceramics as a practice worldwide in recent years, several higher education institutions, such as University of the Arts, London (UAL) and School of The Arts (SOTA) in Singapore, have already embraced ceramics as a medium for creative expression (Singapore Arts School Ltd, 2022; University Arts London, 2022). Clay as a 3D printed medium, although expensive, is now appearing in design schools. This is with the intention of enhancing students' experiential learning of materials in their design processes and manufacturing methods beyond solely digital territories.

Embodied pedagogies are even rarer to locate than sensory pedagogies, especially in higher education. Embodied inquiry supports the use of diverse research methods and pedagogical approaches in order to gather data and analyse embodied, lived experiences. Zembylas (2007:20) speaks of the recalibration of bodies and affects in learning spaces as intensities and energies that generate new affective and embodied connections, as knowledge is felt and understood emotionally and through the body. Leigh and Brown (2021:22) proposed a typology highlighting four distinct yet overlapping motivations of embodied inquiry, which can be applied to this context of the learning spaces of design education and educator/ student bodies: lived experiences, the researcher's body in the field, the body as a communicator and the body in interaction. This aligns with the somatic turn as used by Thomas Hanna to describe the mind/body/spirit (or conscious awareness) connection, which describes the holistic nature of bringing conscious awareness to a moving, feeling, owned and present body (Leigh, 2019:151).

Dixon and Senior (2011) situate embodied teaching and embodied learning as being "conceptualised through 'pedagogy as relational' – between teaching and learning and between teacher and learner" (Dixon and Senior, 2011:abstract). They added drawn lines of pedagogic affect to the images they recorded, aligning bodies within learning spaces (indoors and outdoors) to analyse the complex, fluid relationships between people as embodied pedagogy. Dixon and Senior (2011:477) draw upon bodily consciousness whilst teaching, as 'they strive to make connections across physical bodies, presences and affected bodies'. However, visualising embodiment via image-based data does contrast with many existing studies which articulate the use of the written word and spoken accounts as data; seeing is reading with the whole body. Estola and Elbaz-Luwisch (2003:701) explored narratives as having the capability to express the voices of bodies in the classroom and describe the practice of teaching as "the body voices that we encountered through our own experiences seem to be 'feeling voices' of this kind, and to allow a 'greater sense of agency and personal control'". They identified five body positions of teachers in relation to their physical experiences in educational settings. These include the position of presence, the position of control, the positions of care, the position of listening to oneself and lastly, the position of protection (Estola and Elbaz-Luwisch, 2003:711–712).

Creative body-based learning (CBL) draws from drama, role-play, dance, visual arts, outdoor education, music, game-like strategies, and image work as primary to secondary age students engage in cycles of learning and reflection. These activities are aesthetic, cognitive, and affective in context, and designed to stimulate dialogue using the body as a technique in lesson-planning. Robyne Garrett and Belinda MacGill from the University of South Australia in Adelaide, Australia, developed the CBL curriculum initiative as they combined narrative, artistic and embodied endeavours as a means for students to access and understand curriculum material (Garrett and MacGill, 2021:1224–1225). The embodied body as a critical part of curriculum and via CBL is emerging in several similar recent studies (Green and Hopwood, 2015; Meiners et al., 2019; Dawson, 2021). For example, students use their bodies to identify angles in Mathematics classes, use craft supplies to 'create an abstract visual representation of a key concept, theme, or personal belief' as a 3D model, or when 'inviting students to use their collective group of bodies to create and represent shapes, often with string' to activate the senses to heighten the students' learning experiences (Dawson, 2021).

> *What happens when teachers are introduced to pedagogies that explicitly promote physicality, aesthetics and expression of the body, pedagogies that disrupt the conventional spatial relational discipline systems of classrooms?*
>
> *(Garrett and MacGill, 2021:1223)*

In 2021, I discussed the ethos of CBL with Garrett and MacGill. We discussed the key ideas and influences from Katie Dawson's critical and influential work in this field (Dawson, 2021). Garrett and MacGill explained the distinct approaches of CBL were critical to supporting students as they engage with this transformational approach to teaching practice and as a broader learning design. Garrett and MacGill described CBL as a provocation – working with artists and teachers to empower students as they owned and developed the activities through the notion of their bodies. To comprehend CBL activities the students' experienced DAR: first Describing (what did we do in this activity?), then Analysing (was the task easy or difficult? Why?) and then Relating (why might we play this game?). As CBL strategies clearly support thinking and learning processes through the body, I began to consider how these methods could be applied to contemporary design education as a form of embodied pedagogy. Through the lens of CBL, design education could facilitate CBL activities as design-based teaching tools (to generate real-life awareness of stakeholder issues and end-user challenges in design) when invoking sensory affect with physical bodily actions.

Enactive cognition and becoming aware of experience

In this discussion of becoming aware of the body when teaching and learning, cognitive neuroscientist Francesco Varela's (1946–2001) ideas on the first-person emergent self are pivotal to enactive cognition (also known as enactivism) in the dynamic interaction between person and environment (Varela, 1993; Depraz et al., 2003). Varela argued for acknowledgement of the subjectively experienced body and the physical world in which it enacts. In this way, design educators and students can explore their pragmatic day-to-day experiential teaching and learning, and presence in learning spaces, recognising their bodies know best within real-life educational settings.

Depraz et al. (2003:6) structured the pragmatics of becoming aware from a three-layered temporal revolution, which first consists of going through a cycle of epoché and intuitive evidence – the procedural descriptions of becoming aware. As educators and students become self-aware of the external and internal issues in a learning space, they may assume epoché in the reflective process. This is the act of all judgements of the external world becoming suspended whilst judgements are internalised as evidence. The three phases of epoché – suspension, redirection, and letting go – serve as evidence of the cyclical reflecting act (Varela, 1993; Depraz et al., 2003:26). Intuition is the mental capacity to sense an instinct over time; 'The intuitive act is slow – relative to a reflexive act – and that its fulfillment often occurs in steps. . . . Its qualitative order of sensory apperceptive fulfillment so different in each person' (Depraz et al., 2003:54). This thought experience process is described as intuitive evidence. Two tensions exist within intuitive evidence: the basic component of an individual's subjective experience and a universalised, intersubjective knowledge of eidetic distinctions (drawn from Husserl's notion of the instant recall of vivid, detailed mental images). Intuitive evidence is the active play between one's own subjective perception and intersubjective memories and/ or imagination (Depraz et al., 2003:56). Educators and students might reflectively turn their gaze inward and embrace an 'infrastructure of imagination' composed of 'orientation, reflection and exploration' using the cycles of epoché and intuitive evidence alongside the tools of sensory affect (Wenger, 2000:238). This allows educators and students to react and plan future actions as they gather insight, question assumptions and modify their activities within their learning spaces (Brookfield, 1995; Marshalsey, 2017).

Eugene Gendlin: the Felt Sense

American philosopher and psychologist Eugene T. Gendlin (1926–2017) termed the phrase *Felt Sense* to describe our physical bodily orientating sense towards a situation, person, place or event, in a mix of emotional and factual experiences (Gendlin, 2003). The *Felt Sense* defines embodied knowing as a phenomenon of experiential and focused-orientated meaning (Gendlin, 1996, 1997).

> *The knowing is physically sensed in your body and can be easily found. But this bodily knowing can extend much more deeply. . . . Your body "knows". Your body is not a machine, but rather a wonderful intricate interaction with everything around you, which is why it "knows" so much just in being.*
>
> *You can sense your living body directly under your thoughts and memories and under your familiar feelings. Under them you can discover a physically sensed "murky zone," which you can enter and open. This is the source from which new steps emerge. Once found, it is a palpable presence underneath.*
>
> *(Gendlin, 2003:vii–viii, ix)*

Gendlin was a humanistic psychologist who linked the whole body and physical bodily experience to language and thought: 'the total brain-mind environment as we sense it' (Gendlin, 2003:xv). In 1962, he published his key text, *Experiencing and the Creation of Meaning* (Levin, 1994). Gendlin drew influence from many philosophers to form his theories on lived human experience. These influences included Aristotle (384BC – 322BC), Wilhelm Dilthey (1833–1911), phenomenologists

Husserl and Martin Heidegger (1889–1976), Richard McKeon (1900–1985), Ludwig Wittgenstein (1889–1951) and French phenomenological philosopher Merleau-Ponty among others (Sharma, 2011). Merleau-Ponty located sensation at the heart of human experience, as the body determines the nature of our sensory and motor capabilities to recognise the world in particular ways (Moran, 1999). He conceived of the manifestation of embodiment when he described the bodily character of experience as speaking 'to all my senses at once' (Merleau-Ponty, 1962:203). He positioned the human body at the centre of the sensory experiential world as a two-way, intertwined affiliation, indivisible, conversant, and creating embodied presence in the daily environment. Gendlin continued Merleau-Ponty's ideas of the lived experience further 'articulating precisely how one's bodily felt sense can enter between each step of thought and the next, so that there can be a shift in meaning and concepts can be used in a new way' (Levin, 1994:349). From 1951 onwards, and prior to Gendlin's definitive *Felt Sense*, psychologist Carl Rogers (1902–1987) also referred to bodily sensing as experiencing the world through sensory, visceral, and physiological channels. Rogers continually developed his ideas, and later drawing influence from Gendlin and his concept of experiencing (Ikemi, 2005).

Gendlin examined how shifting between what is already expressed and what is yet to be articulated enables a new kind of thinking through the body. Despite Gendlin agreeing with the basic components of deconstructionism as elevating rationalism through language and literary texts, and being key to forming assumptions, knowledge, opinions, and actions, he developed his reasoning into a new direction. He attested we can move further beyond language alone to understand subjective human experiencing and emotional responses when we listen to the body (Sharma, 2011). Gendlin argued the *Felt Sense* meant feeling a situation, person, event, or setting more profoundly via a bodily, physical awareness, and not primarily through mental experience (Levin, 1994; Gendlin, 2003). This thinking begins from the complexity of felt meaning and returns to it repeatedly (Gendlin, 1997). Gendlin sought to comprehend our subjective free will, individual needs and self-efficacy via the *Felt Sense*, and as a method to understand our life world through bodily experience (Sharma, 2011). He endeavoured to identify the fluid and active sources of subjective experiencing to understand how we form our meanings. Developing a reflective mind-set and enacting embodied knowing without conscious thought can also be described as the *Felt Sense* (Rappaport, 2013). In this way, design educators and students should attempt to foreground their awareness of the processes of the *Felt Sense* (using thought, language, and actions) to reach self-actualisation. Through Gendlins' notion of experiencing, design educators and students can express and reach their highest level of engagement and potential in experiential learning and learning spaces today. Therefore, knowing how and when the body absorbs and translates our lifeworld by experiencing and consciously acknowledging sensory affect in our immediate learning spaces.

As Sharma (2011) states, the body has its own wisdom, and it is the conduit by which we understand our situated place in the world. Our bodies tense when our immediate conditions and stimulus are detrimental to our wellbeing and our bodies release this tension when we realise these experiences are neutral or positive situations. This embodied knowing and becoming aware identifies and changes the way that thoughts and emotions are held within the body, which can instigate dramatic shifts in our understanding and insight of the meanings we can attribute to our experiences. For many years, it has been recognised that educators and students' awareness of their own conscious, embodied, and qualitative teaching and learning experiences arise via the perspective of being reflective practitioners but we need to take this even further through bodily experience (Schön, 1984; Moon, 2004; Mewburn, 2012). Depraz et al. (2003) proposed the basic reflective structure of becoming aware involves an iterative cycle of reflection and affection. In the context of design education, this is with a view to iteratively reflecting and understanding the role of sensory affect in educators and students own experiential practice, social interactions, and contemporary learning spaces. Through this sensory, embodied felt lens, educators and students may be better prepared to make the positive changes necessary to improve and enhance their engagement, social, cultural, and relational interactions, curriculum, pedagogy, and experiential learning within learning spaces today.

Foregrounding sensory affect using the felt sense

The body shift happens when the bodily felt sense has been acknowledged and listened to and a definitive change occurs in thinking and doing. Tension is then released as a physical sensation, as once-hidden awareness of the impact of sensory affect is revealed to the conscious mind to form a plan of action, relief, or response (Gendlin, 2003). There are several steps to focusing on sensory affect, as the *Felt Sense* is acknowledged, and a body shift occurs in the process of foregrounding awareness (Gendlin, 2003). These phases involve slowing down our bodies in time, staying quiet and carefully participating in the following steps at the beginning of planning teaching and learning within a learning space:

1   *The Preparation stage: Clearing and making a space.* This can be physical or non-physical sensing within the body. This step is essentially a moment to relax, get comfortable, remove immediate irritations, ground yourself, breathe deeply, close your eyes and to take in the vicinity of the whole situation, person, place, or event from an outsider viewpoint.

2   *The Felt Sense.* Select one central aspect of an issue to feel (not think about) and focus on (this could be spatial, sensory, pedagogical or something else). The issue can emerge as internal (an issue within yourself) or external (a challenge in the environment or with others). Despite feeling several interconnected facets of the problem; what does the issue feel like without form? Focus on a single feeling that this issue suggests.

3   *Finding a handle.* From this felt sense, what words, images, or phrases come to mind that encapsulates the feeling of this issue? Try not to rationalise, justify,

solve, or explain the feeling you recall. Instead, describe the feeling as a range of different handles.

4   *Fitting the handle.* Does the handle fit? Stay true to the feelings of the bodily *Felt Sense* until a specific handle is generated that describes and fits the issue perfectly. This verbalisation of unseen sensory affect as a handle, emerges from acting upon the felt sense: the formation, transformation, and dissolution of an issue until a handle is accepted as the most suitable one. A suitable handle emerges from a process of drawing ideas, language, and sensations in three-dimensional space. Avoid analysing or dissecting the issue and its handle at this stage. This is the first step in a bodily shift towards foregrounding the issue.

5   *Resonating.* Iteratively move back and forth between the handle and the *Felt Sense*, checking if the handle (the word, image, or phrase) really does fit the feeling associated with the bodily experience being sensed. Say the handle aloud as you resound the appropriateness of the handle with the issue. Does the handle accurately capture the issue associated with the situation, person, place, or event?

6   *Asking.* Then, ask the inner bodily *Felt Sense* if the handle describing the issue associated with the situation, person, place, or event, is accurate. What is its quality (the word, image, or phrase)? Listen to and trust the body. Sense this quality again, and ask what is it that makes this quality fit with the handle? Ensure the answer is slowly considered and that there is a small shift in the body from a deeper, thorough level. Quick answers to asking should be recognised as fleeting responses and disregarded. Return to the bodily *Felt Sense* and reflect, delving deeper as you return to the previous steps several times.

7   *Receiving.* Whatever is received from this process accounts for an inner bodily shift, as you sense and touch the issue at hand and identify the problem through this awareness of bodily sensed affect. This process can be iterative as you circle back around to revisit of address new and multiple issues and as more change and movement occur.

(Paraphrased and adapted from Gendlin, 2003:ch. 4, 5)

First, we draw from, then form and interpret sensory affect from Gendlin's original focusing technique and using the *Felt Sense*. This process of foregrounding sensory affect using these key steps when focusing on the *Felt Sense*, draws out a physical sense of meaning and heightens awareness of the issues and challenges in contemporary design education and its learning spaces. Second, the critical lens of sensory affect also largely draws influence from Juhani Pallasmaa' *Eyes of the Skin* and architectural phenomenology. The practical steps I have described are also influenced by Kolb and Kolb's (2005) continual cycle of reflective thinking-by-doing to consider and evaluate educators and students' experiences of their design education.

Generally, there are many layers and complexities within design education, its experiential forms of learning and learning spaces. These include intellectual, spiritual, and moral intentions, independence, social, personal, information processing, behaviour, wellbeing, achievement, diversity, inclusiveness, differentiation, and respect for others. The focusing cycle helps to foreground sensory affect and can identify challenges emerging from the active interactions between educators, students, peers, and their environment. Supportive and disruptive influences can arise from engaging with real-life design education and learning spaces in this way, as educators and students think, feel, perceive, behave, and sense to support their reflection, engagement, and cognition. An awareness of the experiential impact of sensory affect using the focusing and *Felt Sense* process will help to recognise the factors interrupting engagement in a repertoire of settings (Kolb and Kolb, 2005:194). Meaning making emerges from design educators and students as they process, understand, and make sense of experience, knowledge, their relationships, and themselves in this context of their design education through these phases:

1   Develop an awareness of the bodily senses (as listening through the body).
2   Reflect and evaluate the impact of sensory affect on their bodies, focus and engagement as they consider their learning spaces, social interactions, curriculum, pedagogy, knowledge and understanding, experiential practice and processes, among others.
3   Place value judgements on these newly acquired insights.
4   Apply and embrace this new awareness in terms of improving ones' own subjective focus and engagement within design education, experiential learning, and learning spaces.

Summary

Chapter 2 has presented this book's critical questions: What is sensory affect? And why is sensory affect relevant to teaching and student engagement within experiential learning and learning spaces in design education? This chapter provided a brief overview of the complexity and landscape of sensory affect. This chapter began by offering interpretations of the senses and sensory affect in multiple ways. Briefly, the scientific character and structure of the senses, sensation and perception were also explored to shape the broader meaning of sensory affect, as an umbrella term. Then, a consideration of theoretical, educational, and creative perspectives aligning with sensory experience was unpacked to provide a diverse framework of bodily experience. Many existing studies examine sensory and affective experience, yet few address bodies, spaces, and learning as one intertwined cycle of experience. Therefore, I elucidated a small emergent range of historical and contemporary pedagogies including sensory-based teaching practices, embodied pedagogies, and BBL and inquiry. Then, Eugene Gendlin and his notion of the *Felt Sense* was discussed to support the inclusion of sensory affect, leading to an enhanced body-space awareness, and providing a baseline for body-space engagement. In summary, design educators and students must identify and consider the positive, neutral, and negative signals their bodies sense in the context of teaching, experiential learning, and learning spaces within design education today.

References

Ackerman, D. (1992) *A Natural History of the Senses*. New York: Vintage Books.

Ahmed, S. (2020) 'Happy Objects', In Gregg, M. and Seigworth, G.J. (eds), *The Affect Theory Reader*. Durham: Duke University Press. doi: 10.1515/9780822393047/HTML.

Andersen, P.A. and Guerrero, L.K. (2008) 'Haptic Behavior in Social Interaction', in *Human Haptic Perception: Basics and Applications*. Basel: Birkhäuser, pp. 155–163.

Bachelard, G. (1994) *The Poetics of Space*. Boston: Beacon Press.

Bell, C. (1833) *The Hand: Its Mechanism and Vital Endowments as Evincing Design*. London: William Pickering.

Bolkan, S. (2015) 'Students' affective learning as affective experience: Significance, reconceptualization, and future directions', *Communication Education*, 64(4), 502–505.

Bolt, B. (2006) Materializing pedagogies. *Melbourne*. Available at: sitem.herts.ac.uk/artdes_research/papers/wpades/.

Braithwaite, N. (2017) 'Sensing creativity: The role of materials in shoe design', *Senses and Society*, 12(1), pp. 90–94.

Brookfield, S. (1995) *Becoming a Critically Reflective Teacher, Higher and Adult Education Series*. San Francisco: Jossey-Bass.

Bull, M. (2019) 'Sensory Media: Virtual Worlds and the Training of Perception', In Howes, D. (ed), *A Cultural History of the Senses in the Modern Age*. London: Bloomsbury Academic, pp. 219–241.

Carvalho, L., Goodyear, P. and Laat, M.de (2016) *Place-Based Spaces for Networked Learning*. New York: Routledge.

Cerbone, D.R. (2006) *Understanding Phenomenology*. Chesham: Acumen Publishing Ltd.

Chaves, J. and Taylor, A. (2021) *Creating Sensory Smart Classrooms, Creating Sensory Smart Classrooms*. Abingdon: Routledge.

Classen, C. (2020) 'The senses at the national gallery: Art as sensory recreation and regulation in Victorian England', *Senses and Society*, 15(1), 85–97.

Daniels, H. (2001) *Vygotsky and Pedagogy*. London: Routledge, Falmer.

Dawson, K. (2021) Drama-based instruction. Teaching strategies, *The University of Texas at Austin*. Available at: https://dbp.theatredance.utexas.edu/teaching_strategies.

Deal, C. (2020) 'Body of knowledge: Sunderland museum and art gallery and the blind imagination', *Senses and Society*, 15(2), 156–169.

de Freitas, E., Rousell, D. and Jäger, N. (2020) 'Relational architectures and wearable space: Smart schools and the politics of ubiquitous sensation', *Research in Education*, 107(1), 10–32.

Depraz, N., Varela, F.J. and Vermersch, P. (2003) *On Becoming Aware: A Pragmatics of Experiencing*. Amsterdam: John Benjamins Publishing Company.

Dewey, J. (1936) *Experience and Education*. New York: Macmillan.

Dewey, J. (2009) *Art as Experience*. New York: Perigee Books.

Dixon, M. and Senior, K. (2011) 'Appearing pedagogy: From embodied learning and teaching to embodied pedagogy', *Pedagogy, Culture and Society*, 19(3), 473–484.

Erlauer, L. (2003) *The Brain-Compatible Classroom. Using What We Know About Learning and Improving Teaching*. Virginia: Association for Supervision and Curriculum Development (ASCD).

Estola, E. and Elbaz-Luwisch, F. (2003) 'Teaching bodies at work', *Journal of Curriculum Studies*, 35(6), 697–719.

Facer, K. (2011) *Learning Futures: Education, Technology and Social Change*. Abingdon: Routledge.

Felicia, P. (2011) *Handbook of Research on Improving Learning and Motivation Through Educational Games: Multidisciplinary Approaches*. Hershey, PA: IGI Global.

Foley, H.J. and Matlin, M.W. (2010) *Sensation and Perception*. Boston: Allyn & Bacon.

Fors, V., Bäckström, Å. and Pink, S. (2013) 'Multisensory emplaced learning: Resituating situated learning in a moving world', *Mind, Culture, and Activity* 20(2), 170–183.

Garrett, R. and MacGill, B. (2021) 'Fostering inclusion in school through creative and body-based learning', *International Journal of Inclusive Education*, 25(11), 1221–1235.

Gascoyne, S. (2011) *Sensory Play*. London: Practical Pre-School Books.

Gendlin, E.T. (1996) *Focusing-Oriented Psychotherapy: A Manual of the Experiential Method*. New York: Guilford Press.

Gendlin, E.T. (1997) *Experiencing and the Creation of Meaning*. Evanston, IL: Northwestern University Press.

Gendlin, E.T. (2003) *Focusing*. London: Rider.

Given, L.M. (2008) *The Sage Encyclopedia of Qualitative Research Methods* (Edited by Lisa, M.G). Thousand Oaks, CA: Sage Publications Ltd.

Goldblatt, P.F. (2006) 'How John Dewey's theories underpin art and art education', *Education and Culture*, 22(1), 17–34.

Gray, C. and Malins, J. (2004) *Vizualizing Research: A Guide to the Research Process in Art and Design*. Aldershot: Ashgate Publishing Limited.

Green, B. and Hopwood, N. (2015) *Professional and Practice-Based Learning The Body in Professional Practice, Learning and Education. Body/Practice*. London: Springer International Publishing.

Grunwald, M. (2008) *Human Haptic Perception: Basics and Applications*. Basel: Birkhäuser.

Gumtau, S. (2011) *Affordances of Touch in Multi-Sensory Embodied Interface Design*. Portsmouth: University of Portsmouth.

Harris, A. (2020) *A Sensory Education*. London: Routledge.

Harris, E., Frankel, L., Arnaud, C.St. and Bamber, A. (2019) 'Puzzling pieces: A sensory design learning tool', *Senses and Society*, 14(3), 351–360.

Highmore, B. (2020) 'Bitter After Taste', In Gregg, M. and Seigworth, G.J. (eds), *The Affect Theory Reader*. Durham: Duke University Press. doi: 10.1515/9780822393047/HTML.

Hiris, E. (2007) 'Detection of biological and nonbiological motion', *Journal of vision (Charlottesville, Va.)*, 7(12), 4.

Holl, S., Pallasmaa, J. and Pérez Gómez, A. (2006) *Questions of Perception: Phenomenology of Architecture*. Tokyo: A + U Publishing.

Howes, D. (2005) 'Skinscapes: Embodiment, Culture and Environment', In Classen, C. (ed), *The Book of Touch*. Oxford: Berg Publishers, pp. 27–40.

Howes, D. (2014) 'Introduction to sensory museology', *The Senses and Society*, 9(3), 259–267.

Ikemi, A. (2005) 'Carl Rogers and Eugene Gendlin on the bodily felt sense : What they share and where they differ', *Person-Centered and Experiential Psychotherapies*, 4(1), 31–42.

Ingold, T. (2002) *The Perception of the Environment: Essays on Livelihood, Dwelling and Skill*. London: Routledge.

Jury, D. (2011) *Letterpress: The Allure of the Handmade*. Hove: Rotovision.

Kant, I. (1781) *Critique of pure reason*. Available at: www.gutenberg.org/files/4280/4280-h/4280-h.htm.

Kensinger, K.M. (1991) 'A Body of Knowledge, or, the Body Knows', In *The Gift of Feathers Exhibition, The University Museum, University of Pennsylvania*. Pennsylvania: University of Pennsylvania, pp. 37–45.

Kolb, A.Y. and Kolb, D.A. (2005) 'Learning styles and learning spaces: Enhancing experiential learning in higher education', *Academy of Management Learning & Education*, 4, 193–212.

Kozulin, A., Gindis, B., Ageyev, V.S., Miller, S.M. (2003) *Vygotsky's Educational Theory in Cultural Context*. New York: Cambridge University Press.

Kurt, S. (2009) 'An analytic study on the traditional studio environments and the use of the constructivist studio in the architectural design education', *Procedia – Social and Behavioral Sciences*, 1(1), 401–408.

Lauwrens, J. (2019) 'Seeing touch and touching sight: A reflection on the tactility of vision', *The Senses and Society*, 14(3), 297–312.

Lederman, S.J. and Klatzky, R.L. (2009) 'Haptic perception: A tutorial', *Attention, Perception & Psychophysics*, 71(7), 1439–1459.

Leigh, J. (2019) *Conversations on Embodiment Across Higher Education: Teaching, Practice and Research*. Abingdon: Routledge.

Leigh, J. and Brown, N. (2021) 'Embodied Inquiry', In *Embodied Inquiry*. London: Bloomsbury Academic.

Lengel, T. and Kuczala, M.S. (2010) *The Kinesthetic Classroom: Teaching and Learning Through Movement*. California: Corwin Press.

Levin, D.M. (1993) *Modernity and the Hegemony of Vision*. London: University of California Press.

Levin, D.M. (1994) 'Making sense: The work of Eugene Gendlin', *Human Studies*, 17(3), 343–353.

Levine, M.W. (2000) *Levine & Shefner's Fundamentals of Sensation and Perception* (3rd edn). New York: Oxford University Press.

Lillard, A.S. (2008) *Montessori: The Science Behind the Genius*. New York: Oxford University Press.

Malnar, J.M. and Vodvarka, F. (2004) *Sensory Design*. Minneapolis, MN: University of Minnesota Press.

Marinetti, F.T. (2005) 'Tactilism', In Classen, C. (ed), *The Book of Touch*. Oxford: Berg Publishers, pp. 329–332.

Marshalsey, L. (2017) *An investigation into the experiential impact of sensory affect in contemporary communication design studio education* (Thesis). The Glasgow School of Art. Available at: http://radar.gsa.ac.uk/5894/.

Marton, F. (2014) *Necessary Conditions of Learning*. London: Routledge.

Massumi, B. (2002) *Parables for the Virtual: Movement, Affect, Sensation*. London: Duke University Press.

Meiners, J., Dawson, K., Garrett, R. and Wrench, A. (2019) 'Childhood education creative body-based learning: Not just another story about the arts and young people', *Childhood Education*, 95(6), 66–75. doi: 10.1080/00094056.2019.1689069.

Merleau-Ponty, M. (1962) *Phenomenology of Perception by Merleau-Ponty, M* (Translated From The French by Colin Smith). London: Routledge.

Mewburn, I. (2012) 'Lost in translation: Reconsidering reflective practice and design studio pedagogy', *Arts and Humanities in Higher Education*, 11(4), 363–379.

Minogue, J. and Jones, M.G. (2006) 'Haptics in education: Exploring an untapped sensory modality', *Review of Educational Research*, 76(3), 317–348.

Montessori, M. (1964) *The Role of Play and of Social Training in Montessori Education*. Amsterdam: Association Montessori Internationale.

Montessori Primary Guide. (2013) *Montessori – Sensorial – Introduction*. Available at: http://www.infomontessori.com/sensorial/introduction.htm.

Moon, J.A. (2004) 'Using reflective learning to improve the impact of short courses and workshops', *The Journal Of Continuing Education in the Health Professions*, 24, 4–11.

Mooney, C.G. (2000) *Theories of Childhood: An Introduction to Dewey, Montessori, Erickson, Piaget and Vygotsky*. Minneapolis. MN: Redleaf Press.

Moran, D. (1999) *Introduction to Phenomenology*. New York: Routledge.

Moszkowicz, J. (2009) *A re-evaluation of historical precedents in the age of new media* (Thesis). Bristol: University West of England.

Otero-Pailos, J. (2010) *Architecture's Historical Turn: Phenomenology and the Rise of the Postmodern*. Minneapolis: University of Minnesota Press.

Pallasmaa, J. (2012) *The Eyes of the Skin: Architecture and the Senses*. Chichester: John Wiley & Sons.

Papadopoulou, A. (2019) 'Sensing creatures: Tools for augmenting our sensory awareness of space', *Lecture Notes in Computer Science (including subseries Lecture Notes in Artificial Intelligence and Lecture Notes in Bioinformatics)*, 11587 LNCS, pp. 286–303.

Park, C.W. and Alderman, J. (2018) *Designing Across Senses*. Sebastopol: O'Reilly Media, Inc.

Patch, C. (2020) *Sensory Play for Toddlers and Preschoolers: Easy Projects to Develop Fine Motor Skills, Hand-Eye Coordination, and Early Measurement Concepts*. New York: Skyhorse Publishing.

Piaget, J. (1952) *The Origins of Intelligence in Children*. New York: Norton.

Piaget, J. (1955) *The Child's Construction of Reality*. London: Routledge.

Rael, R. and San Fratello, V. (2018) *Printing Architecture : Innovative Recipes for 3D Printing*. New York: Princeton Architectural Press.

Rappaport, L. (2013) 'Trusting the felt sense in art-based research', *Journal of Applied Arts & Health*, 4(1), 97–104.

Reychav, I., Warkentin, M. and Ndicu, M. (2016) 'Tablet adoption with smart school website technology', *Journal of Computer Information Systems*, 56(4), 280–287.

Russ, S.W. (1998) *Affect, Creative Experience and Psychological Adjustment*. Ann Arbor: Taylor & Francis.

Satpute, A.B., Kang, J., Bickart, K.C., Yardley, H., Wager, T.D. and Barrett, L.F. (2015) 'Involvement of sensory regions in affective experience: A meta-analysis', *Frontiers in Psychology*, 6, 1–14.

Schön, D.A. (1984) *The Reflective Practitioner: How Professionals Think in Action*. London: Basic Books.

Schwartz, B.L. and Krantz, J.H. (2016) *Sensation & Perception*. Thousand Oaks: Sage Publications Ltd.

Scott-Webber, L. (2014) 'The Perfect Storm: Educations Immediate Challenges', In Scott-Webber, L. et al. (eds), *Learning Space Design in Higher Education*. Faringdon: Libri Publishing, pp. 151–167.

Seamon, D. and Mugerauer, R. (2000) *Dwelling, Place and Environment*. Malabar: Krieger Publishing Company.

Seo, M-G., Barrett, L.F. and Bartunek, J.M. (2004) 'The role of affective experience in work motivation', *Academy of Management Review. Academy of Management*, 29(3), 423–439.

Sharma, R. (2011) 'Carrying forward: Explicating Gendlin's experiential phenomenological philosophy and its influence on humanistic psychotherapy', *Journal of Humanistic Psychology*, 51(2), 172–194.

Simm, D. and Marvell, A. (2015) 'Gaining a "sense of place": Students' affective experiences of place leading to transformative learning on international fieldwork', *Journal of Geography in Higher Education*, 39(4), 595.

Singapore Arts School Ltd (2022) *Visual arts*. Available at: www.sota.edu.sg/sota-education/sota-curriculum/artistic-programmes/visual-arts.

Stein, S.N. (2013) Architecture and the senses: A sensory musing park. *University of Maryland*. Available at: http://drum.lib.umd.edu/handle/1903/14615.

Steiner, R. (1996) *The Education of the Child and Early Lectures on Education*. Hudson, NY: Anthroposophic Press.

The Montessori Foundation (2021) *The Montessori Foundation*. Available at: www.montessori.org/

Tuan, Y-F. (1978) *Space and Place: The Perspective of Experience*. Minnesota, MN: University of Minnesota Press.

University Arts London (2022) BA (Hons) ceramic design, *UAL*. Available at: www.arts.ac.uk/subjects/3d-design-and-product-design/undergraduate/ba-hons-ceramic-design-csm.

Varbelow, S. (2015) *Growing into the size of your feet: A narrative inquiry into the role early educational experiences play throughout life* (Thesis). Corpus Christi: Texas A & M University-Corpus Christi.

Varela, F.J. (1993) *The Embodied Mind: Cognitive Science and Human Experience*. London: MIT Press.

Vygotsky, L.S. (1978) *Mind in Society: The Development of Higher Psychological Processes, Mind in Society The Development of Higher Psychological Processes*. Cambridge: Harvard University Press.

Webb, S. (2020) 'Kant as a Revolutionary', *Journal of Philosophy of Education*, 54(6), 1534–1545. doi: 10.1111/1467-9752.12531.

Wenger, E. (2000) *Communities of Practice: Learning, Meaning, and Identity*. New York: Cambridge University Press.

Wolfe, P. (2010) *Brain Matters: Translating Research Into Classroom Practice*. Virginia: Association for Supervision and Curriculum Development (ASCD).

Woolner, P., McCarter, S., Wall, K. and Higgins, S. (2012) 'Changed learning through changed space: When can a participatory approach to the learning environment challenge preconceptions and alter practice?', *Improving Schools*, 1–14.

Zembylas, M. (2007) 'The specters of bodies and affects in the classroom: A rhizo-ethological approach', *Pedagogy, Culture and Society*, 15(1), 19–35.

3

SENSORY AFFECT IN DESIGN AND DESIGN EDUCATION

Introduction

This chapter briefly reviews the broad discourse of the senses in design and design education of the past and present to frame the need for an awareness of sensory affect in experiential learning and learning spaces today. To begin, the diverse inclusion of the senses in design are explored through a fleeting historical chronology. Sensory design can reach beyond purely thought to connect bodily experience to design, as the senses work in tandem to establish deeper levels of cognition and communication between the body and mind. Then, a few notable examples of sensory design are discussed in urban, playful, technological, and installation contexts. Next, the notion of sensory affect emerging in design education began with the material-led basic courses and studio learning spaces of the Bauhaus and Black Mountain College, in conjunction with the active, experiential pedagogies of Josef Albers and Johannes Itten, among others. Then, contemporary sensory-led learning spaces are discussed, as is an exploration of playful TEL spaces in design education. This chapter, by exploring sensory affect in design and design education, blends the lessons learnt from the past with the technological innovation of the future to emphasise the central sensory and experiential discourse of this book.

A brief history of the senses in design

Historically, the senses have been represented in a multitude of ways across art, design, and architecture. Art and the senses have a long-standing partnership, which has evolved from mainly visual processes of sensing and depicting events; luscious periods and times of hardship, skilfully rendered by those telling the visually rich stories of historical love and war, to the more multisensory conceptual telling of narratives in contemporary sculpture, digital installations, craft, photography, and

DOI: 10.4324/9781003175988-3

performance art, among others. As a newer 20th century development, design has seen a more recent turn towards the senses, emerging from the early days of print culture to the consistent inclusion of the senses in modern day processes such as biomimicry (the design and production of artefacts taking influence from and resembling nature) to touch graphics and UI (user interaction) design. Criticism on the senses in art and design can be drawn from prominent art critic Clement Greenburg's (1909–1994) argument of ocular dominance in visual art to Pallasmaas' architectural monograph *The Thinking Hand* (Jones, 2008; Pallasmaa, 2009). In this chapter, the value of the senses and sensory affect in design and design education is explored, and in recognition of 'the fertile territory of multisensory design' in our life worlds (Caroline Braumann, cited in Lupton and Lipps, 2018:6).

To begin, design evolved from the early origins of print culture, which developed over centuries and progressed towards contemporary forms of visual and non-visual design practice we know today. These transformative developments to print flourished when Johannes Gutenberg (1395–1468) invented moveable type c.1450 and with the advent of the Western printing press the mechanisation of visual reproduction began (later evolving naturally into graphic design in the 20th century). He notably printed the Gutenberg Bible, which demonstrated the possibilities of printing as a reproduceable medium. The subsequent introduction of the printed written word spread quickly throughout Europe. Then, in the early 1800s, the shift from oral to print culture continued as a direct consequence of the Industrial Revolution and with the age of steam, canals, and factories occurring between 1750 and 1850 (White, 2009). At this time, newspaper production thrived, representing a rising population and economy, increased literacy, and political interest, helping to define social classes and cultures (Musson, 1958; Mizruchi, 2008). Furthermore, in 1891, William Morris (1834–1896) encouraged better standards of production in the UK when he founded the Kelmscott Press in Hammersmith, London; a renewal in the craftsmanship of fine printing, binding, and papermaking had begun. With mass production and the application of photographic images into editorial and advertising communications now possible, the accompanying rise of consumerism began. The extensive use of commercial art in early advertising and promotion unleashed a flood of colourful visuals onto packaging and advertising (Meggs and Purvis, 2011). Therefore, print culture was established representing all forms of printed materials. Advertising, propaganda, and publishing were examples of disseminating visual communication quickly and effectively at this time (Eisenstein, 1980, 2012; Meggs and Purvis, 2011).

In the first half of the 20th century, the advent of higher quality printing presses further improved the legibility, clarity, and design of commercial typography and typesetting. This is in part due to the need to communicate specific messages quickly (and to obtain a desired response or initiate transactions) through knowledge transfer, political propaganda posters, and pictorial modernism, among others (Frascara, 2004; Armstrong, 2009). Key movements, such as Dada, Surrealism, Futurism, Constructivism, and de Stijl influenced the development of modernist design in the first half of the century. This gave way to an era characterised by industrialisation, social change, consumerism, and scientific innovation (Meggs and Purvis, 2011). The evolution of print culture continued into the 1950s and 1960s, when the lens of design focused on the move from formal and representational concerns towards explorations in semiotics and meaning making. Corporate identity and visual symbolic design began to develop. At this time, Raymond Loewy became the forefather of industrial design and product consumerism, developing trains, planes, cars, white goods, and the Coca Cola bottle (CMG Worldwide, 2020). Modernism also emerged in everyday domestic objects and appeared in world fairs across interior design, architecture, furniture design, and product design. The famous Modernist adage, 'form follows function' emerged as the purpose of the intended design became the starting point in the creative process and not primarily aesthetics (Greenhalgh, 2012).

In the latter half of the 20th century, Postmodernism emerged as a revolution against the legible ideas of Modernism, with visual forms of deconstruction, funky furniture (see Memphis Furniture as an example) and grunge typography developing (Moszkowicz, 2009; Meggs and Purvis, 2011). Postmodernism encompassed many design movements of the time and released a veritable sensory explosion of colour, form, and pattern in design. In the 1980s and 1990s, changes to the role of the traditional designer emerged as designers became authors, producers, activists, creative entrepreneurs, curators, and collaborators (Blauvelt, 2008; Steven McCarthy, 2013). Later in the 20th century, the digital revolution ignited, accelerated further by the arrival of the Internet, networked and interactive computer technology, meaning designers could investigate new technological and experimental processes in their creative practice. In the late 1990s, American designer April Greiman (1948–) was the first graphic designer to recognise the potential of Apple Mac computers as a new medium from which to experiment with hybrid imagery and digital printing techniques (Hillner, 2009). The influential design magazine, *Émigré*, also placed the affordances of computer-based design central to its brand. *Émigré's* founder Rudy Vanderlans (1955) sought to combine 'conventional methods of reproduction such as Xerox and letterpress technology with computer graphics and digital typography' (Hillner, 2009:87). The late 1980s and 1990s saw wide-ranging cultural investigations of the relationship between the body and electronic technologies 'from cyborgs to digital flâneurs to networked hive minds' (Jones, 2006:1). Creative expression began to change across design. Design shifted towards socially responsible, sustainable, wider socio-cultural, and citizenship accountabilities across interdisciplinary sensory practices via art and science, design and biology, and, of course, design and interactive, immersive technology (Resnick, 2016).

In sensory terms, technology has mainly afforded digital vision and screen-based haptic engagement, moving to the forefront of experiential design practice and education. Consequently, contemporary design practice now exists across a wide range of media and contexts, including interaction design, moving image, ambient advertising, human-centred design (HCD), interior environments, graphic design, product/industrial design, visualisation design (Virtual Reality (VR), Augmented Reality (AR) and Mixed Reality (MR)), User Experience (UX), User Interface

(UI), Customer Experience (CX) design, tactile fonts, sound design, and sonic branding. The future of design will continually be shaped by the ever-evolving technological apparatus at our fingertips, expanding the speculative boundaries of design production, creativity, and knowledge into speculative processes that are still emerging today (Dunne and Raby, 2014). Design now embraces cutting edge hybrid practices, as cross-, multi- and inter-disciplinary experimentation and exploration are key to current and emergent design methods. The blending of analogue and digital products alongside sensory-led processes also creates new aesthetic and functional opportunities for expression. Post-digital design, bio-design, and wearable design each address complex forms of new media and medical intervention, incorporating technology and the body (Yock et al., 2010; Myers, 2012; Maeda, 2020). Accordingly, designers today frequently adapt their cultural and contextual practice, as the discipline continually moves between, 'anonymity and authorship, the personal and the universal, social detachment and social engagement' (Armstrong, 2009:9). Furthermore, the boundaries between design disciplines are becoming blurred, driven by technological innovation and the need for merging the human body and experiential forms of 'feeling' design. In this mixed landscape of hand-driven, digital, human-centred, speculative, critical, and sensory design, designers are continually redefining human perception and interaction with the world (Schwartzman, 2011, 2015).

The senses in design today

The senses mix with memory.
The senses move us through space.
The senses merge and mingle.
The senses are unique to every person.
The senses trigger and amplify other senses.
The senses are plastic.
The senses chatter constantly with one another.
The senses have long been dominated by vision.
Sensory design rebels against the tyranny of the eye.
Sensory design enhances health and wellbeing.
Sensory design is inclusive.
Sensory design embraces human diversity.
Sensory design considers not just the shape of things but how things shape us – our behaviour, our emotions, our truth.

(Lupton and Lipps, 2018:10–15)

Sensory practice emerged in the 1960s as creative intersections formed between design and the body, and as design futures became 'sense-altering' (Schwartzman, 2011). Of course, vision, audio, and tactile experiences in design remain prolific with smell and taste continuing to be less present. Design often attempts to hybridise our experiences of the senses into a brand, product, system, or experience.

Design can encompass sensory techniques with immersive advertising campaigns using virtual or augmented reality to draw the consumer in, and interaction design systems embedded into our smartphone designs. Within these fluid, cross-disciplinary practices, there have many successful attempts to combine sensory craft processes and hand-driven material techniques with emerging digital realms.

Combining craft with technology

L'Artisan Electronique, created by Unfold Studio and Tim Knapen in 2010, combines one of the oldest artisanal techniques for making utilitarian objects – pottery – with new digital media through creating a virtual pottery throwing platform (Figure 3.1) (Unfold Studio and Knapen, 2010). Here, participants can experience the manual skills of pottery and working with clay making using technology; exchanging the slower wet-based messy process normally associated when throwing clay for a convenient, quicker dry-based digital form of production. The printing process imitates the traditional coiling technique used by ceramists, in which the form is built up by stacking coils of clay. The virtual pottery wheel, on the other hand, is a digital tool to 'turn' forms and objects in thin air (Unfold Studio and Knapen, 2010). In Figure 3.2, two gallery visitors throw a digital vase on the virtual pottery wheel during the 2010 Salone del Mobile in Milan, Italy. When your hand intersects the laser line, its profile is mirrored on-screen, and you can then virtually push your hand into the digital clay matter (Unfold Studio and Knapen, 2010). Then, fired and finished *l'Artisan Électronique* vases in porcelain and stoneware are produced and displayed as part of the installation. The

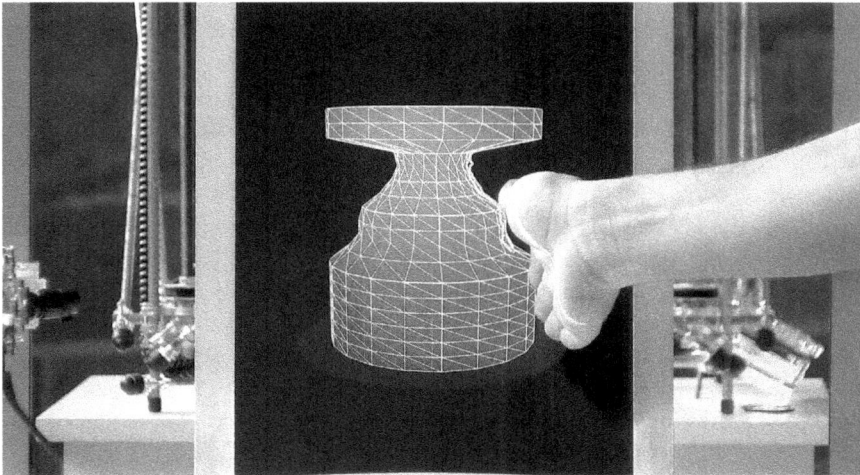

FIGURE 3.1   L'Artisan Électronique. Throwing a digital vase, ready for 3D printing in clay.

Source: © Unfold Studio and Knapen (2010), photo by Unfold Studio.

FIGURE 3.2 Throwing a digital vase.

Source: © Unfold Studio and Knapen (2010), photo by Peter Verbruggen.

sensory-based design of *l'Artisan Électronique* is undisputedly clever, highly visual, and haptic in its methods of engagement. The technological fabrication of coding attempts to imitate tactile sensory experience for the participants in a contemporary way (Unfold Studio and Knapen, 2010). *L'Artisan Electronique* was commissioned for the exhibition 'Design by Performance' by Z33, an arts institution in Hasselt that works at the intersection of art, design, and architecture (Z33, 2020).

Similarly, letterpress (printing from a raised solid image with pressure applied by hand using heavy rollers) thrived in design production from the 1900s through to the later decades of the 20th century. The physicality of using letterpress as a relief method in analogue forms of design and typography, can invoke strong nostalgic connotations when printing on older, heavy Heidelberg machinery, and with the potent smell of inks, wood, and metal. When touching the raised wooden and metal letter forms used for printing (the moveable typesetting invented by Gutenberg c. 1450) the fingertips feel the different grades of paper from which to print on. Letterpress has seen a healthy revival in the last few decades, despite letterpress workshops and facilities being rare to locate, especially in design education. A notable practitioner of letterpress and design, Alan Kitching (1940) turned to printing by hand as the world turned to digital creation. Kitchen established The New Typography Workshop in Somerset in 1989 (Kitching, 2022). He also taught letterpress and printmaking at the Royal College of Art in London, UK and his early printed letterform works in this field are highly regarded (Kitching et al., 2017). Very few design schools still host this technique in the changing face of contemporary design education. This is partly due to cost pressures and space provision in modern universities, and the larger student body now accessing higher education (Rigley, 2005). Design students who are fortunate enough to undertake a physical letterpress printing experience develop a strong material and aesthetic awareness. Glasgow School of Art in the UK is one of the few institutions still providing students with access to a dedicated letterpress room – the Case Room (Figure 3.3): '. . . with the Case Room, you print. The only way to see if you have something worthwhile is to print it, look at it and do it again. I like the idea of the hands-on aspect' (Design student cited in Marshalsey, 2017:259).

In 2011, and as a representation of traditional letterpress, John Bonadies launched *LetterMPress*, a Kickstarter-funded iPad app offering a detailed digital and visually realistic representation of letterpress printing (Figure 3.4) (Bonadies, 2020). The ingredients of letterpress printmaking are visually evident in the technology Bonadies developed, from the mixing of inks to the selection of paper, and the motion of hand-rolling is clever. The realistic, skeuomorphic design creates the illusion of real and alternative ways of engaging with letterpress via digital user experience (think 3D analogue TV controls on a digital screen) (Schwartz, 2017). Digital vision and touch replicate the experience of letterpress, mimicking the hands-on, and experiential learning technique, normally explored through the hands, eyes, ears, and nose.

FIGURE 3.3 The Case Room at Glasgow School of Art.

Source: © Lorraine Marshalsey.

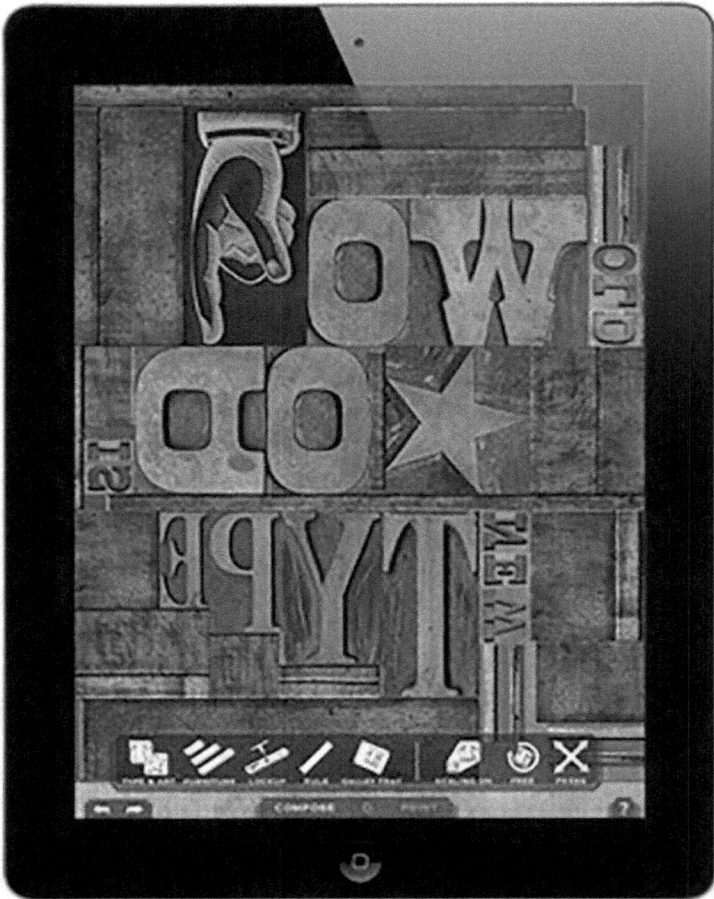

FIGURE 3.4 John Bonadies' *LetterMPress* app.

Source: © Bonadies (2020).

The body in digital contexts

The body as a tool in digital contexts, and as a technique used in immersive and interactive experiences, utilises approaches designed to appeal to the senses. Romy Achituv and Camille Utterback's *Text Rain* (1999) is an interactive installation, which provides a sense of playful digital gesture as participants catch falling type using their hands, bodies, arms, and tongues, 'to do what seems magical – to lift and play with falling letters that do not really exist' (Achituv and Utterback, 2009:online) (Figure 3.5). This installation responds to participant movements as words and phrases can form or fall when the body, or part of the body, is introduced or removed.

FIGURE 3.5   Romy Achituv and Camille Utterback's *Text Rain*, pictured at Virginia Museum of Contemporary Art, Virginia Beach, VA, 1999.

Source: © Achituv and Utterback (2009), Photography by Glen McClure.

In the Text Rain installation participants stand or move in front of a large projection screen. On the screen they see a mirrored video projection of themselves in black and white, combined with a colour animation of falling letters. Like rain or snow, the letters appear to land on participants' heads and arms. The letters respond to the participants' motions and can be caught, lifted, and then let fall again. The falling text will 'land' on anything darker than a certain threshold, and 'fall' whenever that obstacle is removed. If a participant accumulates enough letters along their outstretched arms, or along the silhouette of any dark object, they can sometimes catch an entire word, or even a phrase. The falling letters are not random, but form lines of a poem about bodies and language. 'Reading' the phrases in the Text Rain installation becomes a physical as well as a cerebral endeavour.

(Achituv and Utterback, 2009:online)

In the same way, Austrian graphic designer, Stefan Sagmeister (1962) often invokes the senses in his designs through the body. Sagmeister frequently invites participants to perceive diverse pleasurable and uncomfortable experiences in his physical and digital posters, book designs, and interactive installations. This can be seen in the tactile *Oubey Mindkiss* book with its pronounced three-dimensional raised book cover and the *Being Not Truthful Always Works Against Me*, an interactive digitally woven spiders web consisting of this phrase (Sagmeister and Ammer, 2006; Sagmeister and Woyde-Koehler, 2010). This interactive web breaks and re-assembles itself in response to participants severing the sticky web strands with hand, arm, leg, or body. Playful as this artwork is, many of Sagmeisters' works provoke uncomfortable reactions when he uses the body (often his own) as a canvas. His most controversial work was his 1999 *AIGA Detroit lecture poster*. In this work, Sagmeister is photographed fully nude and with words of the *AIGA Detroit* lecture event cut into the skin of his torso skin with a razor blade. His creative objective with this poster was to externally visualise the pain that accompanies many of his client-led design projects.

Scaling the senses via design can be seen in Kenichi Okada and Chris Woebken's series of wearable devices for children, *Animal Superpowers*. This series of works embodies and 'scales up' the sensory abilities of animals, insects, and birds, including giraffes and bats for children to experience. In the series, *Ant Apparatus* (Figure 3.6), the senses of an ant were magnified 50× for the child to see in real-time through microscope antennas. This apparatus allows the inquisitive child to see and move with their hands as they explore the world from the perspective of an ant, making the sensory and navigational abilities of animals accessible for them to experience (Okada and Woebken, 2008).

Smell and design

Smell is as surprising as it is ambiguous and part of our lifeworld navigation. Our olfactory sense can provoke us to interrupt, engage, or subconsciously recall a nostalgic or memory-laden experience through design. Smell is also the sense that most people are reluctant to engage with voluntarily, as an unknown entity and as a first-person experience – mostly due to the inability to identify if the smell will be foul or pleasant prior to the experience. Norwegian artist Sissel Tolaas (1959) collects, catalogues, and mimics the chemical compositions of smell as she

FIGURE 3.6 Ant Apparatus by Kenichi Okada & Chris Woebken.

Source: © Okada and Woebken (2008).

investigates and explains the language of odour. Tolaas uses scent-analysing technology to deconstruct smells into their chemical formula and for simulated reproduction. In 2005, at the Tirana Biennale, Tolaas collected the bodily smells of a group of men, who demonstrated altered bodily states because of being afraid of something or someone. Tolaas reproduced these smells and mixed them with wall paint for installation in her exhibition *FEAR of smell – the smell of FEAR* (Arning, 2006). Likewise, Dutch experience design collective Polymorf created *Avant Garden*, a speculative multisensory olfactory exhibition experience designed to activate human cooperation with smell. Polymorf used pioneering technologies to shape seven commissioned interactive olfactory installations. These exhibition installations endorsed future thinking around fine perfumery and sought to explore 'the possibilities of smell to facilitate meaningful human interaction' and asked 'How does scent fit into the technological revolution that is blurring the lines between the physical, digital and biological spheres?' (Polymorf, 2021:online).

Bio-design

When designing using the senses, bio-design (also known as biomanufacturing, bioprinting, or biological design) takes a radical approach, seeking to hybridise design, printing, manufacturing, and engineering with the living organisms of nature and science. Mycelium (a vegetable-based fungus) is an example of the organic matter used in bio-design to create architectural structures.

Bio-design harnesses living materials, whether they are cultured tissues or plants, and embodies the dream of organic design: watching objects grow and, after the first impulse, letting nature, the best among all engineers and architects, run its course.

(Myers, 2012:7)

Architects utilise biological materials as living structures, radically rethinking the vast potential of natural materials and sustainable practice when designing and building urban environments. *Fab Tree Hab* (Figure 3.7) draws upon technology and numerically produced scaffolding for the fabrication of houses, with structures inherently generated from a variety of slow-growing native trees 'Home, in this sense, becomes indistinct and fits itself symbiotically into the surrounding eco-system' (Terreform ONE [Open Network Ecology], 2022:online). The process of construction is deliberately unhurried as trees and plants are woven together, naturally growing over a removable computer-designed framework (Myers, 2012). This notion of living and growing trees at the centre of interior spaces functions not only as a core component of the architecture, but also as stronger connections are made between nature, space, and people. *Fab Tree Hab* was conceptually designed as an 'alternative to sterile, stand-alone homes that are at odds with their immediate environment' (Myers, 2012:58). Similarly, in 2009, Why Not Associates and artist Gordon Young "created a 'forest' of oak columns which are sited throughout the library and installed from floor to ceiling like supporting pillars" (Young, 2020:online). They produced a series of 14 non-growing oak typographic trees, using digital techniques to design the typefaces, which were then sandblasted into the timber. They then displayed the cut words onto the timber columns, which were chosen from library users' favourite books, places and memories, and

FIGURE 3.7 Fab Tree Hab, Terreform ONE, 2005.

Source: © Mitchell Joachim, Terreform ONE [Open Network Ecology] (2022).

FIGURE 3.8 Bio-digital Barcelona Chair, CCCB, 2010–2016.

Source: © Alberto T. Estévez, GENARQ/iBAG-UIC Barcelona (2022).

the varied literature nearby and installed within Crawley Library, Sussex in the UK (Young, 2020; Why Not Associates, 2022).

In Barcelona, a Bio-digital urban passage, featured the *Barcelona Chair* (Figure 3.8). This chair, designed by Alberto T. Estévez, was parametrically designed to combine a grassy field and a public bench, asserting that 'new ecologic-environmental architectural design does not imply creating in nature but creating with nature' (Estévez, 2015:20). Estévez (2021:12) works with natural 'software' (DNA), with live elements and with the application of real genetic processes to architecture, intended for 'automation' and natural growth. Second, he works with artificial 'software' (DNA) with computing elements, applying cybernetic processes to architecture, with digital design and production seen as a genetic process. Parametric design uses algorithmic thinking to devise required design outputs from a set of design intents and specified key parameters that suggests precise shapes and materials (Estévez, 2022).

This brief selection of sensory-led design examples is mainly nature-based interventions placed in architecture, museums, exhibitions, and public spaces to invoke a sensorial experience of nature in urban and residential locales. Resting our bodies and hands on tree structures or the grass of a bio digital chair signals to our bodies that nature is near, and sensory affect is activated as a positive interactive experience. The direct experience of physically touching natural materials, produced by craft and technological approaches, triggers affective maturation, 'focusing on the emergence of emotional and feeling capacities' (Kahn and Kellert, 2002:120). Sensory-led exploration, practice and production are already embedded in design education through a balance of craft and digital forms of experiential learning. Both approaches must be robustly supported to continue and not dissipate as let-terpress has, as these craft resources are critical and should not be universally pushed aside by TEL. Slower craft and faster digital methods of experiential learning can work in tandem to enrich the student experience of design. Sensory-led designed experiences, objects, structures, and furniture can be foregrounded and included in the learning spaces of design education for the benefit of educators and students. Now, this is rarely considered for the benefit of educator and student engagement despite the wealth of educational furniture and spatial designs in contemporary higher education. Objectives such as storage, colour, and layout, are taking prec-edent over ergonomic considerations and sensory affect – these human factors need to be taken further. Can we, as educators and students, actually sit on that swivel stool for hours? Can we stand at the smart whiteboard together in a group, with clear access for all of us, equally engaging as a team? Education is a core aspect of our life's journey, and we must attempt to answer this question – do the expe-riences, objects, structures, and furniture present in our specialised and generic learning spaces in design education support the senses? If so, how? If not, why not? How can we adjust and improve these for better participation and engagement? In support of sensory affect in experiential learning and learning spaces, and listening to the body in design education, we must remind ourselves of those lessons learnt from the history of design education and notable contemporary learning spaces, curriculum and educators who have previously driven an integration of the senses in teaching and learning, then and now.

Historical and contemporary sensory-led learning spaces, curriculum, and educators

The Bauhaus and Black Mountain College

It is widely recognised design education is student-centred and invokes Project-Based active Learning (PBL), balancing both individual and group work (Knaub et al., 2016). This approach to design education emerged from the experimental studio-based and student-led pedagogy noted in the basic courses that were held at the Bauhaus (a German art school which operated from 1919 to 1933) and at Black Mountain College (USA, 1933–1957). The Bauhaus effectively shaped a new modern design aesthetic and is arguably the most influential design movement and school to have emerged from the 20th century (Saletnik and Schuldenfrei, 2009). The Bauhaus curriculum taught the fundamentals of art and crafts educa-tion in a hands-on education (the pillar basic course), and then specialist craft train-ing would follow as expert-led workshops (in time the workshops moved from an artist and a craftsman led approach to one singular master-educator) (Goad et al., 2019:26–27). Collaborative practices, the broad 'learning by doing' approach, and the manual experience of materials was encouraged across all creative disciplines with students benefitting from, and supported by, creative practice-led educators and technical specialists at the Bauhaus. The material rudiments of the foundational this 6-month curriculum included classes in sculpture, carpentry, metalwork, pottery and ceramics, stained-glass construction, and weaving. Then, the students would progress to instruction in one workshop area of choice for the next 3 years. The list of workshops included furniture, metal, weaving, typography, wall-painting (mural), sculpture, stage and performance, and applied photography. Within these workshops, the students explored three critical aspects: (1) the study and analysis of nature using observation; (2) descriptive geometry, technique of construction, drawing plans and making models, as forms of representation; and (3) the theories of space, colour, and design to form compositions. Practical/manual and intellectual/theoretical studies were studied side-by-side, 'to release the creative powers of the student' (Bayer et al., 1938:26). The Bauhaus' objective was the connection of all processes of creation situated in one school through intellectual, manual, and technical methods 'to permit the development of every kind of talent' (Bayer et al., 1938:24–30).

Growing out of the demise of the Bauhaus after it was closed by the Nazi Government in Germany in the 1930s, Black Mountain College (BMC) continued the Bauhaus legacy in North Carolina, USA. BMC's underlying belief was to learn through experience via the acquisition of skills and techniques to make acquaintance with a changing world using a 'democratic, experimental spirit' (Harris, 2002:7). The key strength of BMC was its capacity to let creativity and production happen naturally without pressure from a rigid curriculum and, in doing so, it increased the chances for spontaneous and imaginative events to transpire. The educators of BMC were also highly experimental in their teaching practices and drew from John Dewey's principles of progressive education. These educators emphasised hands-on 'learning by doing', experiential projects, problem solving, creative and critical thinking, group work, collaboration and the development of social skills and community responsibility. Personalised learning journeys and individual goal setting were also key via a variety of learning resources and evaluation scenarios made available to the students. The experiential learning approach enabled and facilitated at these two institutions encouraged students to form their own practices and identities and to embrace new ways of learning by exploration (Katz et al., 2013:15). Bauhaus and Black Mountain College are historical examples of approaching design education with an enriching and sensory, yet exploratory material-led 'escalation of experience' and this experiential learning manifests in contemporary design education today (Füssl, 2006:81).

Johannes Itten and Josef Albers

Two of the most influential educators of the 20th century were Johannes Itten (1888–1967) and Joseph Albers (1888–1976). Itten initiated his teaching practices at the Bauhaus with his fundamental notion of the body as a sensory stimulus. The

Bauhaus basic course, originally developed by Itten then later by László Moholy-Nagy (1895–1946) and Albers, was a critical introduction to key knowledge and skills for designers. Within this course, Itten instilled rigorous first-hand experiences of working with a wide range of materials and techniques, across active exploration and experimentation, aimed at increasing the value of the student's perceptive influences (Heywood, 2020). Notably, Itten encouraged the students to approach the basic curriculum course from three directions; with their senses, with their intellectual responses, and with their synthetic realisations (Itten, 1975; Droste, 2006; Saletnik and Schuldenfrei, 2009). Itten began class by introducing morning exercises and encouraging the students to focus on their breathing, their bodily rhythmic movements and their vocal exercises to awaken the senses (Heywood, 2020).

> *Visual and tactile appreciation of rhythm in design, perhaps best understood as an aspect of a specific propriocentric sensory mode, was taught through bodily exercises akin to dance. The aim was to translate the experience of concentrated attention on flowing movement into hand and arm actions through which marks and drawings were made.*
> *(Heywood, 2020:5)*

Josef Albers was the link between the Bauhaus and Black Mountain College. He drew upon Dewey's learning theories to inform his own teaching practice at both institutions, encouraging independence and open-ended experimentation in his students, learning through investigation and constructions (Horowitz, 2006). Albers positioned the basic materials preliminary course at both the Bauhaus and Black Mountain College as a form of investigative play and he encouraged experimentation over study as a playful beginning develops confidence (Dearstyne, 1986:92). He advocated for the wide-ranging utilisation, application, and study of materials to improve eye to hand dexterity and for peer learning by teamwork with fluid open-ended time and ample space to do so (Füssl, 2006:83). Albers often used the entire learning space for lessons, which encouraged the body to move and assimilate with a range of teaching and learning styles (Sayal-Bennett, 2018). For example, Albers used the floor for critiquing three-dimensional paper constructions. The wall-painting (mural) workshop meant that students would directly paint onto the walls for lessons, with no paper or board in between hand and surface. The experiential learning practices and spaces, curriculum, and pedagogy of the Bauhaus and Black Mountain College and its ground-breaking educators, enabled the open-ended creative experimentation of material exploration, which is vital to design education. Itten and Albers championed creativity as the ability to produce something novel and original, and which actualises something real that was previously only potential and unreal (Shaw and Runco, 1994).

Singapore polytechnic's the writers room: playful learning

In more recent years, playful learning spaces are emerging in higher education. Singapore Polytechnic's *The Writers Room* was created for students of the Diploma

FIGURE 3.9 The Writers Room at Singapore Polytechnic

Source: © Singapore Polytechnic (2022).

in Creative Writing for TV and New Media (DTVM) within the School of Media, Arts and Design (Singapore Polytechnic, 2022) (Figure 3.9). This pioneering learning space fosters ideation and conceptualisation of story-writing without judgement. This room encourages the development of written narratives, characters, and plots through students playfully engaging with the environment of *The Writers Room*, which includes toys, sloped floors, soft cube furniture, and writable walls.

A place, a space, a room to explore
Ideas you could have, like never before
Doodle or crawl or jump or just stare
Whatever it takes, for the walls are bare
Toys and pens let you create
Your very own world, with your own trait
A classroom today, a castle tomorrow
A place to play, a hole to burrow
Cushions as chairs, blocks as tables
Let you produce, characters and fables
Sounds good, you think? Then let us groom
The creative mind in The Writers' Room.
© Gamar Abdul Aziz,
Singapore Polytechnic (2012)

This playfulness can be understood in the ways that students let their thoughts roam and go back and forth between varieties of affective processes and their cognitive abilities when material and spatial conditions engage them fully. Russ (1993, 1998), Brophy (2009), Cseh et al. (2014) address the importance of affect in creativity, the affective components and mechanisms of the creative process and the need to remove oneself from reality for our playfulness to emerge:

> *Play and playfulness encourage exploration and creativity and stimulate social interaction and competition. Play often provides satisfaction through a direct reward for one's successful actions and, most importantly, entertains and allows us to 'escape' from the realities of everyday lives.*
>
> *(Tsekleves and Darby, 2020:49)*

Specific processes occur including affect-laden thoughts of thinking and play; openness to affect states, such as anxiety and comfort; and affective pleasure in challenge and problem-solving. The cognitive abilities involved in creativity include divergent thinking, transformative capabilities, sensitivity to problems, practising with alternative solutions, a wide breadth of knowledge and insightful evaluation – which can be empowered in the appropriate spaces for learning through unrestricted play. Yet the personality traits, cognitive and affective processes that facilitate a student's creative abilities might be interrupted in learning spaces that do not support specialised play or supportive forms of play and sensory affect. Experimental play is critical to the creative process and the affective interactions educators and students experience through their bodies. In contemporary design education, we must instil the sensory exploration of hands-on and playful 'learning by doing' within teaching, learning, and learning spaces. There is an urgent need for design educators and students to be allowed to invoke playfulness as a sensory-led tool in learning spaces, for better teaching and learning experiences.

Playful Technology-Enhanced Learning (TEL) spaces in design education

The student population now experiences flexible forms of blended, online and distance curriculum delivery, and adaptable TEL in their learning spaces. TEL spaces have replaced many conventional SBL spaces in design education today (or the 'studio' has been reconfigured, becoming a computer-based 'lab'). In these digitally immersive physical spaces, teaching and learning experiences can now incorporate playful Augmented Reality (known by the acronym AR) and use smartphones to digitally access real-world settings as the impetus for engagement, or Virtual Reality (known by the acronym VR) using entirely computer-generated content. These approaches require VR headsets and digital tools to access virtually produced simulations. Moving forward, design education will continue to align and work in parallel with new directions in technology – moving from physical to purely non-physical learning spaces – as 'the next wave of technology is one you can feel'

FIGURE 3.10   CAVE2 Visualisation learning space at the University of the Sunshine Coast, Queensland, Australia.

Source: © Lorraine Marshalsey.

(Ultraleap, 2021). The future-focused acceleration of technology will bypass the current need for wearable devices, remote controllers, and touchscreens in education, generally – and reduce the spread of surface viruses.

The CAVE2™ Visualisation space at the University of the Sunshine Coast in Queensland, Australia, provides 2D and 3D teaching and learning experiences (Figure 3.10) (Danvel 360 Photography, 2021). The CAVE2™ utilises an 320°, 80-screen viewing podium, which dominates the viewer via visual and audio embodied engagement in the space. The entire body of the educator or student participates involuntarily as it turns towards the wall of screens. Interestingly, the CAVE2™ is situated in "its own bespoke building featuring ample room for 'break-out' sessions and separate presentation areas. Outside the building are covered study and meeting areas surrounded by stunning architecture and lush Queensland foliage" (University of the Sunshine Coast, 2022). This discourse suggests that the CAVE2™ is the communal epicentre of a much broader educational and natural environment, and mindful of diverse human needs inclusive of technology, community, the outdoors, and private space. However, I do wonder how widely accessible the CAVE2™ is to design educators and students, as new and innovative technological spaces are expensive and precious to university governance and often kept securely under lock and key. In terms of teaching and learning, the requirement to cap student numbers in the space would reduce the flexibility of learning tasks when only small groups of students can use the 2D or 3D features. Although, as a panoramic wall of screens upon which to present to others, CAVE2™ fulfils this requirement. In future iterations of similar learning spaces, how might these spaces be responsive to human embodiment and sensory affect? Can this space evolve to work directly with our bodies in teaching and learning while sitting on the floor, watching projections on the ceiling, and so on, as is seen in many immersive installations in museums, planetariums, and exhibitions? The carpeted floor and dark ceiling of CAVE2™ projects a distinctly cinematic rather than pedagogical experience.

The Immerse Studio learning space at the same Australian university felt more diverse and useable as a two-way interactive teaching and learning experience. The digital screens of the Immerse Studio were placed on four 90° angles rather than the panoramic curve of the CAVE2™ space. However, the control room, attached to this space, is operated by an educator or technician, and removed any direct interaction between student and space, reducing creative control. When I visited this space, I observed that a student could provide a single vector file pattern for display in the Immersive Studio. This small vector pattern could be repeated uniformly on every screen of this learning space, replicating, and duplicating the design repeatedly, and projecting a realistic visualisation of a textile or wallpaper design. The Immerse Studio learning space was also demonstrated as a real-time driving experience with the controls of a car visualised on screen using VR tools (Figure 3.11).

Summary

This chapter has provided a very brief overview of the landscape of sensory design and the senses in design education from a fleeting contextual perspective; indeed, this entire subject could fill this volume several times over. The intention here was

FIGURE 3.11 Immerse Studio learning space at the University of the Sunshine Coast, Queensland, Australia.

Source: © Lorraine Marshalsey.

to provide a transitory snapshot of the inclusion of the senses through time in both design and educative experiences. In summary, the senses in creative practice have moved from oral to visual histories through the mechanisation of print, to the ocular dominance of vision across hundreds of years in art, design, and architecture – from reading the printed written word to touching and engaging with digital screens. Sensory affect in design education emerged within the material-led hands-on and experiential tuition provided to students as part of the basic courses at the Bauhaus and Black Mountain College, led by progressive educators such as Josef Albers and Johannes Itten, among others. The 20th century saw an explosion of design as the Bauhaus and the Black Mountain College (among others) sought to shape design education, then several movements including modernism and post-modernism formed future iterations of design as we know it today. In today's inter-disciplinary design fields, the fluid boundaries afforded by time and innovation means the senses in design are now vital when developing solutions and interventions to health, transport, the climate crisis, urban, technological, and education contexts. Designers are turning to nature to reconnect our bodies with our life worlds and providing unique experiences for our beneficial wellbeing, using the latest technological developments to do so.

While design has seen a chronological and outward expansion throughout recent centuries, most noticeably in the 20th century, design education continues to move in and out of focus, depending on a range of societal challenges and technological developments. However, sensory teaching and learning methods today tend to inculcate technological advancement, respond to university-as-a-business pressures, and often limit the inclusion of true authentic experiential learning or ignore the playful potential of those spaces provided for learning. This chapter, by briefly exploring sensory affect in design and design education, acknowledges these lessons learnt from the past while being mindful of the technological advancements still very much a part of our continuing design and educational futures. The following three chapters unpack three distinct themes (*all-surface use, empowerment and lastly, flexibility*) as a series of actionable strategies for educators and students, who face the challenges of cost pressures, more teaching for less, the balancing of craft and digital practice, who seek playfulness, experiential learning and better engagement in their teaching and learning spaces, offline and online.

References

Achituv, R. and Utterback, C. (2009) *Text Rain, Romy Achituv – Selected Projects and Sketches*. Available at: http://gavaligai.com/filter/all/Text-Rain.

Armstrong, H. (2009) *Graphic Design Theory: Readings From the Field*. New York: Princeton Architectural Press.

Arning, B. (2006) 'Sissel Tolaas', In Jones, C.A. (ed), *Sensorium: Embodied Experience, Technology and Art*. Cambridge, MA: MIT Press.

Bayer, H., Gropius, W. and Gropius, I. (1938) *Bauhaus, 1919–1928*. New York: The Museum of Modern Art.

Blauvelt, A. (2008) Towards relational design, *The Design Observer Group*. Available at: http://designobserver.com/feature/towards-relational-design/7557/.

Bonadies, J. (2020) *App design: Virtual letterpress for iPad*. Available at: https://bonadiescreative.com/app-design-virtual-letterpress-for-ipad.

Brophy, K. (2009) *Patterns of Creativity (Consciousness, Literature & the Arts)*. Amsterdam: Rodopi.

CMG Worldwide (2020) *Raymond Loewy*. Available at: www.raymondloewy.com/.

Cseh, G.M., Phillips, L.H. and Pearson, D.G. (2014) 'Flow, affect and visual creativity', *Cognition & Emotion*, 1–11. doi: 10.1080/02699931.2014.913553.

Danvel 360 Photography (2021) *Visual learning, university of the sunshine coast*. Available at: www.panowalks.com/embed/Pd5NZbOxuBPd41MPkduvYbdrN2b2/.

Dearstyne, H. (1986) *Inside the Bauhaus*. New York: Rizzoli International Publications.

Droste, M. (2006) *Bauhaus: 1919–1933*. London: Taschen.

Dunne, A. and Raby, F. (2014) *Speculative Everything: Design, Fiction, and Social Dreaming*. Cambridge, MA: MIT Press.

Eisenstein, E.L. (1980) *The Printing Press as an Agent of Change*. Cambridge: Cambridge University Press.

Eisenstein, E.L. (2012) *The Printing Revolution in Early Modern Europe*. Cambridge: Cambridge University Press.

Estévez, A.T. (2015) *Biodigital Architecture & Genetics. Writings 1*. Barcelona: Universitat Internacional de Catalunya (UIC).

Estévez, A.T. (2021) *Biodigital Architecture & Genetics. Writings 2*. Barcelona: Universitat Internacional de Catalunya (UIC).

Estévez, A.T. (2022) Projects and works, *Genetic Architectures Group & Office – iBAG-UIC Barcelona*. Available at: http://geneticarchitectures.weebly.com/projects-office.html.

Frascara, J. (2004) *Communication Design: Principles, Methods, and Practice*. New York: Allworth Press.

Füssl, K-H. (2006) 'Pestalozzi in Dewey's Realm? Bauhaus Master Josef Albers among the German-speaking Emigrés' colony at black mountain college (1933–1949)', *Paedagogica Historica*, 42(1–2), 77. doi: 10.1080/00309230600552013.

Goad, P., Stephen, A., McNamara, A., Edquist, H., Wünsche, I. and Perren, C. (2019) *Bauhaus Diaspora and beyond : Transforming Education through Art, Design and Architecture*. Melbourne: The Miegunyah Press, Melbourne University Publishing Ltd.

Greenhalgh, P. (2012) *Modernism in Design*. London: Reaktion Books Ltd.

Harris, M.E. (2002) *The Arts at Black Mountain College*. Cambridge.: MIT Press.

Heywood, I. (2020) *Sensory Arts and Design, Sensory Arts and Design*. London: Routledge.

Hillner, M. (2009) *Virtual Typography*. Lausanne: AVA Publishing SA.

Horowitz, F.A. (2006) *Josef Albers: To Open Eyes: The Bauhaus, Black Mountain College, and Yale*. London: Phaidon Press Ltd.

Itten, J. (1975) *Design and Form: The Basic Course at the Bauhaus and Later*. London: John Wiley & Sons.

Jones, C.A. (2006) *Sensorium: Embodied Experience, Technology and Contemporary Art*. London: MIT Press.

Jones, C.A. (2008) *Eyesight Alone: Clement Greenberg's Modernism and the Bureaucratization of the Senses*. Chicago: University of Chicago Press.

Kahn, P.H. and Kellert, S.R. (2002) *Children and Nature: Psychological, Sociocultural, and Evolutionary Investigations*. Cambridge, MA: MIT Press.

Katz, V., Brody, M., Creeley, R. and Power, K. (2013) *Black Mountain College: Experiment in Art*. London: MIT Press.

Kitching, A. (2022) *The new typography workshop*. Available at: www.newtypographywork-shop.com/.

Kitching, A., Walters, J.L., Sayer, P. and Birdsall, D. (2017) *Alan Kitching: A Life in Letterpress*. London: Laurence King Publishing.

Knaub, A.V., Foote, K.T., Henderson, C., Dancy, M. and Beichner, R.J. (2016) 'Get a room: The role of classroom space in sustained implementation of studio style instruction', *International Journal of STEM Education*, 3(1), 1–22. doi: 10.1186/s40594-016-0042-3.

Lupton, E. and Lipps, A. (2018) *The Senses: Design Beyond Vision*. New York: Princeton Architectural Press.

Maeda, J. (2020) 'Design education in the post-digital age', *Design Management Review*, 31(1), 41–48. doi: 10.1111/drev.12201.

Marshalsey, L. (2017) *An investigation into the experiential impact of sensory affect in contemporary Communication Design studio education* (Thesis). The Glasgow School of Art. Available at: http://radar.gsa.ac.uk/5894/.

Meggs, P.B. and Purvis, A.W. (2011) *Meggs' History of Graphic Design*. Hoboken, NJ: John Wiley & Sons.

Mizruchi, S.L. (2008) *The Rise of Multicultural America: Economy and Print Culture, 1865–1915*. Chapel Hill, NC: University of North Carolina Press.

Moszkowicz, J. (2009) *A re-evaluation of historical precedents in the age of new media* (Thesis). Bristol: University West of England.

Musson, A.E. (1958) 'Newspaper printing in the industrial revolution', *The Economic History Review*, 10(3), 411–426. doi: 10.2307/2591261.

Myers, W. (2012) *Bio Design: Nature, Science, Creativity, Museum of Modern Art*. New York: Museum of Modern Art.

Okada, K. and Woebken, C. (2008) *Animal superpowers, chriswoebken.com*. Available at: https://chriswoebken.com/ANIMAL-SUPERPOWERS.

Pallasmaa, J. (2009) *The Thinking Hand: Existential and Embodied Wisdom in Architecture*. Chichester: John Wiley & Sons.

Polymorf (2021) *Avant garden*. Available at: www.polymorf.nl/interaction/avant-garden/.

Resnick, E. (2016) *Developing Citizen Designers*. London: Bloomsbury Academic.

Rigley, S. (2005) 'Thinking in solid air. Design educators are finding that letterpress nurtures creativity and visual abstraction', *Eye Magazine*, 15(57). Available at: www.eyemagazine.com/feature/article/thinking-in-solid-air.

Russ, S.W. (1993) *Affect and Creativity: The Role of Affect and Play in the Creative Process*. Hillsdale: L. Erlbaum Associates.

Russ, S.W. (1998) *Affect, Creative Experience and Psychological Adjustment*. Ann Arbor, MI: Taylor & Francis.

Sagmeister, S. and Ammer, R. (2006) Being not truthful always works against me, *The Art Institute of Chicago*. Available at: www.artic.edu/artworks/197545/being-not-truthful-always-works-against-me-edition-1-10.

Sagmeister, S. and Woyde-Koehler, D. (2010) *OUBEY Mindkiss*. Berlin: Deutscher Kunstverlag.

Saletnik, J. and Schuldenfrei, R. (2009) *Bauhaus Construct: Fashioning Identity, Discourse and Modernism*. London: Routledge.

Sayal-Bennett, A. (2018) *Posthuman pedagogy: Affective learning encounters in studio art practice* (Doctoral thesis). Goldsmiths, University of London. doi: 10.25602/GOLD.00024089.

Schwartz, E. (2017) *Exploring Experience Design*. Birmingham: Packt Publishing.

Schwartzman, M. (2011) *See Yourself Sensing: Redefining Human Perception*. London: Black Dog Publishing.

Schwartzman, M. (2015) *See Yourself X: Human Futures Expanded*. London: Black Dog Publishing.

Shaw, M.P. and Runco, M.A. (1994) *Creativity and Affect*. Norwood: Ablex Publishing Corporation.

Singapore Polytechnic (2022) *The writers' room*. Available at: www.sp.edu.sg/sp/about-sp/visit-us/VirtualTour.

Steven McCarthy (2013) *The Designer as . . . : Author, Producer, Activist, Entrepreneur, Curator, and Collaborator: New Models for Communicating*. Amsterdam: BIS Publishers.

Terreform ONE [Open Network Ecology] (2022) *Fab tree hab*. Available at: https://terreform.org/fab-tree-hab.

Tsekleves, E. and Darby, A. (2020) 'The Role of Playfulness and Sensory Experiences in Design for Public Health and for Ageing Well', In Ian, H. (ed), *Sensory Arts and Design*. London: Routledge.

Ultraleap (2021) *Digital worlds That feel human. World leading hand-tracking and haptics*. Available at: www.ultraleap.com/.

Unfold Studio and Knapen, T. (2010) *l'Artisan Électronique*. Available at: http://unfold.be/pages/l-artisan-electronique.html.

University of the Sunshine Coast (2022) *CAVE2™ and the community, Visualisation and simulation*. Available at: www.usc.edu.au/study/life-at-usc/facilities/visualisation-and-simulation/cave2-and-the-community.

White, M. (2009) The industrial revolution, Georgian Britain. *The British Library*. Available at: www.bl.uk/georgian-britain/articles/the-industrial-revolution.

Why Not Associates (2022) *Crawley library, Why not associates*. Available at: https://whynotassociates.com/environmental/crawley-library.

Yock, P.G., Makower, J. and Zenios, S.A. (2010) *Biodesign: The Process of Innovating Medical Technologies*. Cambridge: Cambridge University Press.

Young, G. (2020) *Typographic trees, gordonyoung.info*. Available at: https://gordonyoung.info/typographictrees/.

Z33 (2020) *Z33*. Available at: www.z33.be/en/.

4

ALL-SURFACE USE IN DESIGN-BASED LEARNING SPACES

Introduction

Identifying and recognising the critical properties of sensory affect to empower reflective teaching and experiential learning in design education, and associated learning spaces, can be complex and challenging. In the previous three chapters, this book has addressed a small portion of a much bigger landscape, in terms of discussing design education of the past and present, sensory affect as its own entity, and aspects of sensory affect fused with design and design education. The first half of this book has, effectively, set the scene and defined sensory affect, experiential learning, learning spaces, and design education, alone and in combinations of each other. Now, the latter half of this book turns towards action. The following chapters dynamically embrace sensory affect in experiential learning, learning spaces and design education through reflective teaching approaches, methods, and strategies.

This chapter, and the following two chapters, unpack three distinct actionable themes, as a series of strategies for design educators to reflect upon; *all-surface use, empowerment*, and *flexibility*. First, I start with the fundamental 'skeleton' of design education – the physical space itself and the materials, boundaries, and surfaces available to teaching and learning. This chapter explores physical, specialised, online, communal, legacy, and outdoor learning spaces, concluding with practical implications of *all-surface use* in design-based learning spaces. Chapter 5 addresses *empowerment* in design education via a sense of place, environmental stressors, restorative environments, and structures of shared power in the Co[D]P (Wenger, 2000). This chapter addresses the 'heart' of design education; empowering the things we feel, embody, nurture, and believe in as human educators and students. This chapter closes with a series of diagnostic methods and strategies to identify sensory affect in design-based learning spaces. The subsequent Chapter 6 focuses

DOI: 10.4324/9781003175988-4

on the 'brain' of design education; our inherent abilities to indicate our need for flexibility and freedom of choice. Chapter 6's discourse focuses on *flexibility* and the capabilities of choice to adjust sensory affect within experiential learning. Through the lens of sensory affect, I activate these three themes through a series of strategies and recommendations in the second half of this book. In this way, we can be vested in choosing our ideal educational environments, our preferred conditions for teaching and learning, and be empowered to model our curriculum and pedagogies in design education in our own way.

Starting with a blank canvas

Every empty room or outdoor space can evolve with human participation and activity into a learning space, and the furniture, objects, and resources we place on walls, the ground, the windows and hang from the ceilings provide character and identity to the space. University directives assign a role and purpose for teaching classrooms, corridors, and campus spaces, often by academic need and specialism, and student numbers. In higher education, an empty generic classroom, specialised workshop or studio, online platform, legacy, communal or outdoor space is a blank canvas as a learning space for design education. We (as design educators) must figure out how to make the most of the space, when considering its intended purpose. Educators are central to this embodied dialogue of learning spaces and student engagement, as Brown (2019:93) says, 'To understand what I do in the teaching situation, I need to experience, feel and be grounded in my body'. How do educators transform an empty learning space or area into an engaged space for learning in design education today? Clearly, educators need to prepare the tools, strategies, and environments to makes spaces for learning inclusive, engaging, and diverse: 'Specific objects of learning have specific keys, and, without them, the intended learning cannot take place' (Marton, 2014:xii).

Empty studios instil a sense of excitement and enthusiasm in those artists or designers about to populate these specialised spaces at the beginning of their creative journeys. Can we foster the same feelings in university-led learning spaces in design education? How can we support design educators and students to fully invest themselves in their learning spaces (specialised or generic, creative, or non-creative) throughout a 3- or 4-year design degree in higher education today? If we start with an empty space, how can it be turned into a successful, thriving sociable design-based learning space, embedded with the necessary conditions for authentic, practice-based teaching, learning and engagement? Foregrounding an awareness of the impact of sensory affect in experiential learning and learning spaces can improve the practical and conceptual teaching and learning activities to take place there, therefore engaging students. New concepts and discoveries emerge and 'thinking-by-learning-by-doing' becomes increasingly visible via objects, artefacts, drawings, ideas, and collaborations. Today, these concrete happenings are normally instigated by a pre-planned (yet often squeezed) design curriculum, timetabling, and pedagogy. Cognition, arising from experiential learning and practice, and the community of practice (CoP) instigated within a learning space emerges from within these parameters (Wenger, 2000). As Nair and Doctori (2019:11–13) say, we must first live comfortably and relax there, then we play, experiment and actively engage in order to finally create, perform, and present finished solutions and artefacts. The role of the learning space is a critical lifeworld for students' design practice and education.

The prepared environment

The prepared environment serves as a bridge between teaching and learning, bringing real life into the design studio via knowledge, processes, production techniques, resources, artefacts, and projects, and all within reach of the student. Although aimed at early years education, Montessori proposed the educational environment should be attractive, in both aesthetics and practicality, and should appeal to different age groups. The environment should be resourceful, and inviting to stimulate interest and purposeful activity, to foster experimentation and development via personal abilities and preferred speeds of learning. These environments should also reflect organisation and order, for the community of practice to function properly, 'to allow every individual the freedom of independent activity, without interfering with that of others' (Montessori, 1970:5). Montessori described this as like a traffic system; containing all objects and students in a way that can respectfully interact and deviate at the sections of physical flow. There should be 'ample opportunity in the environment to be practised, worked through and integrated . . . limitations as well as possibilities should be taken into consideration' (Montessori, 1970:5).

As Corazzo (2019:1255) noted, studies of the material space and preparedness of design education environments are rare to locate, although the material space of the studio is critical to learning together and 'enables or constrains activities, experiences and interactions'. University leaders may have utilised research-funded, cutting-edge educational environments (such as smart-schools and creative innovation labs) as showcase spaces for corporate events, keynotes, symposiums, visiting international groups and so on, but these are rarely used for day-to-day educative purposes. In design education, educators and students experience prepared environments in higher education as open plan and large generic-based closed learning spaces (meant for large groups of people to work together but alone), clean, carpeted and with TEL installed.

Open-plan learning spaces mimic office-like layouts with the benefits and challenges of these spaces for specialised design education still being questioned. Since the 1970s, open plan teaching and learning spaces have become increasingly widespread as designed educational environments, yet equally contested as unproductive layouts. A wealth of literature continues to argue for and against this layout. In these spaces, educators and students often describe constant noise disruption, visual disruption, a lack of concentration and the challenges of hosting one-on-one discussions or to maintain whole class engagement. Educators and students can feel watched and analysed in open plan learning spaces, which also erodes confidence and concentration. Open plan designed learning spaces sit uncomfortably with conventional design studio circulation, where both educators and students mingle freely. It also becomes challenging to host a studio critique, as a central element of design studio pedagogy. Critiques can occur spontaneously or planned, formally or informally, individually or in groups, at desks, on the floor or in corridors in design education – in any accessible and suitable space. Commonly, these open plan spaces contain groups of desk islands or are divided and partitioned into cubicle stations, with an overabundance of moveable furniture and desks that become obstacles. Students twist in their chairs to look at the educator positioned at the front-and-central projection screen and often do not have enough space to branch out and work on the walls or floors.

Similarly, sizeable glass partitioned learning spaces are often meant for groups of students to be seen working as an industrious collective, separated yet connected (Figure 4.1). However, glass-walled learning spaces can foster distraction among educators and students, especially as linked open plan environments. These types of learning spaces are notoriously unpopular with many design educators due to the noise levels from neighbouring classes. Sensory affect can originate from internal and external stimuli and experiences, within the community of practice, and from the physical environment. The connotations of sensory affect within design education and these prepared learning spaces of higher education,

FIGURE 4.1 Glass partitioned learning spaces where design is taught.

Source: © Lorraine Marshalsey.

manifesting as loud noise, silence or visual distractions intermittently disrupt or support students' natural flow and creativity (Csikszentmihalyi, 2013). This is the prepared environments of design education today, leaving many design students adrift and disengaged.

Prepared interior spaces in contemporary design-based learning spaces in university settings reflect the same ingredients as offices, and the more attractive the learning space looks, assumptions are made that the space works well. However, design-based learning spaces require different interpretations of these criteria. In renovated, pre-prepared campus spaces, the popular criteria for contemporary interior design in higher education include:

1   Visual attractiveness of the space
2   Tall ceilings
3   Open plan
4   Physical and digital connectedness
5   Technology-Enhanced Learning (TEL) capabilities
6   Multi-usage layouts
7   Adaptable configurations
8   Brightly coloured furniture and furnishings
9   Ample seating of variable heights
10 Display areas
11 Communal workspaces
12 Free movement around the space
13 Natural light and clear visibility
14 Plentiful resources
15 Sufficient storage
16 Comfortable and warm temperatures
17 Clean and neat environments
18 Visual inspiration
19 Meditative, natural surroundings (preferably looking out the windows to trees and parkland).

In addition to these criteria, design education needs prepared and specialised studio learning environments with assigned individual workstations for educators and students, fully accessible specialist resources, unique and accessible workshop facilities (managed by technicians), outdoor areas for creative expansion and teaching opportunities, and fluid seminar rooms with plenty of wall space and whiteboards. Furthermore, sufficient storage may not necessarily be high-volume small lockers but instead be large-scale physical and online storage facilities for numerous prototypes, scaled furniture design or drying facilities for printmaking or textile design. Visual inspiration could take the form of fully scaled prototypes, influential design posters and students' messy work-in-progress pinned to the walls rather than colourful walls and fabrics. Clean and neat often sits at odds with essential creative mess in design production and practice. Plentiful resources may be defined as specialist, diverse, state-of-the-art, natural, or man-made materials produced and assembled using newer digital and older analogue machinery.

The following sections explore a range of further questions and potential suggestions when seeking to understand educational environments in design education today. However, I have purposely not included visual or diagrammatic configurations, layouts, or solutions to the arrangement of learning spaces as one size does not fit all. Every learning space needs to be approached and addressed with a fluid mindset, and through the lens of the felt sense to understand the experiential impact of sensory affect disturbing that exact environment. Educators must first *feel* the space and then take appropriate action to address the issues present in their own educational environments in design teaching and learning. We must return to the naturalness and humanness of space sensed through the bodies of those people using these learning spaces every day.

The ideal studio through student eyes

In early 2015, as a research method to understand design students' perspectives on their studio learning spaces, I asked a group of 50 third-year design students, who were enrolled in a design program at a university in Queensland, Australia, to draw their ideal studio in less than 15 minutes. This was an ethnographic research method, as a visual deviation of Photovoice, a form of arts-based visual ethnography in action. It elicits responses from individuals as an image-based discovery and action method of storytelling (Delgado, 2015). Students were asked to devise their ideal studio learning space by drawing scenes. This visual method enables a powerful expression of subjective perceptions, as the responsibility to create their preferred images of studio as a site for learning is placed directly in the hands of the students.

I gave the students no prior information or parameters on what the studio as a site for learning or learning space should look like in design education. This was an exercise conducted during a regular class to gather the students' subjective thoughts and perceptions of what their preferred studios might look like, and as an indication of their favoured conditions for better engagement. Their current learning space was dark, carpeted, with intermittent motion-activated timed lighting and with small windows, with a large screen at one end of the room for their educator to deliver content. Their produced drawings contained many elements not seen in normal learning spaces. These elements included indoor plants (trailing plants and plants in pots), visual inspiration on the walls and ceilings (periodic table of typefaces on the ceiling, the front covers of design magazines and large artwork on the walls), stacks of books and 'instaframes' (digital photo frames enabling a carousel of images to be shown) displayed on shelving. Light was key and the students included large wall-size windows with views outdoors to palm trees and cactus. For working areas, a desk was crucial, equipped with over-size double monitors and a laptop, and a desk stool or chair with wheels. Comfort areas for breaks, thinking or reading were also visible in the drawings and included swinging chairs hung from the ceiling, hammocks, rugs, and beanbags. Floors were not carpeted but wooden or polished concrete and the walls were exposed brick or colourful with mirrors. Light fittings were large, designer downlights and not harsh, fluorescent strip lighting. The students may have designed their ideal studio spaces in the manner of replicating professional studios or their own preferred home-based studio in this task. Nonetheless, comfort and the visibility of creative influences, light and nature were key themes. My point is that students *know* what would engage them in a learning space – generally, a designated, private area for them to work which provides relaxed settings, fresh air and light, and visible sources of inspiration were critical conditions for working.

A few years later, I asked a different group of third-year design students in this same university in Queensland, Australia, to analyse their existing day-to-day learning spaces on campus using an iPad®. Photos were taken of each learning space they occupied, and I asked them to digitally draw on top of the image, using illustration software Procreate®, as a method of analysis. No other directions were given. From these images the design students identified their central working areas as grouped tables with dense triangles of colour. No wall, floor, or ceiling surfaces were selected or considered for analysis. Small sporadic groups of marks indicated the transient areas of the carpeted high-turnover, timetabled learning space. The PC Lab with rows of fixed computing stations (in the mark making, dark lines were added in rows to represent this), the students had drawn storm clouds and rain drops to signify the low temperatures in this very cold room as the air conditioner could not be locally adjusted. Interestingly, this learning space was also deemed to be a silent working space; 'shhhhhh!!' (Figure 4.2). The students designated Work-Integrated-Learning (WIL) drop-in design studio was seen to be the most busy

FIGURE 4.2 A student's interpretation of their PC Lab.

Source: © Lorraine Marshalsey.

and productive space with room for movement, sensory-led comforts, and relaxed surroundings vis the astro-turf rugs, coffee tables, bookshelves, blackboard painted walls, sofa, and computing desks.

Often, learning spaces do not align with the ideal studio-based environments students prefer despite several studies addressing the effectiveness of classroom and learning space design on students' performance and learning (Barrett et al., 2015; Ariani and Mirdad, 2016). Many of the aspects identified by students as beneficial for their learning and engagement in design education are missing on campus but are present to a degree in many home learning environments.

Indoor learning spaces

Design educators and students have the power to arrange their learning spaces at home, based on their preferences, but they have no say in the design of their physical, online, and distance learning spaces on campus. On campus or at home, generally, often the size and layout of a room or platform identifies its appropriateness as a learning space. At home, design educators and students tend to choose the smallest room, alcove, or corner of a larger room to situate a physical desk and organise their study materials. Very few homes have enough space for actual home-based design studios. If they do, these are in the garage, shed or other garden-based room. These spaces are often not fully specialised learning spaces and without adequate resources and machinery. Additionally, small rooms do not always equate to quieter, focused learning spaces and large, open plan rooms do not always support group learning. Today, design teaching and learning ensues across a blended mix of physical, online and distance education, in a combination of campus and home-based learning spaces. Regardless of the location, design educators and students must learn to first *sense* their chosen environment through listening to their bodies, to first identify the preliminary advantages and disadvantages of a learning space. Second, in conjunction with intended purpose and practicality, they should use their bodies as a guide via the following sensory lenses and identify the appropriateness of their preferred educational environments in these contexts.

Thresholds and entrances

As we know, physical thresholds and entrances separate the internal learning space from external spaces, and act as an intervening barrier for the potential noise and visual interference from people external to the learning space. Thresholds and entrances provide an important tangible, physical entrance to cross, signalling to the design educator or student they are stepping into a creative workshop, seminar space or home-based study room from which participation in learning is activated. Therefore, thresholds and entrances should have a barrier to cross, which does not entirely exclude the world but holds it at arms' length. This clearly signals the crossing of a boundary into an educational period of time to focus and the students know to expect their immersion in teaching and learning tasks and their participation within a community of practice (physical or online) (Wenger, 2000).

However, design students face several challenges when setting up and securing a reasonably productive learning space at home. The interior of a student's home is not normally designed for rigorous and creative design study and practice with readily available specialist design resources. Apart from the potential inclusion of a small study space in a bedroom in the home, there is often little or no space to set up a private and permanent design workstation, especially in shared houses. A similar yet scaled down notion of crossing thresholds and entrances should apply to home-based learning spaces but often this is more difficult to achieve. Thresholds to delineate these as spaces for learning are normally solid bedroom or study doors, designed to afford privacy and concentration, excluding the intrusion of pets, housemates, and family who may share the home. I briefly surveyed my own students a few years ago on the actual learning spaces they used at home. The three scenarios they identified as home-based learning spaces included (1) a dedicated workstation in their own private bedroom or similar space, which was theirs to own and kept reasonably tidy, (2) a shared workstation in a communal space in the house, which was kept reasonably tidy with materials and resources tidied up at the end of each learning episode, or (3) teaching and learning materials strewn across their own bed or bedroom floor, which were tidied up at the end of each learning episode (or sometimes, not at all). These learning spaces are still not ideal for design education as specialist resources, materials, techniques, processes, and surfaces are not always to hand. Being physically separated from the social community of practice is also challenging for students.

However, a design student should still strive to plan and create a personal learning space of their own, which affords them a threshold and entrance separating them from the non-studying people of the home. Private and productive in intention, home studio learning spaces can instil concentrated spaces of learning and engagement at times when social interactions and specialist resources are not needed. Doors are closed to the outside world, especially in times of thinking, researching, and writing. Crossing the thresholds of temporary physical learning spaces, such as those within museums, libraries, and cafes are more difficult to substantiate and define as educational environments yet these spaces can often provide accessible dedicated semi-private spaces, and function as spontaneous short-term learning spaces for design research, for example. Thresholds in these circumstances can take the form of claiming an unoccupied table and chair, or a private upholstered furniture pod, or a bench in the corner of a museum or gallery.

In a physical campus learning space, a substantial door must be clearly signposted to a learning space, made from rigid, natural, and warm materials, soundproofed, easy to push and pull, and which closes softly. At this point, I remind myself of Husserls' phenomenological notion of double-touch – when you touch a door handle, or push and pull, the surface of the door also touches you in return in a dual structure of experience. Semi-opaque doors are preferable as they allow the population inside the room to look outwards but with elements of privacy (and

FIGURE 4.3 Semi-windowed walls between learning spaces, Gerrit Rietveld Academy, Amsterdam, the Netherlands.

Source: © Lorraine Marshalsey.

sound reduction as a sensory affect) intact. This fosters a subconscious awareness of the continuing happenings beyond the learning space and reminds us to connect with the ongoing social and real-life contexts outside. A semi-opaque entrance also reduces potential claustrophobia in the students and diminishes the notion of being totally separated from the outside world. It then becomes relatively easy for external populations to view work-in-progress happening within a class if the windows and/or doors can allow viewing of the creative activities inside to the outside audience. This extends an invitation to prospective observers outside of the space to participate, even if only as peripheral spectators. Additionally, providing semi-windowed walls between learning spaces can foster a feeling of light and togetherness across groups of students, even if they are not directly in the physical spaces together (Figure 4.3).

Size and layout

As design educators sense and reflect on their own embodied positions in their teaching and learning spaces, they can identify their subjective levels of comfort or discomfort relative to the walls, doors, floors, ceilings, size, and layout in their immediate surroundings. This is the first step to deduce if the size of the physical learning space is suitable for the class population and the intended design activities to be held there. Will their students experience levels of experiential comfort or discomfort while participating in learning? How will design students be able to adapt and engage with their preferred design specialism in the space? Where will the design educator stand to talk, present, or present the lesson and how will they circulate around the space to engage with their students? Will their movement be free-flowing, akin to a conventional studio environment, or restricted within a learning space populated with rows of static computers? Educators must also reflect on how design students might feel or work when seated or standing. Overall, how will an awareness of sensory affect help design educators and students to engage spatially, socially, and materially within their assigned or chosen learning spaces?

To answer these questions, initial impressions on the body do count: does the space feel oppressive or relaxed when empty? Does the body feel at ease or tense? In what ways does the sensory affect present in the space impress on the body and mind? Design educators should also reflect on the action of crossing the threshold the entrance and physically being in the learning space. How do you feel when facing to the entrance and when facing inwards, in the learning space itself? Frequently, in the first few minutes of inhabiting new, clean, bright, and aesthetically pleasing educational environments, our rational minds attempt to ignore any negative bodily signals and buy into the perceived newness or cleanliness. Does the size and layout of the learning space *feel* right? There is often no direct channel or communication between those design educators and students intensively occupying learning spaces daily and those designing the size and layouts of learning spaces from a distance. The experiential impact of sensory affect between the body and the space is subtle; the loud voice in our minds often overrides the quiet voice of the body. Our minds tell us the space works because we concur with new and pleasing interior and architectural appearances. Yet the body may be noticing subtle shifts in our subconscious as we delve deeper into our teaching and learning needs in design education. Space is often characterised by 'being there' and duration. Therefore, there is a need to consider the 'phenomenological belief in the centrality of bodily and physical engagements in the constitution of human perception' in educational environments, particularly in design education (Moszkowicz, 2009:144). If, on first inspection, the learning space feels mainly supportive for the intended teaching and learning activities and the bodily needs of educators and students, then we must examine the constituent parts of the space and the available surfaces. No surface should remain ignored or unused in a design-based learning space.

When evaluating the size and layout of a learning space, educators need to triangulate the intended purpose of the learning space, the style of teaching required there and the needs of the students. Educators know a learning environment greatly impacts their teaching approaches and students' educational experiences and outcomes. The number of students occupying a learning space must not exceed the capacity of the allocated learning space – often this is a prerequisite of university room-booking and timetabling, with no further consideration of the close relationship between student numbers and needs, space for teaching and learning activities, and educational function. Educators' choices of physical spaces are limited to table centric classrooms (seminar or tutorial rooms, open plan office-like rooms, computing labs), workshops (digital studio labs, or practical, messy workspaces), conference facilities (small boardrooms with networked audio-visual capabilities), or lecture theatres. Ideally, the sensory consideration of an intertwined fusion of need, space, and function – drawing out the effects of these three elements on the senses, emotions, and feelings – would be more effective for identifying the impact of design teaching and learning spaces on the stakeholders using them.

Fundamentally, in either open or closed learning spaces, there should be ample space around and between bodies, furniture, tools, and walls. The physical flow of the learning space should cater for multiple numbers of students and not feel cramped. An obstruction free, spacious layout will foster better movement and engagement. Inflexible, fixed layouts (such as rows) must become fluid and portable. Design educators can then physically engage better with individual students and groups as layout arrangements can be altered, and without much exertion. Students should also be able to move towards others, or be able to share their learning spaces, for peer or team learning opportunities and discussions. Free-flowing circulation within the learning space allows educators and students to circulate without restrictions as they critique, work and process learning on every available surface. There should be no physical interruption or inaccessible surfaces for the design educators and students using the space (squeezing past others, chairs touching or bumping into furniture) from awkward learning space layouts.

Walls

In home-based or campus learning spaces, walls, floors, ceilings, and windows can be extensive surfaces to display on and work from, and a design educator or student should naturally feel the freedom of taking ownership of all these surfaces in their practice. Walls are critical as visible platforms, as teaching and learning can be made more evident via vertical display surfaces than on flat desks; content does not have to be restricted to whiteboards or screens. The wall space can function as an extension of a horizontal desk surface.

- Are the walls large enough to work on, for the intended task?
- Can the body physically engage with a wall with no restrictions?
- Can the wall be touched with ease and is there adequate space for the body to move the length of the wall?
- Can the arms be extended vertically and horizontally to reach a reasonable height and width on the wall?

Walls don't have to be in particularly good condition, but I do tend to avoid walls that are intentionally designed to be 'clever' – those walls integrated with magnetic pin board or carpeted surfaces (instinctively, I find these surfaces very

FIGURE 4.4   Writable blackboard walls, Sandberg Instituut, Amsterdam, the Netherlands.
Source: © Lorraine Marshalsey.

non-creative), smart boards or with too many screens covering the walls, or walls that are set with built-in cabinets.

- Are the walls suitable for working on?
- Can 2D or 3D maquettes, work-in-progress or large sheets of paper be attached to the walls surface?
- Is there enough wall space for the whole class to work on or share surfaces as one cohort, and at the same time?
- Can the wall be pinned into, or stuck on (a flat wall is better than a textured wall surface)?
- Can the wall surface be written on? Chalkboard paint on the wall surface or even writing directly onto one entire whiteboard wall can be options for surface engagement in learning spaces (Figure 4.4).

Flexible boundaries and settings

Impermanent, flexible boundaries, such as moveable partitions, roll-down felt sections or hanging fabric can extend or reduce the size of a learning space, and open or close the environment as required. The flexible boundaries present in the learning spaces of the Sandberg Instituut in Amsterdam, the Netherlands, were exciting to see: the multifunctionality of using fabric dividers rather than heavy moveable wall partitions meant design-based learning spaces could be divided easily and quickly. Thick felt-based rolldown walls and doorways provided degrees of warmth, soundproofing and privacy to design educators and students using the spaces. Even thin muslin-type fabrics hung from the ceilings provided lenient yet effective boundaries for working, masking visible interruptions in a soft, opaque manner. In contrast, cold fixed glass walls act as rigid boundaries and feel sharp and severe in learning spaces. This material is only softened when creative artefacts, such as paper, are attached to glass, fabric adorns the glass structure, or if the glass is directly written or painted on. There is little room for flexibility with glass walls and student engagement can be challenging in glass-walled teaching and learning spaces: a very public two-way reality or hot sun shining in, makes the conditions uncomfortable. Too much glass built into the structure of a space should be avoided for these reasons. The placement of furniture can also be used to diffuse any sort of rigid boundary. Instead, the distributed, flexible nature of communal and individual tables and chairs can invoke freer, tolerable ways of working between people and design disciplines, if they are empowered to re-arrange them as they prefer.

Furthermore, alternative spaces can be created in temporary overspill areas, such as corridors, halls, or other transient spaces, for example, under stairs, in corners or alcoves, in picnic areas. It is advantageous that design-led critiques can be conducted relatively anywhere; work can be displayed on the ground or walls in classrooms and corridors (Figure 4.5), on windows, on desks (why not tip over a desk and use the vertical surface as a display area?) or on portable, wheeled boards. Design educators and students should feel they can identify and adapt their own preferred spaces for learning by utilising any available areas for teaching and learning activities. Improvised spaces for learning can also evolve over time into more regular short- or long-term break-out areas, adding to a repertoire of available specialist workshops and classrooms. The motion and movements of bodies, and the passages and places they move in, between and around, take on more importance in the formation of a design student's character and practice than we may imagine (Nottingham, 2017:abstract). It is important for design educators and students to migrate between formal and informal spaces without duress, and to ensure the opportunities impermanent spaces and fluid boundaries can afford for design education are not ignored. This strategy also provides an opportunity for the wider population to view work-in-progress and critique or comment on activities in passing.

Floors and windows

Floors are often overlooked as a surface for teaching and learning, as many educational research studies examine the floor plans and layouts of learning spaces, but no one really talks about the floors themselves. When using floors, design students can move their bodies freely and be more dynamic in their movements and be actively engaging in practice-based learning – physically rotating around larger displays or

FIGURE 4.5 Critiquing work in the ground floor corridor, Reid Building, Glasgow School of Art.

Source: © Lorraine Marshalsey.

prototypes. Reading, researching, ideation, drawing, planning, collaborating, and discussing can all be done on the floor, with soft cushion pads or beanbags, which do not elevate far from the ground and are key to comfort while working. Second to walls, floors are my favourite spaces for design-based teaching and learning. There are no scale restrictions – I can add sheets of paper, sketch, draw, and build as far as I can beyond regular desk boundaries. As an educator, don't be afraid to get down on the floor beside students. Without furniture or chairs to act as barriers, floors foster togetherness and inclusiveness. As Garrett and MacGill (2021:1222) say 'affect, aesthetics and embodied pedagogies' can act as a base 'for transformative action' when considering all-surface use in a learning space. Consider the teaching of Josef Albers at the Bauhaus: working and displaying work on the floor was integral to his lessons. Floors can also be acoustically softened with rugs and specialised floor coverings, and zoned for different teaching and learning activities, from silent to social engagement, individual to group working. Floors should be designed to cater for high traffic with low maintenance, be clean and easy to clean, and relatively soft. Carpet tiles, vinyl or polished concrete with non-slip rugs or mats are best for floor working.

Apart from the necessary inflow of fresh air, daylight, ventilation, protection from weather elements and external noise, windows can be activated as display, teaching, and learning surfaces using Post-it® notes, temporary glass writing pens, for fixing 2D blank sheets or 3D fabric and paper structures to. However, if windows are small and positioned at a high level, the main function is to filter light. Modern windows can be inaccessible due to position or height, or difficult to open. If windows are medium to large, and positioned at body level, then windows filter light and generally can be opened, becoming a two-way conduit to the world and nature outside (activating the senses we already know through our bodies of the seen world: the smells outside, the sky, the sound of trees and wind, etc). Vertical or slanted, whole sheet glass or divided windows can still afford opportunities for engagement and become surfaces for working on. The traditional studio normally has older glass structures in place, often with tall or vast walls of windows, with metal rimmed frames (Figure 4.6).

Ceilings

Our primary focus tends to fall on the appropriateness of the furniture and the suitability of the layout of the learning space at first glance. We, as educators, consider the condition of the walls (preferably white, blank, and freshly painted). We deliberate on the flooring (preferably wood or even polished concrete). Less so, we consider the windows. Even less so, do we consider the ceiling as a surface to utilise within a learning space. Yet, together as a whole, ceilings, walls, floors, windows, and furniture are the fundamental components of a learning space. Ceilings can be low, high, or pitched and have artefacts hanging from the ceiling, revolving mobiles, or for attaching audio speakers, lighting, 2D and 3D fabric, signage, mobiles, and paper structures to. Ceilings can be digitally projected on to and the visuals can be experienced by physically laying on the ground – why should this form of cinematic experience be reserved for people visiting planetariums and museum exhibitions? Ceilings within learning spaces are not only decorative platforms, for installing illumination devices, for fitting acoustic padding or to separate of levels to a building. High ceilings promote creativity and provide a sense of airy freedom. Low ceilings provide a certain sense of intimacy and snugness to a learning space.

FIGURE 4.6 Studio windows, London College of Communication (LCC), London, UK.
Source: © Lorraine Marshalsey.

Furniture and physical storage

Several decades ago, McLean (1980:36) depicted the ideal basic and advanced furniture arrangement for each designer to effectively work within a design studio environment, with 'a minimal use of equipment, working at a steady solid desk with an ergonomically designed chair, and having ample storage and a wallboard for display purposes'. These arrangements included drawing materials, an extensive work surface and specialised storage, such as a plan chest. Storage is critical to design education as the production of artefacts and their delicate and secure storage of these and their associated tools and materials is necessary. However, I have seen lots of storage in learning spaces but most of these are locked and inaccessible to the educators and students using these spaces every day. Many do not even know where the key is held or by whom. If the key is held by a known member of staff, then often it is seen as a privilege to access the storage – meant for few and generally not students. This is a barrier to engagement. All educators and students must have lockable storage for personal, work, and communal use on campus. Storage must also be of a decent size to be useable – most educational lockers are not big enough to hold numerous materials or large-scale prototypes or furniture designs.

Today, many institutions do not offer even these basic furniture formations (offering transient, laptop enabled spaces instead) and many students prefer to arrange their own configurations at home. Nevertheless, at HDK-Valand in Gothenburg, Sweden, each student was assigned their own workstation with storage drawers, angle poise lamp, and an office-like desk and chair, resembling McLean's preferred model.

In traditional SBL spaces in design schools and departments, desk and wall dividers are used to separate open plan space into equal, reservable working sections for year groups, classes, and students (Figure 4.7). Individual desk dividers set the

FIGURE 4.7 Allocated desk arrangements for individual students, HDK-Valand, Academy of Art and Design, Gothenburg, Sweden.

Source: © Lorraine Marshalsey.

boundaries between a design students' own space and that of others, allowing them to feel a sense of physical and psychological comfort, privacy and empowerment while still being part of the community of practice. I observed one design student fix a mirror to the inward facing side of their vertical desk divider, effectively doubling their visible desk space, while others attached shelving. In Figure 4.8, the partial enclosure of the dividers is low enough that a quick glance over the top of them permits a student to scan the studio (to observe the population, to listen into or contribute to nearby conversations, to catch the attention of the educator or to find friends for a break). In this way, spontaneous discussion can take place, yet the student is still contained within their own private area. These dividers also add display space for exposing work-in-progress, showing an intimate gallery of creative influences, and embedding acts of personal place-making, such as exhibiting artefacts and photographs. It is critical that a design student feels a sense of place and control over their workstations, and that they feel secure and safe in their own individualised learning spaces in the wider community of practice.

Up until now in education, when design studios mimic industry ones, the layout resembles office structures. Still, in these times of post-pandemic design education, furniture and furnished working spaces for privacy and collaboration must be re-imagined. This turn reflects much of what is critical in the hybrid delivery of higher education and educational learning design today. Consequently, personalised and divided individual workspaces are now less common in design education and instead, a high turnover hot-desking or no-desking impersonal practice prevails today in higher education. The modular delivery of a hot-desking and no-desking culture should be avoided, if possible. Groups of desks and chairs are a common sight in many learning spaces, providing places for students to be seated

FIGURE 4.8 Dividers separating students' desks, Glasgow School of Art, Glasgow, Scotland, UK.

Source: © Lorraine Marshalsey.

with places to work individually and together at static workstations. These group-ings are normally placed near other table islands, yet further enough away from the interference from neighbouring working groups. Educational furniture is often expensive, colourful, plastic, or wooden and cleverly designed in terms of features (e.g. storage built into the bottom of a chair or hidden compartments in tables). For areas of focused work and privacy for online classes and collaboration, pods and compartments are becoming more common to see in university settings. Until now, these pods are mainly found in library settings and across general campus spaces for use by anyone to shield studying students from noise and visual inter-ruptions. However, every educator and student want their own dedicated space to work. In contemporary times, it is challenging for students to create a sense of belonging and place in a learning space when no desk is formally assigned to them. Their place-making is temporary for a few hours or a day at most, with students reluctant to use the surfaces of the furniture, walls, and floor in their own personal way due to lack of ownership of the furniture or the space.

Older and informal furniture and spaces may be just as functional as newer ones yet hold less value in the university managements eyes, but these could provide a much-needed workspace for a design educator or student. The learning spaces in which design takes place should also be formal and informal yet follow a studio footprint of old and new, digital and analogue, and in the way we approach teaching and learning in and around these spaces. This arrangement encourages intentional and spontaneous connections with others, a sense of place and can break down per-ceived or physical barriers between educators and students, and student-to-student. The flexible use of informal furniture (not originally intended specifically for higher education) does alter the way people behave in learning spaces and can foster a sense of homeliness and belonging, albeit for a short time. Sofas, armchairs, and other informal furniture can act as a central place to conduct informal or formal critiques and discussions in a design-based learning space. The fabric and ergonomic surfaces of a sofa become a lateral, multi-directional platform for the educator and students to gather informally. There is no front and centre teaching rostrum. Sofas soften the learning space and mimic a breakout or reception area in educational settings or industry studios, putting educators and students at ease. Allowing free choice over bodily movement in a learning space lets the student sit on the arms of the sofa, stand behind or to the side of the sofa, sit in front of it with backs leaning against the sofa as well as the primary intended use of sitting on it. The same notion can be applied to all surfaces in a learning space, for example, sitting on a table, leaning against the walls, or sitting on the floor. Encouraging preferred forms of movement, standing, and sitting across all surfaces, furniture, walls, and floors raises comfort, attentive-ness, and engagement levels. Bodies will naturally gravitate towards the best sensory comfort and ergonomic position for each person, fulfilling this human need before engagement with teaching and learning. When students actively move around the learning space then brain function improves, implicit learning is reinforced, basic human needs are met, attention and engagement can be refocused, stress is reduced as the senses are engaged (Scott-Webber, 2014:161–163).

Specialised studio and workshop learning spaces

Specialised studio and workshop resources and learning spaces are fundamental to design education. From machining and woodworking, wet-based illustration, analogue photography, metalwork, plaster mould-making, printmaking to letter-press printing spaces, such as the Caseroom at Glasgow School of Art in the UK (Figure 4.9). In this learning space, the experiential impact of sensory affect is felt through the hands–on machinery, creative mess, inks, rollers, handles, and specialised furniture (e.g. the wooden drawers filled with lead and wooden type). In recent decades, digitally enabled VR (Virtual Reality), AR (Augmented Reality), MR (Mixed Reality), 3D-printing, CNC-machining (Figure 4.10), and additive manufacturing populate specialised design-based learning spaces. The experiential impact of sensory affect is felt through digital learning spaces is dry, clean with minimal furniture and screen-based tools in a technology-abled specialised educational environments.

The time allocated for design students to access these specialised learning spaces in a formal timetable varies enormously from institution to institution. Some students may have periods of pre-booked access with technicians doing most of the actual work for them, while others have long periods of workshop rotations embedded in their curriculum to reinforce their own ability at using the facilities available

FIGURE 4.9 Letterpress printing in the Caseroom at Glasgow School of Art, UK.

Source: © Lorraine Marshalsey.

FIGURE 4.10   Workshop CNC machine at HDK-Valand, Academy of Art and Design, Gothenburg, Sweden.

Source: © Lorraine Marshalsey.

to them. When students are openly introduced to long spells of active studio and workshop time driven by their own autonomy, then design becomes an exploratory creative practice underpinned by the sensory affective processes of handling and playing with materials, robust real-world techniques, and specialist methods. Some design institutions focus on a strong practical skill set to complement conceptual thinking, while other design institutions flexibly adapt the design students' journey so they can cater to their own design and study preferences. But all design students should have access to a diverse range of dynamic and experiential materials, surfaces, processes, and equipment (both analogue and digital). This is reflective of design students developing an all-round desirable 'thinking-by-learning-by-doing' skillset. Within a specialised studio learning environment, the layout and furniture should mirror the activities and resources required of the learning space.

The physical, face-to-face presence of design educators, workshop technicians and students in teaching and learning is often cited as integral to the signature pedagogies of design, guided by space, people, surfaces, materials, practice, and social interactions. However, the practice, processes and possibilities of design-based teaching and learning can be supported, and analogue or craft-orientated activities occasionally substituted, by the ever emerging technologies of TEL and Networked Learning (NL); 'we often try to alternate between context and content to talk about the influence of technology on society and vice versa, but we are not yet expert at weaving together the two resources into an integrated whole' (Latour, 1990:111). Maeda (2020:45) says 'I find it strange that a technical act cannot be creative, and that a creative act cannot involve technology', which may be contentious for many conventional design educators, who instil valuable analogue and craft design skills and knowledge to students.

Online learning spaces

Networked Learning (NL) environments extend into physical spaces, digital realms and across unseen boundaries, often using asynchronous yet formal learning strategies and platforms to do so. In design education today, NL is often distributed via TEL in generic classrooms and portable devices. This NL can be mobilised at home and in library study spaces as forms of online and distance design education, but the possibilities are broader than this. In recent years, the use of networked devices has clearly expanded the possibilities for design-based learning and facilitated the use of non-traditional learning spaces. Consequently, the learning spaces and surfaces in design education can extend far and wide, likened to a digital and unseen rhizome. Deleuze and Guattari (Holland, 2013) say the rhizome represents an advancing vine-like form of multi-layered, connected, and non-hierarchical compositions, breaking through boundaries in its exploratory growth. Despite the complex fabric of contemporary technologies and connected learning, and the metaphoric rhizomes of online affordances, design educators and students may struggle to engage with, and co-construct, knowledge and practice across spaces and surfaces. Yet, Ingold (2002:140) positions this notion of rhizomes as 'giving us a way of beginning to think about persons, relationships and land that gets away from the static, decontextualising linearity . . . and allows us to conceive of a world in movement'. This also describes the tendrils of Networked Learning (NL) and TEL as these expand the abilities of design educators and students to digitally connect with teaching and learning surfaces, spaces, and platforms and within a continually evolving online mass. Portable surfaces and spaces for NL learning today include museums, parks, galleries, coffee shops, outdoor landscapes, and home environments.

Online thresholds and virtual entrances still have the sense of crossing into learning through a threshold. No matter what the virtual platform is, the construct of clicking the mouse or a trackpad of a laptop to join an online class signals participation. A physical threshold into learning means the student is committed to learning. Often the crossing of the threshold is quiet and unassuming – generally, students web cameras are switched off and participant audio silenced. Then, when the student observes that friends and familiar peers are in the online space, then cameras will be turned on, or at the request of the educator. Nonetheless, online learning spaces can make the students less visible and their participation in learning can be obscured. If bodies are not visible, as cameras and audio may be turned on and off throughout the class, then the student could have cognitively withdrawn from the learning space, despite signs of a digital presence. An online threshold into learning leaves opportunities for students to slip in and out of participation unless they are directly working in design-orientated digital platforms such as Miro or Padlet (online visual collaboration platforms currently used widely in education, resembling physical surfaces and tools such as artboards and Post-it® notes). Smartphones have also become a new threshold into online and distance learning in recent years. Students can use smartphones as entrances into online classes and as exits from learning into social media, for example. Smartphones, as interactive surfaces, have the dual purpose of allowing students to access channels to learning but also to disengage with learning in both physical, home, and online spaces, for periods of time – in minutes or hours. And critically, the ability to use multiple surfaces and spaces in online learning can become one-dimensional and limited in sensory engagement, when hands-on learning-by-doing is limited to a degree.

Within online learning spaces the design student relies on the educator instigating and tutoring the tasks initially, which has caused changes to the ways courses are being taught and received by students in the variety of networked environments (and digital surfaces) available (de Laat et al., 2006). Educators and students generally find networked, online learning and educational delivery tiring and wooden. That is, lacking ease and fluidity in both space and surface use, limiting the social engagement of communal design practice and production: "Online learning is more time-consuming, more tiring and engagement is difficult when the protocol stipulates 'mic/camera off'. Bodies in space, people, energy responding to each other provides real connection" (quote from 1st year Design undergraduate 2020). How might online, distance and virtual design-based learning be developed utilising Networked Learning (NL) through the lens of sensory affect, and seen as an opportunity and opening to facilitate design student engagement rather than an encumbrance? This notion needs deep reflection by design educators and educational developers. There is not a clear-cut digital and physical division of labour, especially when the complex psychosocial learning experiences key to a student's sense of place and meaningful involvement in their degree are traditionally situated within a conventional, physical studio (Kahu et al., 2020). Carvalho et al. (2016:3) centred their Activity-Centred Analysis and Design (ACAD) framework on the argument that in order to understand and design for learning we must '(i) pay close attention to human activity: to what people actually do – mentally, physically, emotionally, perceptually; and (ii) examine the relations between this activity and the structures within which it emerges'. Carvalho et al. (2016:4) classified the types of elements required for the design of Networked Learning (NL) as 'set design' (tools and resources for practice, the arrangement and layout of physical furniture or online learning platforms); 'social design' (social structures and roles); and 'epistemic design' ('informed by ideas about the nature, form, and structure of knowledge, appropriate sequencing and pacing, relations between different kinds of knowledge and different ways of learning'). Design education is a complex and entangled web of learning spaces, social, cultural, and relational interactions, curriculum and pedagogies, and experiential learning. In the delivery of online, distance, virtual and other networked forms of learning for design education – and in the use of fluid and transferrable platforms and surfaces – Boys (2016:59) considers 'spaces, objects, our bodies, and our encounters are utterly intermeshed, and need to be analysed as dynamic practices'.

Communal and community learning spaces

Shared and communal spaces for learning on campus include university libraries, breakout rooms, student eating spaces such as cafes and Work-Integrated-Learning (WIL) spaces. Off-campus these learning spaces comprise public libraries, museums, parks, shared houses, and art galleries. Both on-campus and off-campus learning spaces can align to a formal or informal teaching and learning context in a wide sphere of activities. As Oblinger (2006:1) clearly states, built pedagogy is the 'the ability of space to define how one teaches'. The diversity of shared and communal learning spaces on campus allows design educators to adapt teaching strategies into flexible contexts for learning, based on space and resources, among others but they have less involvement in off-campus learning spaces favoured by design students.

University libraries

In traditional academic libraries, space is divided into rows of static or moveable rolling shelving for categorised books per topic and small breakout areas of chairs and the occasional table for studying quietly and privately. Today, contemporary university library design has evolved into bright open plan spaces with high ceilings, smaller and fewer bookcases, e-catalogues replacing many books, clusters of soft fabric chairs, stools, benches, and sofas, which are arranged over multiple floors. Communal open plan areas for learning are now integral to university library design, branching from main entry areas on the main floor of each library, often to several floors above, with sub-rooms or pods are provided as segregated, quiet spaces for individual or group use.

All-surface use in modern academic libraries is inherently restricted to sitting at laptop-sized tabletops with the floor, walls, dividers, or ceilings of a library rarely used for design-based study or experiential working. Even if only for short, concentrated study or for long periods of time, design educators can break out from their normal learning space constraints; from pinning work to the walls of individual pods for critique purposes, gathering in groups sitting on the carpeted floors between shelving units to conduct activities in design teams. Libraries can become centralised learning spaces for all, including for design practice, research and thinking workshops. Glass walls or windows can be written on with glass pens, use large sheets of paper or Post-it® notes on any visibly vertical working surface. Structural features in libraries such as columns, display cabinets, unoccupied corners, alcoves, and community pinboards can also be used for these hands-on teaching and learning activities.

Yet, expectations on behaviour and seeking permission are barriers to these types of engagement in library settings. Permission from university governance can be an issue on campus to work in any space beyond the allocated, timetabled one – spaces need to be pre-booked and are not designed for creative mess. Inflexible pre-bookable systems for learning spaces are a challenge when seeking to incorporate all surface use in library (or similar) environments. The library generally has a portion of reservable silent or small group seminar spaces but much of the library is freely available. Design educators and students may be reluctant to relax their methods of working to include all surfaces and spaces within a campus library for fear of being asked to move on to more suitable practice-based learning spaces. Most pods and breakout areas in libraries are bookable spaces, which are reserved in advanced or conversely, unreserved spaces are full of students working on assignments from early in the day. The spontaneity of educators and students being able to use either university or public libraries as individuals, or for small or large group working is a challenge, especially as library populations have risen significantly in recent years in the communal working areas. If space is available (bookable or not), each space must still be felt and sensed as suitable beforehand – design educators and students should walk around and envisage their preferred surfaces for working on in the library. Any surface or space chosen for design-based teaching and learning activities must be considered in the context of safety, as cables and materials crossing into open spaces and surfaces may cause risk to others.

- Are the study tables too close to walls for wall working?
- Can the seating or tables be moved into a better arrangement?
- Does the space give a feeling of being 'out of the way'?
- Does the position of the space reduce sight lines of visual interruption?
- Is there enough surface space to work on without feeling too cramped or too open?
- Can a vertical space nearby be used to extend the learning space?
- Can the floor around a structural column be utilised as a surface for sitting and working on?

- Can open, communal surfaces and spaces be divided or sectioned for better use?
- Again, does the intended space for working *feel* right?

Libraries can offer many positive sensory affective conditions and opportunities for engagement through the naturally studious environment, carpeted floor space, soft furnishing, curved sofas, and glass walls. There is something rather lovely about working on the floor of a library, nestled between two bookcases filled with knowledge and influence – I have a distinct memory of being a student at art school and being surrounded by books on the floor of the library in a warm, and darkened space. Books are surfaces to work from: individual books laid open from their spines, books stacked into columns or arranged in vertical rows on bookshelves. Books of original design knowledge and authenticity – old and new – are to be touched and experienced by the hand and eyes. In the past, design books have been treasured items – fundamental tomes of design history, knowledge, management, processes, and practice. Mostly, the necessary learning materials for design activities and classes are physically taken from a library and used elsewhere on campus or at home. Today, there are fewer physical books than ever to purchase or access with an increased catalogue of digital books and e-resources a preferred economical method, which grants access to key texts for hundreds or thousands of students on one course within higher education.

Shared public spaces: human and non-human

Shared public spaces can be pre-planned or ad hoc spaces for social and communal learning in design education. Informal learning spaces such as these are dynamic places of opportune discussion, meetings and social gatherings underpinned by a shared domain of interests and study between students. Spaces can be converted into learning spaces, using regular everyday surfaces to facilitate a learning experience. These spaces can be situated in any generic location occupied by others, such as public cafes, waiting rooms or within university breakout areas. I have hosted a design class within a local café in a shopping mall, and while this location had its challenges due to noise, this space allowed us to come together in real-life settings, which informed the lesson I had planned. Design, after all, seeks to solve real-world issues and situating the students at the heart of public and populated places such as this, and hospitals (design and health), community gardens (design and wellbeing), galleries and museums (design and education), local industry sites (collaborative design) and others, can be beneficial for teaching and learning. Using portable technology and the laptop as an online learning space blended with the physical space, can broaden the educational experience and as students work to observe others and work with actual stakeholders in situ via design.

Nottingham (2017:41) discusses learning graphic design in 'non-human' places such as corridors and hallways, can trigger sensory affect to be activated between body and place: 'it is the student work pinned on the walls that is capable of triggering

FIGURE 4.11 Communal learning space at the University of the Sunshine Coast, Queensland, Australia.

Source: © Lorraine Marshalsey.

a series of affective relations with human bodies passing by'. A hallway can become a critique-led gallery, producing learning. This notion "enables non-human objects – such as a hallway or a blog – to 'reciprocate or co-participate in the passages of affect' (Gregg and Seigworth, 2020:2), and for affect to become attached to these kinds of non-human entities" (Nottingham, 2017:41). At the University of the Sunshine Coast in Queensland, Australia, communal spaces for students are large, open spaces with ample seating and leather sofas yet with few table surfaces to work on. In this image (Figure 4.11), the sofas don't look like they were designed for sitting on for long periods of time as the back supporting structure is low. Instead, the height of the sofa structures and the with low dividing segments shown here allows brief communication between and across either side of the sofa and encourages students to limit their time here. Growing from this notion is the opportunity to utilise the non-human spaces nearby such as the vast glass windows, circular concrete structure, or lino floor as workable surfaces, providing creative opportunities to extend teaching and learning into this area. Any shared public spaces (human or non-human) such as corridors, communal hallways, public benches, and transient paths can be used to connect design educators and students with teaching and learning. Their bodies trigger sensory affect – in the interactions between themselves and the surfaces on offer – and stimulate these non-human places into learning spaces.

Work-Integrated Learning spaces

Work-Integrated Learning (WIL) is a common feature in design programmes, providing the steppingstone between industry and student-led collaborative projects.

Purpose made WIL spaces are found as dedicated environments for design education in university-built environments. These spaces tend to work better in bigger cities where footfall is greater, and students can access and build partnerships
with key external stakeholders more readily. WIL spaces are designed to replicate
real-world collaborative professional practices, with students designing to actual
briefs set by industry partners and to function as a drop-in shared working space
for design students of any year. In WIL, the rooms are furnished with desk-based
workspaces, bookcases, rugs, low setting sofa furniture, framed images on the walls,
wall and ceiling hangings, and Mac stations, with a Staff Manager on-site to oversee
the relationships between students and their industry partners, and the financial
transactions. In the Liveworm studio, the upper years in the design program also
had to undertake internship hours to achieve a course assessment requirement.
WIL studio spaces are also a showcase platform for students as emerging designers
to exhibit their work in a professional studio environment; almost like an innovation start-up hub with critical exposure to mentoring while working within budg-
etary and client constraints on live design briefs.

Legacy buildings as learning spaces

Legacy buildings, such as museums and art galleries, are one of the richest sources
of engagement for design education and these environments provide opportunities to connect with historical and contemporary influences in the buildings and
resources. Europe is well known for historical architecture and art schools were
often housed in older buildings, such as at the renowned Glasgow School of Art's
Mackintosh Building (now sadly destroyed by fire) in Scotland. In Sweden, older
SBL spaces can be seen at HDK-Valand's Academy of Art and Design in Gothenburg (Figure 4.12). Tall ceilings and large, architectural windows provide light
and space, providing beneficial sensory affect. Expansive concrete wall and floor
space allows for all-surface use on a greater scale. University management systems
and rules tend to assign less value to these older learning spaces, which allows for
greater creative mess and opportunity.

As further examples of legacy buildings in Sweden as learning spaces, external
buildings in the wider community are utilised for creative engagement for the
public, schooling, and university students. Since 1916, the Röhsska Museum in
Gothenberg has specialised in curating and exhibiting over 50,000 historic and
contemporary design and craft objects, with a focus on design, fashion, and applied
arts (Göteborg and Co, 2022). The Studio space within the Röhsska Museet is a
clean multi-purpose space on the ground floor, used for small events such as children's workshops and exhibition launches (Figure 4.13). It was typical of Swedish
design in its interior and was very much catered for the younger generation as a
steppingstone into design and craft education. This space almost felt like a modern
family apartment to me, with spotless kitchen areas, rugs, contemporary lighting,
and small child-sized chairs hanging on the wall. Clean surfaces it may have yet
it was not fully engaging as a space for prolonged creative mess, or alternatively,

FIGURE 4.12 Legacy studio learning space at HDK–Valand, Academy of Art and Design, Gothenburg, Sweden.

Source: © Lorraine Marshalsey.

the mess created by children's workshops would be very minimal and short-lived. However, the Museum itself was a fascinating resource for learning about design and the floor, public furniture, and wall surfaces within the Museum, alongside the products and artwork, could foster a strong alignment between design student and experiential learning, connecting the past with present.

FIGURE 4.13   The Studio @ Museum of Design and Craft, Röhsska Museet, Gothenberg, Sweden.

Source: © Lorraine Marshalsey.

In 2020, on a Wednesday afternoon in Gothenberg, I joined the 2nd year student cohort from the Master of Fine Arts (MFA) in Design at HDK-Valand and their Senior Lecturer, Dr Thomas Laurien for a critique. Here, students do not pick a specialism as their graduation portfolio aims to reflect who they are as a designer for employment purposes, so there are no majors, minors, or specialism streams. In terms of space, several communal specialised workshops hold a large footprint, which is much larger than the SBL space footprint itself (where individual workspaces are provided for students) at this institution. Wide-ranging interdisciplinary facilities are provided for all on one floor, and every student is assigned a desk regardless of year in the studio space, with all year groups mixed. There are few classroom boundaries with lots of large-scale flexible spaces provided for several weeks at a time for the production and experimentation of specialist production or large-scale work, for example, furniture or textile design. In studio, the students never deliver digital presentations. All presentations and critiques are roundtables with work-in-progress artefacts or performative displays in front of the actual work. The tutors also work in teams with not a single educator taking all responsibility for the classes. This allowed a 'broadening out' across staff collaboration for the assigned tasks, which also involved professional design agencies off-campus. Lectures are rarely conducted and normally only by guests.

Thomas had told me the critique he had planned would be held off-campus at a design studio in the Western side of the city. When we arrived at Gathenhielmska Huset, where the critique was to be held in collaboration with the design agency based here, I was astonished that this would be the host building for design agency, never mind a university-led design critique. I spent much of my time here considering why I was so surprised and delighted that a heritage building such as this could offer the conditions necessary for design education. Gathenhielmska Huset in Gothenburg was built during the 1740s and became a listed building in 1964. Fast forward to April 2020 and the Swedish Historical Agency took over Gathenhielmska Huset with 'a vision to create a place for artistic and cultural activities' (Gathenhielmska Huset, 2020:online). After a development phase, the building opened its doors as a 'culture house', hosting events such as concerts, experimental cultural heritage, artistic co-creation, and film screenings to performance works specifically written around the context of this building (Gathenhielmska Huset, 2020). In addition, Gathenhielmska Huset offers resident studios for creative practitioners.

The critique was held around this solid table in the main reception room of Gatenhjelmska Huset, surrounded by antiquities and portrait paintings linked to the history of the house (Figure 4.14). I worried about the fragility of such a space, yet Thomas told me that the design degree show had previously been held in this house. I wondered – did they affix things to the walls for the degree show? Did they leave the furnishings in situ? Was anything damaged? Weren't there rules and restrictions governing such a space? What an incredibly rich, authentic, and spiritual place to hold a student exhibition! The surfaces and artefacts embodied the history of the house and became an influence on the contemporary work created there. There were no 'do not touch' signs, everyone was respectful of the buildings and its contents. We even used the outdoor walled garden to conduct a student's design performance, which was critiqued by peers. The unrestricted use of this building and grounds opened my eyes to the possibilities afforded by all spaces and surfaces – old and new – for teaching and learning in design education. This example sits in direct opposition to the contemporary yet bland 'online filing cabinet: aesthetically dull and utilitarian' digital learning spaces of today (Nottingham, 2017:39) or the design studios of the 1970s as a series of 'faceless filing cabinets' that ignored the qualitative needs of human presence or experience (Bloomer and Moore, 1978; Woolner, 2010). Anthropologist David Howes (2005:25) expresses a not too dissimilar view of modern university spaces: 'in the modern university . . . walls are flat and smooth, corridors are clear, the air is still, the temperature is neutral'.

Outdoor space: natural and urban spaces for learning

Natural, forest, urban, and place-based learning spaces are widely known to be advantageous to early years and primary outdoor schooling, and for secondary physical education, but are often not utilised enough in other areas within higher

FIGURE 4.14   Gatenhjelmska Huset, Gothenburg, Sweden.

Source: © Lorraine Marshalsey.

education, or indeed, in design education. In the UK, the Forest School is an emerging area of interest in informal and outdoor settings as regular, timetabled learning environments in early years and primary education (Harris, 2018). Natural and urban environments should also be thought of as learning spaces of sensorial delight and affect – museums, galleries, libraries, and cafes should not be the only option beyond the campus boundary. Climate does play a large part in the consideration of teaching and learning outdoors depending on the weather conditions in each locale. In this context, sensory affect is dominated by the natural elements in relation to the useability of available open-air settings across seasons. However, the surfaces on offer for teaching and learning are endless, despite weather conditions. In Australia, yes, the favourable weather plays a large part on outdoor living and schooling, and less so in the windy rainy conditions of Edinburgh, Scotland (I belong to both countries), but both offer distinctly experiential locations, spaces, and surfaces for students to engage with. One of the best photography sessions I ever did was in a wet, rainy graveyard, which added enormously to the atmosphere and creative end result. When the conditions are favourable for teaching and learning external to the regular classroom and campus structures, natural (not only grass landscapes) and urban environmental experiences should be considered – and not just for field trips or close to the universities' boundaries.

As an example, Firth et al. (2016) used the beach as a classroom to conduct two product design classes with design students at university level in Edinburgh, Scotland. They cast melted pewter into the sand to form structures, using the fire from found timbers as the heat source, underpinned by a sustainable discourse. The flexibility of being able to move freely to a diverse range of accessible outdoors spaces also exposes the students to different contexts, materials, and surfaces for learning. The rigid boundaries of the classroom are dissolved, and the experiential impact of sensory affect takes on a whole new perspective when outdoors in the natural world – breezes, bright and dull, smells, textures, plants and trees, man-made materials, warmth, and coolness, wet and dry, among others. Dynamic activity and movement are encouraged, the students noise levels are tolerated better, and teaching and learning takes in the context of the terrain. Place-based outdoor learning environments provide an 'intermission space for transition and recreation . . . spaces that are not deliberately intended for creative design work but connect the other space types, for example, hallways, cafeterias, or the outdoors and provide spaces for breaks' (Thoring et al., 2018:64). Thoring et al. (2018:71) provide examples of forgotten outdoor spaces for learning – those external areas that can be included in design education – such as outdoor booths, pavilions, parking lots and tree benches, noting 'positive stimulation was achieved through natural sounds and smells while working outdoors'. Nomadic and outdoor learning spaces are learning spaces ripe for exploration, risk-taking and expanding the boundaries of design education beyond the walls of the university-situated classroom, while embracing the positive impact of sensory affects in natural and man-made spaces.

Summary: practical implications of all-surface use in design-based learning spaces

This chapter has been a whirlwind tour of learning spaces and all-surface use in those spaces, opening and expanding the possibilities for the practical implications of teaching and learning in design education today. From starting with a discussion of empty rooms and prepared environments for learning, I moved on to muse the thoughtful drawings created by students as they envisaged their ideal studio learning spaces. Then, a diverse repertoire of learning spaces was conversed; across indoor and physical learning spaces at campus and at home, to rarer specialised studio and working spaces, to the greater debates of the merits of online and distance learning spaces today. The last third of this chapter pitched unexpected plot twists with the consideration of underrepresented areas for all-surface use in design teaching and learning. Why not consider more broader indoor and outdoor communal and community learning spaces? Or rich and authentic legacy buildings as learning spaces? Outdoor natural and urban learning spaces are often seen in early years, primary and secondary education but seldom in design higher education. In a search of literature exploring design education or studio learning outdoors, the results would yield almost nothing as an underutilised area of all-surface use in design education learning spaces. This seems like a missed opportunity for imaginative approaches to all-surface use, while encouraging fresh-air and positive out-of-doors sensory affective settings for experiential learning.

No space or surface should be overlooked in the preparation and planning of studio-like design activities. All surfaces within a learning space, indoors or outdoors, should be treated as potential surfaces for learning; to write, touch, stand, dance, express, draw, ideate, sketch, model, hang materials, explore influences, and suspend prototypes from. The whole design-based learning space should become a 360° multi-surface, diverse 2D/3D/4D entity, and certainly not limited to static individually hung, vertical boards and screens or horizontal desk surfaces. No student will have their back to a peer or educator-led lecture or projection, and a relaxed body position eases tension and anxiety in both teaching and learning. Ceilings can be projection screens and beanbags used as viewing furniture – consider changing the postures of educators and students into comfortable, yet horizontal observational positions.

To summarise, the shifting landscapes of design education posited within higher education, blended with miscellaneous provision of learning spaces and surfaces provided to contemporary design education needs considered with fresh eyes. Foregrounding an awareness of sensory affect, design educators and students can adapt their spaces and surface use for more engaged and experiential learning. This approach will enable discussion of all-surface use in new ways in higher education. This chapter is intended to provoke debate and a richer conception of how to access all available surfaces for design-based teaching and learning, and certainly within our life worlds, beyond existing learning spaces in design education today.

References

Ariani, M.G. and Mirdad, F. (2016) 'The effect of school design on student performance', *International Education Studies*, 9(1). doi: 10.5539/ies.v9n1p175.

Barrett, P., Davies, F., Zhang, Y. and Barrett, L. (2015) 'The impact of classroom design on pupils' learning: Final results of a holistic, multi-level analysis', *Building and Environment*, 89, 118–133. doi: 10.1016/J.BUILDENV.2015.02.013.

Bloomer, K.C. and Moore, C.W. (1978) *Body, Memory and Architecture*. New Haven, CT: Yale University Press.

Boys, J. (2016) 'Finding The Spaces In-Between', In *Place-Based Spaces for Networked Learning*. New York: Routledge, pp. 59–72. doi: 10.4324/9781315724485-5.

Brown, N. (2019) 'The Embodied Academic: Body Work in Teacher Education', In Leigh, J. (ed), *Conversations on Embodiment Across Higher Education*. Abingdon: Routledge, pp. 86–97.

Carvalho, L., Goodyear, P. and Laat, M.de. (2016) *Place-Based Spaces for Networked Learning*. New York: Routledge.

Corazzo, J. (2019) 'Materialising the studio. A systematic review of the role of the material space of the studio in art, design and architecture education', *Design Journal*, 22(sup1), 1249–1265. doi: 10.1080/14606925.2019.1594953.

Csikszentmihalyi, M. (2013) *Creativity: Flow and the Psychology of Discovery and Invention.* New York: Harper Perennial.

de Laat, M., Lally, V., Simons, R.J. and Wenger, E. (2006) 'A selective analysis of empirical findings in networked learning research in higher education: Questing for coherence', *Educational Research Review*, 1(2), 99–111. doi: 10.1016/j.edurev.2006.08.004.

Delgado, M. (2015) *Urban Youth and Photovoice: Visual Ethnography in Action.* Oxford: Oxford University Press.

Firth, R., Stoltenberg, E. and Jennings, T. (2016) 'Using an outdoor learning space to teach sustainability and material processes in the product design', *International Journal of Art & Design Education*, 327–336. doi: 10.1111/jade.12109.

Garrett, R. and MacGill, B. (2021) 'Fostering inclusion in school through creative and body-based learning', *International Journal of Inclusive Education*, 25(11), 1221–1235. doi: 10.1080/13603116.2019.1606349.

Gathenhielmska Huset (2020) *Gathenhielmska Huset Kulturhuset i hjärtat av Majorna.* Available at: www.gathenhielmska.se/.

Göteborg & Co (2022) *The Röhsska Museum, Gothenberg.* Available at: www.goteborg.com/en/places/the-rohsska-museum.

Gregg, M. and Seigworth, G.J. (2020) *The Affect Theory Reader.* Durham: Duke University Press. doi: 10.1515/9780822393047/HTML.

Harris, F. (2018) 'Outdoor learning spaces: The case of forest school', *Area*, 50(2), 222–231. doi: 10.1111/area.12360.

Holland, E.W. (2013) *Deleuze and Guattari's 'a Thousand Plateaus': A Reader's Guide.* London: Bloomsbury Publishing.

Howes, D. (2005) 'Skinscapes: Embodiment, Culture and environment', In Classen, C. (ed), *The Book of Touch.* Oxford: Berg Publishers, pp. 27–40.

Ingold, T. (2002) The Perception of the Environment: Essays on livelihood, dwelling and skill. London: Routledge.

Kahu, E.R., Picton, C. and Nelson, K. (2020) 'Pathways to engagement : A longitudinal study of the first-year student experience in the educational interface', *Higher Education*, 79(4), 657–673.

Latour, B. (1990) 'Technology is society made durable', *The Sociological Review*, 38(1), 103–131. doi: 10.1111/j.1467-954x.1990.tb03350.x.

Maeda, J. (2020) 'Design education in the post-digital age', *Design Management Review*, 31(1), 41–48. doi: 10.1111/drev.12201.

Marton, F. (2014) *Necessary Conditions of Learning.* London: Routledge.

McLean, R. (1980) *The Thames and Hudson Manual of Typography.* London: Thames & Hudson.

Montessori, M. (1970) *The Psychological Background of the Montessori Material Within the Setting of the Prepared Environment.* Amsterdam: Association Montessori Internationale.

Moszkowicz, J. (2009) *A Re-Evaluation of Historical Precedents in the Age of New Media.* Bristol: University West of England.

Nair, P. and Doctori, R.Z. (2019) *Learning by Design : Live Play Engage Create.* Bangalore: Education Design Architects.

Nottingham, A. (2017) 'Feel the fear: Learning graphic design in affective places and online spaces', *International Journal of Art and Design Education*, 36(1), 39–49. doi: 10.1111/jade.12058.

Oblinger, D.G. (2006) 'Learning spaces', *British Journal of Educational Technology*. doi: 10.1111/j.1467-8535.2009.00974.x.

Scott-Webber, L. (2014) 'The Perfect Storm: Educations Immediate Challenges', In Scott-Webber, L. et al. (eds), *Learning Space Design in Higher Education*. Faringdon: Libri Publishing, pp. 151–167.

Thoring, K., Desmet, P. and Badke-Schaub, P. (2018) 'Creative environments for design education and practice: A typology of creative spaces', *Design Studies*, 56, 54–83. doi: 10.1016/j.destud.2018.02.001.

Wenger, E. (2000) *Communities of Practice: Learning, Meaning, and Identity*. New York: Cambridge University Press.

Woolner, P. (2010) *The Design of Learning Spaces*. London: Continuum.

5

ENVIRONMENTAL EMPOWERMENT IN DESIGN EDUCATION

Introduction: environmental empowerment in design education

> *Environments come in vastly different scales, shapes, and materials, and they trigger perception using a range of mechanisms. They focus on the sounds, sights, smell, and touch between the body and another surface and the space in-between, across which the sensory experience is enacted. . . . Some environments reach out and touch, others alter or engulf the body. They provoke questions about the nature of space, enclosure, privacy, control, community, and autonomy using traditional static means — external walls, floors and ceilings, or mechanical means — manipulating body chemistry via hormones, light, and temperature — sparking sensation from the inside out.*
>
> —(Schwartzman, 2011:58)

What does environmental empowerment mean in the context of learning spaces in contemporary design education? This chapter addresses the 'heart' of design education; empowering the things we feel, embody, nurture, and believe in as human educators and students. To further this discussion of sensory affect and learning spaces in design education, I examine the immediate environments in design education as potential places of empowerment. Experience of places can be direct and intimate, or indirect and conceptual. It is important for both the educator and the student to feel at home, and to individually perceive, receive, and be satisfied with, the right conditions for them to engage in their design-based learning spaces. This chapter begins with a discourse on a sense of place, the reality of placelessness, and acts of place-making. Then, environmental stressors, such as noise, overcrowding, and temperature changes are explored before moving into a discussion of restorative environments, such as biophilic-designed learning spaces. Next, structures of shared power in the Co[D]P are debated, leading into

DOI: 10.4324/9781003175988-5

a discussion of why empowering the design curriculum and its resources in learning spaces is important. Lastly, diagnostic methods and strategies are recommended for identifying and addressing sensory affect in design-based learning spaces, with several proposed key themes.

Generally, environmental empowerment can be seen in the control given to enhance physiotherapists' capabilities of preventing falls in older adults or in climate change activism (Worum et al., 2020). Educational empowerment commonly embraces broader areas such as diversity, inclusion, equity, equality, gender, rights to schooling, and technology use. What happens if we adjust this focus to empower educators and students to address the daily issues prevalent in their actual educational environments? Learning spaces are the physical, blended, or digital locales of day-to-day design education as spaces of dynamic interaction between the environment and the educator teachings or the student learnings. Learning spaces in design education offer diverse forms of prospect, refuge, social interaction, and creativity to each educator or student, and as a collective Co[D]P (Wenger, 2000). Therefore, educators and students must have a say in the design and use of their learning spaces, placing the responsibility of environmental empowerment for teaching and learning purposes directly into their hands.

Although educators and students can articulate their ideas of place, it can be challenging to express what is known about place through the senses (Tuan, 1977:6). As Schwartzman (2011:62) states, 'Responsive environments extend elements of the room out to make contact with the visitor or retreat in reaction to motion, temperature or colour'. To enable a strong awareness of a design-based learning space, kinaesthetic movement (in and around the studio and its boundaries), sight (the presence of visuals, equipment, spatial dimensions, furniture, light, artwork, and people in the studio) and touch (handling objects, surfaces, textures, and materials, touching furniture) are the dominant conduits for educators and students to ascertain their experiences of place. Yet, if spaces are subconsciously affecting comfort, concentration, and engagement levels, then we need to turn towards and identify the subtilities of sensory affect impacting on our bodies in design education. There must be connections made between educators' and students' specific and personal needs, and the learning spaces provided to them (and all that these spaces contain) for better engagement. Educators and students must be allowed to diagnose and construct their own meaning making of their learning spaces, to be able to improve their own subjective conditions for teaching and learning. As Boys and Hazlett (2014:44) state:

> *The concepts and terminology design educators and students use in connecting their personal, social, educational, and material experiences; what it is that matters about space for students' feelings of belonging and engagement; and what kinds of changes to university space can improve student belonging and engagement.*

Furthermore, design students' longitudinal experiences of these learning spaces across the duration of their degree, from new undergraduate to seasoned postgraduate student, needs attention (Boys and Hazlett, 2014:50). Learning spaces in design education accommodate transient and collective populations, nomadic and static students who need to focus, be active and engage in a repertoire of preferred yet different daily educational locations. These daily environments can change from year to year, moving from foundational basic workshop training to self-directed design projects. Often, more trust and time is afforded to fourth year design students who have proved themselves capable in specialised design learning spaces earlier in their programme. Boys and Hazlett (2014:49) proposed the affective and emotional attitudes and the performative, learning-by-doing and relational practices are critical in the construction of educational environments, and a sense of place and belonging across the years of a degree.

A sense of place

Embodiment in the built environment

Since the early 1960s, architecture has endeavoured to search for authentic and original embodied experiences in the built environment. This notion was prompted by architectural history as human experience returned to its ontological origins and architectural phenomenology sought to theorise this embodiment in architecture. Philosopher Robert Vischer (1847–1933) denoted a harmonious correlation between body and architecture can be perceived in relation to the gentle curves and movements of the human body as it is reflected in the architecture being sensorially experienced (Otero-Pailos, 2010). Human patterns of activity contribute to the perceived sensory experiences of internal and external environments. Phenomenology is the private and subjective experience of our lifeworld unencumbered by prejudice, the foundations of which were construed by Edmund Husserl (1859–1938), Martin Heidegger (1889–1976), and Italian philosopher Enzo Paci (1911–1976). Architectural phenomenology involves the conscious revelation of those layers of experience and intuition (a form of experience in itself) detected through bodily sensation and perception. Blending sensory experience with architectural history and theory contributed to the thematic makings of architectural phenomenology and were key to the conceptual formation of the lifeworld (Moran, 1999; Cerbone, 2006; Otero-Pailos, 2010). Jean Labatut (1899–1986) and Ernesto Nathan Rogers (1909–1969) were also early advocates of architectural phenomenology as they pressed for the importance of bodily lived experience in architecture (in the moment that space is experienced) and not as disconnected mental inquiry. Rogers considered the experiential aspects of a physical environment to be a fusion of culture and people, containing a constantly evolving process of human activity, cultural, and collective experiences, which affects those immersed in the setting. Architects, such as Labatut and American architect Charles Moore (1925–1993), argued that a buildings' historical importance can only be reliably determined 'through the direct physical experience of the building itself' (Otero-Pailos, 2010:xiii). Labatut also renewed an emphasis on historical design in architecture and from those precedents taught at the École des Beaux-Arts in Paris. However, Maurice Merleau-Ponty (1908–1961), known for his influential work on embodiment and perception, argued there should be less emphasis placed on the historical aspect of architecture and experience (Merleau-Ponty, 1962). Then, the Norwegian architect, architecture historian, and theoretician Christian Norberg-Schultz (1926–2000) proposed Genius Loci, 'the spirit of place', as the experiential origin of meaning in the phenomenological approach to architecture (Haddad, 2010:90). He determined existential space as qualitative, experiential architectural, and natural spaces; understood as 'phenomenology of place' (Haddad, 2010:92). Consequently, this body-based ideal has challenged architects to embrace natural forms and sensory-led sustainable spaces, alongside architectures fast developing technological and material innovation.

Postmodernism prospered from the 1970s onwards and is noted as a highly flamboyant stylistic and intellectual reaction to futuristic and functional mid–century Modernist design, which had been prevalent in architecture until then. At this time, architectural phenomenologists sought to absorb the critical ideas of Postmodernism. For example, they reinvented surface decoration and embraced the visual and experiential impact of buildings as they pushed the limits of phenomenological architecture. Then, in 1990, Walter Gogel (1918–2006) referred to the perceptual experience of three-dimensional space as 'phenomenal geometry', the geometry of perceived space, and argued cognitive factors can affect the spatial sense (Gogel, 1990). Spatial senses can refer to a range of perceptions including occlusion, a key source of an object's distance information; people can construct and navigate their three-dimensional life world effectively via these depth indications, unified with the interrelations present between auditory and visual information (Foley and Matlin, 2010).

American humanistic geographer, Yi-Fu Tuan (1930–2022) (1977:52), who wrote many seminal works such as *Space and place: the perspective of experience*, argued learning spaces, classrooms and other educational facilities should feel 'commodious and liberating to students who go there to enlarge their minds'. Paying close attention to the role of sensory affect received through bodily awareness, and the effect of this embodiment on informal and formal learning spaces (and in the design of those spaces) is critical to the nomadic, distance, and dispersed nature of design education today. To truly experience a learning space is to become aware of, understand and foreground sensory affect emanating from that space, whatever forms that may take, and take action to resolve the affects as a method of empowerment.

Place and placelessness

> The term "place" always refers to a place. One whose composition is highly individual (if not unique). Second, while the composition is individual, the elements that form it are common to the milieu . . . Third, a place is always sensed.
> —(Malnar and Vodvarka, 2004:1–3)

And the higher he climbs, the further removed he feels from the groundedness of place, and the more drawn to abstract sense of space. Conversely, the return trip homeward takes him on a downward movement, through the levels, from space back to place.

—(Ingold, 2011:146)

Literature that focuses on sense of place can be found within ethnography, anthropology, and architectural phenomenology (Bloomer and Moore, 1978; Norberg-Schulz, 1980; Bachelard, 1994; Seamon and Mugerauer, 2000; Relph, 2008; Aravat and Neuman, 2010; Otero-Pailos, 2010; Pallasmaa, 2012). A space may be understood in terms of the affective bond between people and place; as the essence of understanding experiences within space (Aravat and Neuman, 2010). In comparison, place is continually sensed, revealing more of itself as educators and students encounter and inhabit a particular learning space. This is relative to the being whose environment it is (Malnar and Vodvarka, 2004). As such, one cannot exist without the other, as the body and environment shape and develop each other (Ingold, 2002). According to Relph (2008), four themes define how place is experienced:

Firstly . . . relationships between space and place are examined in order to demonstrate the range of place experiences and concepts. Second, the different components and intensities of place experience are explored. . . . Third, the nature of the identity of places and the identity of people with places. . . . Fourth, the ways in which sense of place and attachment to place are manifest in the making of places.

(Relph, 2008, preface)

This search for authenticity of place surfaces from a disconnectedness between person and environment, and this is referred to as placelessness, which is often a result of industrialisation or technology in modern day space. A learning space can never be a place unless an intimate attachment is formed and placelessness within a learning space can foster negative feelings in both educators and students (Seamon, 1996; Relph, 2008). Our perceptual experiences of learning spaces imitating design studios can be momentary, unremarkable or disconnected and feelings of boredom or anxiety may surface in educational environments often containing a high turnover of bodies on a daily basis (Sharp et al., 2016). However, Pallasmaa (2012) positions melancholia as the embedded enigma of all insightful thinking and creative effort; not in a despondent sense, but as an unintentional sensation of being in a place. Likewise, Relph (2008) suggested drudgery will remain an ingredient of place as mundane experiences partner the more invigorating design studio experiences during day-to-day pedagogical processes (Brooks and Brooks, 1993). Placeways, (1998) author E. V. Walter assert that people experience a sense of place in their daily interactions within space (Malnar and Vodvarka, 2004:60). The strongest sense of place experience is what Relph (2008:55) term 'existential insideness'. This is a situation of deep, unselfconscious immersion in place and the experience most people know when they are at home or in their own community. The opposite of 'existential insideness' is what he labelled 'existential outsideness': a sense of strangeness and alienation (Relph, 2008). There is a marked need to create a communal sense of place in a diverse range of learning spaces designed for larger numbers of transient design students. But how can this be achieved? Is it indeed possible to create a sense of place in the context of contemporary design education, especially when it may exist in both virtual and real environments integral to pedagogical space (Davidts and Paice, 2009:10)? As design education has seen a shift from formal craft and skill-related workshop instruction to informal, blended, open plan, online, and distance teaching approaches common in modular delivery, achieving a sense of place is challenging.

Today, educational thinking has shifted towards a student-led, learning-based, flipped approach to teaching and learning, which doesn't always support a sense of place in the learning spaces allocated for this approach. Learning spaces (offline and online, on campus and at home) can limit the activities of studio learning, in terms of social interactions, and affective, cognitive, behavioural, and physical responses of students and educators (Scott-Webber et al., 2014). Students may exhibit differing responses and perceptions of a sense of place in the variety of learning spaces they experience (in both beneficial and unfavourable ways) depending on their previous and current experiences of learning spaces (Heschong Mahone Group, 1999; Boys, 2010). To a degree, social interactions have shifted to online spaces for a significant proportion of teaching and learning in contemporary design education. This shift has seen significant changes and implications on interaction between humans in general, worldwide as global classrooms have co-constructed lessons and activities across cultural divides (Ghassan and Bohemia, 2015; Murdoch-Kitt and Emans, 2020).

Interestingly, when open-plan spaces first emerged, a wealth of literature contended the impact of environments would be minimal (Woolner, 2010). However, alternative smaller studies have suggested that a younger student demographic enjoy the very complex, interwoven nature of an open-plan space (Rasila and Rothe, 2012). Educators remain divided on the matter and it is often the educators' responsibility to structure and operationalise open plan learning spaces to facilitate and engage design pedagogy (Saltmarsh et al., 2015; Cardellino and Woolner, 2020). However, it is common to find research studies which identify intrusive acoustics, light/thermal discomfort, and issues of privacy as being common, unsolved problems in open plan environments (Biddick, 2014; Saltmarsh et al., 2015). This notion also applies to university buildings and online learning spaces, as design educators and students struggle to identify their own embodied place within them. When designing multi-place learning spaces to promote empowerment in design education, first, it is widely known that space can be roughly defined as *room*; a three-dimensional room for people to freely move within and in which to act and related to perceived spaciousness, whereas second, place signals *attachment* (Tuan, 1977). The French poet Charles Baudelaire (1821–1867) noted that in large structures, such as a university, 'there is no place for intimacy' and we must identify 'centres of simplicity' in buildings with many rooms (Bachelard, 1994:29). As Tuan (1977: 34–35) says,

> *Ways of dividing up space vary enormously in intricacy and sophistication, as do techniques of judging size and distance . . . if we look for fundamental principles of spatial organisation we can find them in two kinds of facts: the posture and structure of the human body, and the relations (whether close or distant) between human beings. . . . Body is "lived body" and space is humanly construed space.*

While there has been a renewed interest in design studio inhabitation, habitus and the 'studio-as-pedagogy' model for teaching and learning in recent years, few texts explore design educators and students' authentic sensory-led experiences of place in education itself (Gray, 2013). Studies centre their debate on local and global studio pedagogy, affective physical and digital environments, psychological inhabitation of studio, the roles of studio teaching and learning, and social media-based learning in the design studio (Hannon, 2014; Muhammad et al., 2014; Ghassan and Bohemia, 2015; Güler, 2015; Belluigi, 2016). Non-educational discussions of artists' and designers' situated practice, identity, and place within a studio environment are found in the older research studies of Bain (2004) and Pigrum (2007). Further studies explore an authentic sense of place as a tool for students' design problem-solving but not the actual educator or students lived experience of their daily learning spaces in design education (Henshaw and Mould, 2013; Özkan Yazgan and Akalın, 2019). Consequently, there is a marked need to research individual and a communal sense of place in the choice of spaces offered to design educators and students today, which were designed for larger numbers of transient students.

Therefore, everyday experiences of a sense of place remain immeasurably diverse and challenging to define, despite the distribution of technology connecting people and places. There is a significant gap, predominantly in relation to the impact that learning spaces may have on the connection between educators' senses and teaching, students' senses and learning or, indeed, investigating educational environments through the senses to reinforce a sense of place. Understanding a sense of place is important for design educators and students to foster a deep immersion in teaching and learning spaces, to mediate the feelings they experience in these spaces, and how this might affect their engagement in design education. Developing a sense of place is aligned to both the conscious and unconscious ways in which design educators and students are enabled to work, guided by their senses as an integral part of their being. This is closely linked to the degree to which learners are actively embedded in the communities of practice they inhabit.

Place-making

Place exists as validation of a student's presence and representation in a design-based learning space and, furthermore, through acts of mark-making, socialising, and occupation. Indeed, design students may come to cherish a learning space

FIGURE 5.1   Design students place-making within their studio learning spaces using artefacts.

Source: © Lorraine Marshalsey.

they spend periods of time at. Evidence of place-making may result from their productivity, sociality, meditation, and solitude in their educational environments, as in the places of creative learning and practice. Place-making can assist the ways in which students relate and interact with the specificity of place as well as with each other through objects and actions. In a shared studio environment, creative work in progress is openly shared over longer periods of time in familiar and natural settings, which may foster a communal sense of place among the year group (Boling et al., 2016:16). Students use creative or memory-laden artefacts, such as readymade posters, self-initiated artwork, personal objects, and associated comforts to project their ownership of space within a space (Figure 5.1) (Vyas et al., 2013). These acts of place-making speak of the students' design process, rituals, habits, or self-reflective journeys to improve their experiences of day-to-day studio learning and can be instigated or activated by an individual's internal or external actions. In the context of design education, these can be viewed as psychological and sensory tools that help learners inhabit place, as Bloomer and Moore (1978:54) indicate 'By maintaining recognisable artifacts at key points along the boundaries and in the centre of public places the identity of the human can be projected outward into the community or back into it . . .'.

Contemporary design studio learning has become increasingly transient and fluid, with a less visibly defined footprint in which to create an anchored identity in learning spaces with fewer opportunities for place-making. The subjective actions of populating a learning space with artefacts may be limited in generic, timetabled learning spaces due to the reduction of wall space, small or temporary personal work areas, lack of time and insecure boundaries. For the same reasons, it is challenging to support a critical sense of ownership in hot-desking and no-desking educational environments so common in higher education today. Therefore, the ability to define a sense of place in design-based learning spaces can blocked by institutional systems despite a need for place-making. However, small scale place-making does exist through the arrangement of students' water bottles, laptop, note-pads, and pencil cases, and so on, within short-term learning spaces, even if only for an hour. Nair and Doctori (2019:9–11) posed tough questions that reflect the reality of education still recovering today from a pandemic, which swept much of education into distant and online learning platforms (temporarily or permanently), affecting acts of place-making.

1   How will humans adapt to transformations in the practice of learning?
2   How will learning environments adapt to the challenges of individualisation?
(Nair and Doctori, 2019:9–11)

These are pertinent questions that I suspect will never be completely resolved, although acts of place-making within an ever-evolving education sector may still foster 'existential insideness' in the repertoire of learning spaces available, offline and online (Relph, 2008:55). Given that learning spaces are developing in parallel with the rapid development of new technological tools, processes, places, platforms, and pedagogical practices, encouraging design educators and students to continue in acts of place-making is key.

Environmental stressors

When we feel negative towards a space, then our emotions are heightened, and we assume engagement will be disrupted and the educational experience a potential waste of time due to physical and sensory stressors in the environment. We can initially respond to a learning space through a generalised feeling of affect, such as dislike, without consciously understanding or processing why we react that way (Steg and de Groot, 2019:67). As Ackerman (1992:281–282) says (in her wonderful book *A Natural History of the Senses*), 'There is much more to seeing than mere seeing. The visual image is a kind of tripwire for the emotions'. The affective quality of a 'multi-place' approach to learning spaces in design education can veer between relaxing or exciting to unpleasant or gloomy (Steg and de Groot, 2019:119–120). When we feel positive towards a learning space, our emotions are still heightened yet we judge the risks and disruption to be lower and the probable experience more pleasurably and productive. The same notion of emotional reaction applies when educators and students perceive a learning space in design education to be supportive or unsettling. These emotions can arise as prospective feelings (arising from anticipation of the activity or space) or retrospective feelings (after the activity or space) (Steg and de Groot, 2019). In the realm of sensory affect, these emotional states can be considered as 'the affect heuristic', touching our day-to-day lives in design education (Slovic et al., 2007). This term relates to judging learning spaces and their usefulness, and the decision-making involved in changing the layout, adjusting the conditions or our positions within a learning space. This is environmental empowerment.

Noise, overcrowding, and auditory stimulus overload

Noise in design education is one of the most dominant sensory affect states to be overcome. Noise is the direct consequence of overcrowding within and between learning spaces. Contemporary open-plan learning spaces are the greatest culprits of noise as an environmental disruption to engagement in design education. In a few art and design schools in Europe and Australia I have observed open plan design studio learning spaces side-by-side over entire building floors. This arrangement is fine if one or two of these learning spaces are populated but in the event of busy classroom scheduling when all spaces are utilised it becomes an auditory explosion of disturbance to all educators and students. Visual barriers may separate the learning spaces, but sound still travels beyond these dividers to disrupt many educators and students trying to focus and engage on the task in hand. Noise can arise ubiquitously from people, the environment and machinery in a 360° ambush. This overcrowding and negative noise stimulus leads to a sensory affective stimulus overload with different scales of intrusive noise emerging from whispering students to loud machinery. Personal space is impossible to locate and retain, and social withdrawal are consequential of these challenging circumstances. Therefore, noise can increase anxiety, particularly for the educator, who is trying to maintain a positive learning environment for students. Educators can often feel that control is slipping through their fingers in a learning space if excessive noise blocks their control of the environment. Students will tend to leave class early because of larger student numbers generating noise and their inability to engage with working processes. Educators then feel under pressure to make students stay and then feel guilty if they don't have the opportunity to speak with every student about their work before they leave. They hurriedly deliver feedback and move on quickly to the next student in case they should leave early without a two-way exchange in which to unpack ideas and direction. Noisy learning spaces leave educators and students feeling challenged and unfulfilled.

On the other hand, noise can also indicate productive activity and sound levels should be measured by the educator as being positive or negative influences to teaching and learning. Student teamwork, role playing, debates, discussion and such are robust and sometimes loud affairs, yet dynamic engagement continues as projects are undone, discussed, and re-assembled as learning outcomes. Sound travels from multiple areas in design-based learning spaces: from student voices maintaining a constant background hum as conversational sounds fluctuate or key technical resources such as laser cutters and CNC machines generate productive noise. Sound fluctuates from busy, industrious days when the learning space is populated with students to quiet, less industrious days when the learning space is occupied with only a few students. Design students seem to prefer both conditions as engaged learning ebbs and flow: 'As soon as it becomes deadline it absolutely goes crazy. . . . But in a good way because of the stuff being made – of things created. But it does get a bit overwhelming' (Design student, UK, 2017).

Lack of appropriate lighting, ventilation, temperature, or air

> *Current standards for light environments are based on technical requirements, e.g., luminance, uniformity, and illuminance, and do not necessarily describe all parts of the light experience to ensure visual comfort from a user perspective.*
>
> (Boork et al., 2020)

Lighting in university learning spaces can deviate from harsh, artificial, and auto controlled lighting to soft, natural lighting from large windows. I have observed timed lighting plunging learning spaces into darkness midway through teaching and learning activities, with an educator or student repeatedly having to manually activate the lighting several times in a 2-h timetabled period. I have seen warm natural lighting afforded by large, metal framed studio windows in a design-based learning space. In this instance, lighting was only switched on in the dark of winter or stormy days and sometimes not at all, as students preferred the darker conditions in less populated studios. Darkness does seem to associate with quieter learning spaces and conversely, bright learning spaces become a hub of activity when many design educators and students populate the space at the same time. In sunnier climates, blinds are a necessity to block out the hot, bright sunlight making it impossible to view laptop or projector screens. The light is often dictated by the purpose of the learning space and is only adjustable to a minor degree. In specialist learning spaces, such as film and photography studios, dark lighting is a preferred option. Yet, poor lighting in any learning space can cause headaches, eye strain, and visual interruptions. The ability of educators and students to adjust the input of natural lighting and air can be blocked by an inability to exert manual control, to reach high, small, inaccessible windows or locked windows, or thwarted by broken blinds or no blinds at all.

Thermal comfort and natural ventilations regularly swing from too cold to too warm, or too stuffy to too breezy. I have observed students bringing blankets to lecture theatres as the temperature setting for an entire semester was set to 'cold' with no known way of knowing who controlled this. The air conditioning control is often standardised and set by remote parties in university estate management and generally not accessible by the design educators or students freezing or overheating in the learning spaces. Furthermore, it can be challenging for design educators try to keep lethargic students engaged in stuffy, overwarm learning spaces of which there is no thermostat or temperature control to hand or windows to open. The air in learning spaces tends to be very still. Ventilation is motionless (unless situated within a spray booth or as an extraction system above machinery) and air contamination present. Poor air quality is a common issue in learning spaces, with a high turnover of bodies often situated in open plan spaces and as 'indoor air quality impacts health, comfort and performance' (Andamon et al., 2021). In summary, design educators and students have little control of the lighting, temperature, ventilation, or air conditions and even less control to adjust their environment to accommodate the required changes for better teaching and learning engagement. The power of ownership and the flexibility for design educators and students to manually adjust and change the sensory affects created by lighting, temperature, ventilation, or air conditions is restricted. Design educators and students should be afforded the control to change conditions as necessary for their preferred conditions in design-based learning spaces (Barrett et al., 2015).

Mess and grime

Learning spaces rarely have dedicated spaces for exploratory creative mess and play. In non-specialised learning spaces, design educators and students can exhibit apprehension of their own creative mess in relation to intruding on other spaces for working and in the context of clean, dry, carpeted TEL spaces. In addition, institutional rules and governance in university structures provoke anxiety in design educators and students when making mess. Today, there is little mess, no sink, and no wet materials visible in use in generic high turnover learning spaces, such as paint or ink for creative practice. Creative mess externalises a student's 'thinking-by-learning-by-doing' process and the mess is evidence of a creative process happening in individual students' workspaces and areas. Educators and peers might not be able to interpret a student's creative process if their methods of progression are concealed. Untidiness can be controlled or uncontrolled during the creative process as mess is often tied to tactility and making. A lack of storage, fewer refuse bins and inadequate surface area within a learning space contributes to the physical mess in populated learning spaces. It would appear mess generated from students' design processes is acceptable because of creativity, yet non-creative mess is tolerated less. In this sense, creative mess seems to provoke positive and productive impactful experiences in terms of sensory affect, for example, through touch and smell, yet non-creative mess (such as leftover lunch) does not. Allowing space for creative mess on students' individual workstations and in communal work areas, encourages students to take responsibility for the mess they produce. However, grime plays a more prominent role in multi-use learning spaces designed for many in higher education today – and often these spaces are shared with non-design disciplines. Touch can foster negative connotations via the perceived presence of dirt and grime from large numbers of transient students in learning spaces. Interestingly, cleanliness becomes an issue in learning spaces, as many educators and students reluctantly work in a dirty, unclean learning space: a clean space can foster a productive and engaged mind.

Restorative environments: designing multi-place learning spaces to promote empowerment in design education

Biophilic design and learning spaces

There are many texts exploring the design of places and spaces for health and wellbeing but finding key approaches to designing natural and sustainable learning spaces where educators and students thrive, due to the sensory conditions, are limited. Biophilia and biophilic design looks at people's intrinsic emotional connection with nature, as a biological need (Kellert and Wilson, 2013). Biophilia is a complex mix of learning rules encapsulating several emotional fields, and when humans are removed from the natural environment, then these natural rules are not replaced or replicated by modern non-natural artefacts, 'Instead, they persist from generation to generation, atrophied and fitfully manifested in the artificial new environments into which technology has catapulted humanity' (Kellert and Wilson, 2013:32). As Browning and Ryan (2020:98) say 'throughout history, 'learning from nature' has been a recurring theme', so why aren't adult students learning in restorative and natural, sensory-focused learning spaces? Historically, classrooms were light, airy and naturally ventilated by open windows, with uncluttered views to nature, trees, clouds, water, among others. Generally, early years and primary education students experience these conditions to improve cognition and engagement but not in higher education. Such aspects were believed to be distractions to student learning rather than be supportive peripheral sensory elements. Biophilic design elements (specifically designing to encourage close human interaction with nature) can be brought indoors to learning spaces via natural and nature-duplication via pattern-making of fabrics and decor, when importing natural colours, brickwork, rocks, wood, pebbles, water and murals, or even including a nature-based colour palette in a learning space, and its furniture and surfaces, can help (Browning and Ryan, 2020). Why aren't living walls or moss wall art (also known as vertical gardens or green plant walls) installed or created in learning spaces? Including nature in design education doesn't always mean having to set a nature-themed or climate crisis project studio brief or teaching and learning outdoors (although all are also beneficial to engagement). Smaller adjustments within design-based learning spaces in higher education can foster the feeling of being exposed to nature and its environments; access to fresh air, earthy materials, tree trunk stools and columns, window seating bays and greenery will support the sustainable ethos contemporary design tries so hard to circulate to all. Biophilic design can be included via three critical themes and across 14 biophilic patterns, which focus on psychological, physiological, and cognitive benefits (Browning et al., 2014:5):

i   Nature in the Space Patterns

    1   Visual connection with nature: being able to directly view nature.
    2   Non-visual connection with nature: being able to engage with 'auditory, haptic, olfactory, or gustatory stimuli' that create or refer to 'nature, living systems or natural processes'. Mimicking nature.

3   Non-rhythmic sensory stimuli: random and transient contacts with nature that may not be foreseeable yet able to be analysed via probability patterns, such as unforeseeable weather events.
4   Thermal and airflow variability: subtle changes in air, temperature, humidity, airflow 'across the skin', and 'surface temperatures that mimic natural environments'.
5   Presence of water: viewing, listening to or touching water.
6   Dynamic and diffuse light: 'varying intensities of light and shadow that change over time to create conditions that occur in nature'.
7   Connection with natural systems: a consciousness of 'natural processes, especially seasonal and temporal changes' as the characteristics of a 'healthy ecosystem'.

ii   Natural analogues patterns

8   Biomorphic forms and patterns: 'Symbolic references to contoured, patterned, textured or numerical arrangements that persist in nature'.
9   Material connection with nature: 'Material and elements from nature' that, via 'local ecology or geology', create a 'distinct sense of place'.
10 Complexity and order: 'Sensory information that adheres to a spatial hierarchy similar to those encountered in nature'.

iii Nature of the space patterns

11 Prospect: 'An unimpeded view over a distance for surveillance and planning'.
12 Refuge: 'A place for withdrawal, from environmental conditions or the main flow of activity, in which the individual is protected from behind and overhead'.
13 Mystery: 'The promise of more information achieved through partially obscured views or other sensory devices that entice the individual to travel deeper into the environment'.
14 Risk/peril: a recognisable hazard.

(Browning et al., 2014:5)

These biophilic ideas may be easier to install in a country-based institute rather than a metro or urban context but there is no reason to not consider and include natural aspects into city-based learning spaces in higher education. Literal and implied depictions of nature can be installed into a physical learning space and digital backgrounds in online teaching and learning platforms in design education.

Restorative multi-place learning spaces to promote empowerment in design education

For educators and students to be empowered in design education and their associated learning spaces, they must be given the authority to (1) install their own forms of natural and biophilic design into their educational environments for sensory autonomy in both their wellbeing, engagement, and design practice, and (2) have their voices clearly heard when contributing to the educational design of their diverse multi-place learning spaces in design education. They are the central stakeholders of specialised design-based learning spaces, underpinned by unique studio signature pedagogies, and they know what works best for their teaching and learning engagement. Design educators and students should be given the power to assert their sensory and experiential needs through biophilic inclusive practices in their learning spaces. This notion may not stretch university budgets to begin to demolish and rebuild whole building blocks but surely, the interior of university buildings and their facades can be toyed and played with using a sensory affective approach?

Structures of shared power in the Community of [Design] Practice (Co[D]P)

Students can form their identities in their own practice and activate modes of belonging within their learning spaces in design education (Lave and Wenger, 1991; Wenger, 2000; Coffield and Williamson, 2011). Design is the common interest that connects and holds this teaching and learning community together, connected by the shared practical activities, critiques, and discussions the educators and students undertake in their teaching and learning spaces. Through collaborative activities and shared discussion, the student cohort interacts. In the relationship between body and learning space structures of shared power such as, 'dominance, territoriality, personal space, crowding, privacy, diversity, social dimensions and age groups' are prevalent to the actual inner workings of a successful design-based learning space (Nussbaumer, 2014:3). Learning spaces are experienced and interpreted by students in a complex mapping of shared social and spatial processes: they invoke a shared repertoire of experience together. The students' own practice informs their participation in the community; and what they learn from the community affects what they do in return (Wenger, 2000). In his influential work on Communities of Practice (CoP) theory educational theorist and practitioner Etienne Wenger (2000) calls this 'reification'. That is, making concrete the shared domain of interest in learning, commitment to the learning community and a shared competence of the discipline (Lave and Wenger, 1991; Wenger, 2000). The Community of [Design] Practice (Co[D]P) is unique and draws from Wenger's communities of practice theory, which evidences that learning is a process that takes place in a participation framework, and not exclusively in an individual's mind (Wenger, 2000). Design educators and students concretise their teaching, learning and the sensory affect they are influenced by and immersed in every day within learning spaces, 'we recognise ourselves in each other, in reification we project ourselves onto the world and not having to recognise ourselves in those projections, we attribute to our meanings an independent existence' (Wenger, 2000:58). By viewing teaching and learning in learning spaces as belonging, as doing, as experience, as becoming, and as concretising, educators and students see their experiences as being fundamental to their specialist design community, 'giving form to our experiences . . . to create points of focus around which the negotiation of meaning becomes organised' (Wenger, 2000:58). Therefore, these notions of reification, community, practice, meaning, and identity frame the focus of attempts by the educators and students investing within their Co[D]P.

In learning spaces, the social, cultural, and relational interactions formed over time and shared between educators and students, and each other, are critical to restoring and empowering a healthy Co[D]P. Although the design education community learn together, it is the individual who internalises and manipulates structures to alter their conceptions of learning (Lave and Wenger, 1991:15). Since a community denotes a greater identity through the presence of multiple perceptual bodies than an individual self does, the students learn to value their collective, participatory membership of their learning spaces and as a form of empowerment (Schön, 1984–1990; Wenger, 2000; Relph, 2008). The specialised and communal learning spaces within design education today also provide shared domains for the community to self-reflect on the nature of its own practice. Intersubjectivity – our inherently social being – becomes a bridge between the personal and the shared, the self and the others in the Co[D]P. This is an idea that Boys, (2010:44) emphasises when stating 'teachers, students . . . are . . . all members of . . . two intersecting communities of practice: the educational institution and their own specialist subject or subjects'. Fors et al. (2013:abstract) proposed a theory of 'sensory-emplaced learning' as understanding the correlation between the embodied and environmental in everyday learning processes. The idea of the lived, embodied studio experience being intertwined with community is a powerful notion, as students participate, contribute, and share power with each other. Communities of Practice (CoP) theory combines experiential learning (emphasising the process of learning through experience) and Social Constructivism (emphasising the collaborative nature of learning) in its domain, community, and practice and broad theories such as these can be applied to this notion of empowerment from within the Co[D]P.

The students retain multiple memberships in their community, aligning to their individual and collective preferred creative practice and influences. These memberships could include print or web communities, formal and informal memberships within hidden and open physical or online communities, and in and across friendship groups, working groups, and the wider institutional communities. Many micro and macro memberships overlap depending on the students' own identity, practice-based interests, community, and social preferences, and on the meaning that they assign to learning experiences. The more immersed educators and students become in the Co[D]P within their learning spaces, the more empowered they will become to assert their needs and preferences for better engagement. To reiterate, structures of shared power in the Co[D]P can involve:

- Allocating and allowing educators and students to take ownership/make use of the learning space themselves to inspire a sense of belonging.
- Participating in the community of discovery and serendipity.

- Facilitating more contact between students and educators, formally and informally, as shared narrative of power in learning spaces.
- Social and relational interactions in learning spaces, for example, informal, non-creative areas within or near to the learning space for lunch, rest, spontaneous debate/critiques.
- Encouraging collaboration and teamwork, fostering a sense of inclusion in the Co[D]P via collaborative group projects and learning together.
- Encouraging the benefits of peer feedback on students' creative practice, as building and being part of a community of practice.
- Encouraging ad hoc and spontaneously formed cross-culture learning communities and groupwork across nations, beliefs, and demographics.
- Open-ended time and spontaneous opportunities for learning.
- Familiarity, collegiality, and friendships, nurturing friendly, informal, day-to-day social interactions with peers and staff.
- Asserting confidence to extend 'moments of invitation' (Clandinin, 2013:27) to others on the peripheral of the Co[D]P.
- Social responsibilities in learning spaces, such as taking responsibility for clearing mess, including others, and extending Co[D]P networks.
- Fostering multi-memberships in the community across offline and online participation platforms in the Co[D]P, for example, within a design studio culture, freedom to pursue chosen interests.
- Encouraging diverse and overlapping interests, supported by events and sub-communities in the Co[D]P.
- Demonstrating and visually/verbally reflecting the students' practice-led or practice-based design work back into their Co[D]P to feel valued.
- Displaying student work, to the smaller peer group in the brief period following assessment, and to the college of art community or the wider university population on a broader collective basis, which is necessary to feel valued.
- Governing institutions supporting a stronger sense of Co[D]P identity to design departments, art schools, and colleges of art, especially when situated within mainstream universities.
- Institutional management must adjust university-wide rules and guidelines to support creative and practice-led design studio learning, beyond technology-empowered persuasive experiences.

Design education can be argued to be a specialist networked, multicultural and inclusive community in terms of local and global membership, societal encounters, and collective manifestations. Despite a multicultural and interdisciplinary profiling, there is literally no published text on culturally responsive design studio pedagogy in higher education (Morrison et al., 2019). Promoting a sense of place and structures of shared power in design education must embrace all cultures, races, and identities with:

- Freedom to express and pursue personal histories, languages, cultures, gendered, religious and socio-economic backgrounds, and beliefs. Students should feel empowered to use their voice and display their identities in learning spaces. Educators should provoke the use of multicultural project briefs and socially responsible intentions.

- Freedom to pursue chosen interests across cross-cultural, mutual, and overlapping interests.

Empowering the design curriculum

Providing open-ended curriculum frameworks with flexible timetabling and supportive sensory affective learning spaces, thus facilitating an open-ended fluid curriculum is so needed in design education today. Can the design curriculum in higher education be re-invigorated to allow design educators to provide better educative experiences for students, using inclusive sensory practices? Educators and students should be encouraged to pursue open-ended digital and/or conventional methods of practice, depending on their sensory preferences for practice – dry, clean, wet, messy, large, or small. Governing higher education institutions should also provide specialised and dedicated design studio learning spaces. These are distinct from generic classroom learning environments, and support students' interests across analogue, digital, and specialist resources with preferred tools, methods, and techniques on hand to support sensory exploration and material investigation. A collective reflection of sensory affect within experiential learning, learning spaces and design education will not be preserved or thrive without institutional support.

Diagnostic methods and strategies: identifying sensory affect in design-based learning spaces

Diagnostic medical procedures and assessments are utilised to understand the current state of our health and accurately assess learning needs in education. Diagnostic methods are also needed to understand the presence and impact of sensory affect on teaching, learning, and engagement in design education and its learning spaces. When educators are first assigned learning spaces to work with, we are often already familiar with these spaces from regular use, or we investigate the suitability of unknown spaces we have been allocated for each class in design education. Classes are normally short, timetabled events, which means the learning space is often judged as being potentially suitable with only a brief, cursory glance around the room itself. Educators and students need to spend more time and effort on this task than first thought – not only in preparation of the space, but also in the population and use of the learning space over time, and later, in the retrospective use of the space. There are many sensory methods I have used for research purposes, which can be easily implemented for diagnosing the effectiveness of a space for teaching and learning through the lens of sensory affect. The diagnostic sensory affect method shown in Table 5.1 can be employed to prepare the body for identifying sensory affect in learning spaces.

Diagnostic methods can be used to understand and address the impact of sensory affect intrusions and pacifications on design-based teaching, learning, engagement,

TABLE 5.1 Preparation for identifying sensory affect in learning spaces.

Preliminary diagnostic method	Resources needed	Steps	Objective
Preparation for identifying sensory affect.	Only the body.	1 Breathe slowly. 2 Eyes closed. 3 Slow the mind. 4 Loosen and stretch the body to relax. 5 Slowly move around the space.	To focus on sensing the direct and noticeable effects of learning spaces and immediate environments through the body.

Source: © Lorraine Marshalsey.

and spaces. Key critical questions can be asked and considered, and sensory issues be acted upon from these interrogations including:

- Does sound bounce and/or echo in the learning space?
  - Do contemporary architectural materials such as brick, steel and concrete reduce or increase the sound emitting from people or machinery?
- Are external sounds impacting on the space?
  - Is there traffic or vehicle noise?
  - Or a highly populated area or café nearby?
- Are the sounds made by others disruptive?
  - Are the sounds of loud conversations, noise emitting from open plan learning spaces nearby intrusive?
- Are the sounds made by others supportive?
  - Is the sound a comforting 'hum' of people working or group working collaboratively?
- Are subtle sounds impacting on the learning space?
  - Is sound originating from air-conditioning apparatus or the regular beep of a security alarm?
- Are external smells pervading the learning space distracting?
  - Are there smells of cooking, smoking, or refuse from unemptied bins?
- Are internal smells within the learning space overpowering or noticeable?
  - Is the smell of paint, spirits and inks, food present?
  - Are there smells from lunch brought indoors by students?
- Are the smells in the learning space neutral or pleasant?
- Are visual interruptions few or frequent?
  - Are there people coming and going, which could unsettle students?
- Are visual influences apparent?
  - Is there evidence of colour, nature, and artwork on the walls or in the space?
  - Are there examples of modelled artefacts from design practice, which students can aspire to?
  - Are students visually experimenting with design processes and techniques?

- Are bodily touch sensors activated in positive ways?
  - Are a variety of design materials and tools at hand that invoke haptic engagement?
  - Is creativity supported through touch?
  - Are there natural materials to hand?
  - Is the seating arrangement and furniture appropriate, comfortable and supportive?
- Are bodily touch sensors activated in negative ways?
  - Is there evidence of mould or damp in the space?
  - Is there an absence of haptic stimulation via inappropriate seating arrangement and uncomfortable furniture in the learning space?
- Is the temperature regulated effectively?
  - Is the temperature controlled by the educators and students using the learning space?
  - Is the learning space warm or cool depending on preferred conditions?
- Are drafts acting as fresh ventilation or unsettling chills?
  - Can the windows be opened on a warm day?
  - Is the air conditioning set at too low or too high a temperature?
- Is the overall ambience of the learning space reassuring or disturbing?
  - Is the learning space cramped or bland?
  - What are the supportive or challenging issues in the learning space and why?

Methods for identifying sensory affect in design-based learning spaces

To empower actionable narratives for sensory affect within experiential learning and learning spaces in design education, the following qualitative, reflective strategies can be employed. These can be used by design educators (and students) to investigate their local teaching and learning environments (Table 5.2). The data generated by these methods is mostly narrative in nature and will generate discussion, encouraging the externalised reflection of the experiential impact of sensory affect in everyday blended, online, and distance learning spaces.

Key themes and recommendations for addressing sensory affect in learning spaces

The key themes identified as significant and detected via sensory affect in design-based learning spaces can be addressed to a degree, when applying the following recommendations in learning spaces today (Table 5.3). Design educators and students must be given the capacity to use their preferred tools, methods, and strategies to work with and address the impact of these sensory affects, as mechanisms to aid their participation and engagement in contemporary design education within

TABLE 5.2 Diagnostic methods and reflective strategies for identifying sensory affect in learning spaces.

Diagnostic method	Reflective strategy
Write short descriptive scenarios, when thinking about sensory affect and the body situated in the learning space.	Write a short narrative on how the learning space feels through the bodily senses – from the base of the feet touching the floor up to the ears, eyes, noise. For each aspect of the body, does the narrative outline positive or negative feelings? Why? • Sensory affect can occur in more than one way. What does each sense tune into, in the learning space?
Observing physical traces via notetaking in learning spaces.	Observe physical traces of others in learning spaces. Are there physical traces in the learning spaces of those who have gone before – in the short and long term? Then reflect on this. How does this method make you feel? • Positive? As an example, over years traces of paint has built-up in a communal studio sink, tracings of prior creative practice. • Negative? As an example, leftover takeaway foods and overflowing bins.
Observations of behaviour via notetaking in learning spaces.	Observe students engaging in the learning space. Are students engaging in distinct areas of the learning space but not in others? Is this a regular occurrence? • Consider the room layout and the sensory affective conditions. As an example, sitting next to a cold window can disrupt engagement, too many students cramped around a table with little room for working. • How might students contribute to the self-examination of their habits and behaviours in learning spaces and isolate their preferred conditions for learning?
Sound mapping internally and externally to learning spaces.	Record sound using smart phones or other recording devices and listen back to the audio recording for instances of repetitive or intrusive noise. • Locate where sound originates from by physically moving about the learning space. Are there places of quiet and stillness in amongst the busyness? What do these quiet and noisy spaces do or produce to emit these sounds? • For example, sound mapping can identify the elevated sound levels as resulting from teaching larger student numbers or external interference.
Ethnographic drawing methods (both digital and hand-driven) in learning spaces.	Produce intuitive sound drawings by closing eyes and/ or listening to bodies reacting to sound to externalise feelings about the learning space. • Use PC or Apple® tablets with a pressure-sensitive stylus, or paper and coloured pens/pencils to draw interpretations of the experiences of daily learning spaces onto actual images (or draw representations of these spaces). • Use colour, dynamic shape and line, and words to represent the experiential impact of sensory affect in the different learning spaces occupied every day.

	• Are the drawings representative of sound in their harshness or softness of touch, sharp or flowing, muted or garish? Reflect on this. How does this method make you feel and what does this identify?
Ethnographic image-making methods (photography and video) in learning spaces.	Photograph or video scenes to identify supportive and challenging aspects in learning spaces, to develop both personal and collective change.
	• GoPro® film cameras and mobile phone video applications can be utilised. GoPro® is an American brand that develops, manufactures, and markets high definition (HD) videographic equipment and cameras, known as GoPro's®. These cameras are compact and lightweight and are wearable via chest, head, or wrist harnesses, capturing footage lasting from seconds to hours as design educators and students can film their everyday experiences of learning spaces from their own storytelling perspective.
	• Encourage immediate and spontaneous image-making as opposed to setting up scenes.
	• Analyse, highlight, and ask the students to group, share and reflect on the recurring themes emerging from the collective student-generated images.
	• This visual method enables a powerful expression of experiences, as cameras and videos are placed directly in the hands of the design educators and students. Photography is tool to foreground design educators and student's active voices and perspectives from behind the camera – a term Brandt (2014:621) called 'shooting back'.
Social media using networking tools such as Snapchat® or similar (any photo or video sharing mobile application) in learning spaces.	Use social media-based photo or video messaging mobile applications, in which design educators and students can also add captions and drawings onto images and send them to others in their Co[D]P community.
	• Using Snapchat® (or similar social media app) allows design educators and students to voice their immediate and fleeting experiences of learning spaces from their own, empowered perspective, as they share them with others.
	• Screen grab and save images to reflect upon later.
	• This method produces unbiased data from design educators and students own perspectives, as life happens around them and with them in learning spaces.
Focus group discussion of identified issues emerging from learning spaces.	Informal discussion situated within learning spaces themselves to openly examine and compare the impact of sensory affect impressing on design educators and students.
Manifesto activity of learning spaces.	Ask the students to produce a written declaration or statement outlining their preferred conditions for learning spaces, with a focus on improving their experiences and engagement.

Source: © Lorraine Marshalsey.

TABLE 5.3 Key themes and recommendations for addressing sensory affect in learning spaces.

Key sensory affect theme	Recommendations
Sound. The effects of excessive noise/ sound transference in learning spaces. • Sound originating from technology, machinery, music, people talking and moving, and the architecture. • Noise is mainly a symptom of informal social behaviours. • Social networks perform differently between digital platforms and physical 'face-to-face' interactions in design education.	• Limit the number of people in the learning space. • Isolate the excessive noise. • Students can use noise-cancelling headphones for self-directed working or studying, to overcome negative sensory affect. • Facilitate working in a darkened room for perceived noise reduction. • Facilitate working a light room for increased productive sound. • Facilitate working in an outdoors learning space. • Sound bouncing and/or echoing from architectural materials can be muted by interventions of small adjustments to the building structures, for example, the use of soft furnishings, division of open plan space into segments of learning spaces with physical noise-reducing boundaries or professional acoustic intervention. • Manage background ambient sounds to avoid silence. • Manage sound levels; incorporate temporary and permanent soundproofing or sound-reducing measures and strategies, depending on the learning environment and the number of students present.
Mess. The effects of physical and creative mess generated by others.	• Allow space for creative mess on personal workstations and communal work areas; students should be encouraged to take responsibility for these areas. • Reduce grime and dirt. • Provide refuse bins at each workstation.
Colour The effects of colour on learning spaces.	• Use harmonious and calming colour palettes to support engagement in learning spaces. • Don't paint interior walls in bright or harsh colours such as red.
A sense of place. A sense of place and belonging supported by governance, place-making, the Community of [Design] Practice (Co[D]P), space, display, tools, and resources, and satisfying bodily senses.	*Governance.* Governing higher education institutions should: • Adjust university-wide rules and guidelines to support creative and practice-based specialist design studio learning. Relax rules and guidelines set by the institution as these can often interfere with attempts to maintain the Community of [Design] Practice (Co[D]P) and discovery. • Provide specialised and dedicated design education and studio learning spaces, which are distinct from generic classroom learning environments.

- Provide formal and informal design-based learning spaces.
- Provide open-ended curriculum frameworks and timetabling for design education and studio learning.
- Foster and support a stronger identity to design departments, art schools and colleges of art, especially when situated within mainstream universities.
- Provide greater support and a stronger sense of creative identity to design students within mainstream university structures for the duration of their degree.

Place-making.

- Design educators and students should use artefacts help to instil a sense of belonging/comfort in learning spaces.

Community of [Design] Practice (Co[D]P).

- Establishing membership in learning spaces through familiarity, friendships, collaboration, and teamwork is important to maintain the community of practice and discovery.
- Provide opportunities for design educators and students to foster multi-memberships in the community across offline and online platforms.
- Provide opportunities for design educators and students to foster friendly, informal, day-to-day social interactions with peers and staff.
- Encourage collaborative group projects.
- Encourage the benefits of peer feedback on students' creative practice, as building, and being part of, a community of practice.

Space.

- Support a balance of space between the need for a 'personal zone' and a studio-wide 'free zone'.
- Allocate formal, communal creative learning spaces and individual desk spaces.
- Assigning a personal desk space to students means that they are more likely to implement strategies to engage with the learning space.
- The modular delivery of a hot-desking and no-desking culture should be avoided.
- Design and project-based learning can function in a variety of physical and non-physical spaces, internal and external to the campus environment.

(Continued)

TABLE 5.3 (Continued)

Key sensory affect theme	Recommendations
	• Provide breakout spaces to 'think'.
	• Provide informal spaces to listen, talk and 'debrief'.
	• Allocate informal, non-creative areas within the studio for lunch, rest, spontaneous debate/critiques and allow the student community to take ownership/make use of the space themselves.
	• Make sure the physical layout and furniture is appropriate and comfortable, e.g. suitable chairs, sofas, bean bags, and benches.
	Display.
	• Students should be encouraged to display their work in progress openly and using physical, printed, 2D and 3D artefacts as a form of place-making is a two-way process necessary for learning and to feel valued.
	• Educators should display student work, to the smaller peer group visually/verbally in the brief period following assessment, and to the college of art community or the wider university population on a broader collective basis, for students to feel valued.
	Tools and resources.
	• Readily available tools and resources should be accessible to design educators and students to encourage preferred digital and conventional methods of practice.
	• Provide wet and dry resources to design educators and students in learning spaces, e.g. access to sinks when using paint.
	Satisfying bodily senses
	• Make sure all senses are satisfied while in the space (physical hunger, thirst, etc.).
	• Facilitate communal spaces for eating and have access to food and drink outlets.
Pedagogy and curriculum design and methodologies.	• Facilitate active, experiential pedagogy.
	• Support diverse forms of experiential learning.
	• Facilitate an open-ended fluid curriculum.
	• Facilitate the flexible use of formal and informal, group and individual activities.
	• Set non-medium specific briefs that are open to the student's interpretation and creativity.
	• Encourage diverse and overlapping interests, supported by events and sub-communities.
	• Facilitate more contact between design educators and students, formally and informally.
	• Educators and institutions should support design educators and students to explore their perceptions of design pedagogy, to adjust and learn together.

Time in learning spaces.	• Remove clocks from walls to lessen the pressure and need to continually check the time and adhere to university schedules. This reduces self-consciousness and feeling time pressured.
	• Learning spaces should be accessible for longer periods of open-ended time to design educators and students.
Olfactory conditions/Smell in learning spaces.	• Ensure there is little or no identifiable smell in the learning space, for example, hot food or overpowering fumes such as inks/paints.
	• Maintain a level of pleasant smell; reduce the odours from refuse bins, smoking shelters, and nearby cafes.
	• Make sure there are windows for fresh air, for smell as well as vision.
Vision and visual interruptions in learning spaces.	• Reduce visual interruptions; incorporate soundproof wall-size dividers, fabric barriers and desk partitions to reduce ocular distractions.
Space provision in learning spaces.	• Provide a variety of spaces, which optimise creative practice.
	• Provide a variety of spaces, which optimise ergonomic comfort.
	• Provide a variety of spaces, which provide the choice to socially engage with others.
	• Avoid inadequate storage in a populated learning space.
Temperature in learning spaces.	• Maintain a level of thermal comfort.
	• Be able to self-regulate thermal comfort in learning spaces supports teaching, learning and engagement.
Natural and artificial lighting in learning spaces.	• Provide natural lighting.
	• Natural light supports learning in the daytime.
	• Artificial light might support learning in the evening.
	• Harsh lighting should be avoided.

Source: © Lorraine Marshalsey.

higher education. The strategies noted should not be seen as a conclusive list and further themes and recommendations can be developed with reflection.

Summary: environmental empowerment in design education

This chapter has investigated environmental empowerment in the context of learning spaces in contemporary design education. This chapter began with an examination of a sense of place, embodiment, place and placelessness present in the built environment and acts of place-making. A sense of place is the goal in teaching and learning spaces, which reinforces participation and engagement, even if only for a short time in the fast-moving torrents of higher education. Then, the discourse moved towards identifying aspects of the environmental stressors intruding and supporting experiential learning and learning spaces in design education today, such as the sensory overload generated by crowded environments and poor acoustic provision in open plan learning spaces. Next, a brief survey of the theoretical and practical components of restorative environments was discussed. Many existing design movements such as architectural phenomenology and biophilic design already explore the human-environment sensory connection, but the foci of these values and actions needs foregrounded in educational environments too. This section explored the merits of including biophilic design into learning spaces. Learning spaces are inseparable from the community inhabiting them and structures of shared power in the Community of [Design] Practice (Co[D]P) was deliberated. Lastly, diagnostic methods and strategies were recommended for identifying and addressing sensory affect in learning spaces, and several key themes were suggested to support environmental empowerment in design education.

References

Ackerman, D. (1992) *A Natural History of the Senses*. New York: Vintage Books.

Andamon, M.M., Woo, J. and Rajagopalan, P. (2021) Australian children are learning in classrooms with very poor air quality, *The Conversation*. Available at: https://theconversation.com/australian-children-are-learning-in-classrooms-with-very-poor-air-quality-154950.

Aravat, I. and Neuman, E. (2010) *Invitation to ArchiPhen: Some Approaches and Interpretations of Phenomenology in Architecture*. Bucharest: Zeta Books.

Bachelard, G. (1994) *The Poetics of Space*. Boston: Beacon Press.

Bain, A.L. (2004) 'Female artistic identity in place: The studio', *Social & Cultural Geography*, 5(2), 171–193. doi: 10.1080/14649360410001690204.

Barrett, P., Davies, F., Zhang, Y. and Barrett, L. (2015) 'The impact of classroom design on pupils' learning: Final results of a holistic, Multi-level analysis', *Building and Environment*, 89, 118–133. doi: 10.1016/J.BUILDENV.2015.02.013.

Belluigi, D.Z. (2016) 'Constructions of roles in studio teaching and learning', *International Journal of Art & Design Education*, 35(1), 21–35. doi: 10.1111/jade.12042.

Biddick, N. (2014) 'Working in open plan learning spaces', *Teacher Learning Network*, 21(1), 23–25.

Bloomer, K.C. and Moore, C.W. (1978) *Body, Memory and Architecture*. New Haven, CT: Yale University Press.

Boling, E., Schwier, R.A., Gray, C.M., Smith, K.M. and Campbell, K. (2016) *Studio Teaching in Higher Education*. New York: Routledge.

Boork, M., Nordén, J., Nilsson Tengelin, M. and Wendin, K. (2020) 'Sensory evaluation of lighting: A methodological pilot', *LEUKOS The Journal of the Illuminating Engineering Society of North America*, 1–17. doi: 10.1080/15502724.2020.1813037.

Boys, J. (2010) *Towards Creative Learning Spaces: Re-thinking the Architecture of Post-Compulsory Education*. Abingdon: Routledge.

Boys, J. and Hazlett, D. (2014) 'The Spaces of Relational Learning and their Impact on Student Engagement', In Scott-Webber, L. et al. (eds), *Learning Space Design in Higher Education*. Faringdon: Libri Publishing, pp. 37–51.

Brandt, D. (2014) 'Photovoice', In Coghlan, D. and Brydon-Miller, M. (eds), *The Sage Encyclopedia of Action Research*. London: Sage Publications Ltd, pp. 621–624.

Brooks, J.G. and Brooks, M.G. (1993) *In Search of Understanding: The Case for Constructivist Classrooms*. Virginia: The Association for Supervision and Curriculum Development.

Browning, W.D. and Ryan, C.O. (2020) *Nature Inside: A Biophilic Design Guide*. London: RIBA Publishing.

Browning, W.D., Ryan, C.O. and Clancy, J. (2014) *14 Patterns of Biophilic Design. Improving Health and Wellbeing in the Built Environment*. New York: Terrapin Bright Green, LLC.

Cardellino, P. and Woolner, P. (2020) 'Designing for transformation – A case study of open learning spaces and educational change', *Pedagogy, Culture & Society*, 28(3), 383–402. doi: 10.1080/14681366.2019.1649297.

Cerbone, D.R. (2006) *Understanding Phenomenology*. Chesham: Acumen Publishing Ltd.

Clandinin, D.J. (2013) *Engaging in Narrative Inquiry*. Walnut Creek: Left Coast Press, Inc.

Coffield, F. and Williamson, B. (2011) *From Exam Factories to Communities of Discovery: The Democratic Route*. London: Institute of Education, University of London.

Davidts, W. and Paice, K. (2009) *The Fall of the Studio: Artists at Work*. Amsterdam: Valiz.

Foley, H.J. and Matlin, M.W. (2010) *Sensation and Perception*. Boston: Allyn & Bacon.

Ghassan, A. and Bohemia, E. (2015) 'The global studio', *FORMakademisk*, 8(1), 1–11.

Gogel, W.C. (1990) 'A theory of phenomenal geometry and its applications', *Perception & Psychophysics*, 48(2), 105–123. doi: 10.3758/BF03207077.

Gray, C.M. (2013) 'Informal peer critique and the negotiation of habitus in a design studio', *Art, Design and Communication in Higher Education*, 12(2), 195–209. doi: 10.1386/adch.12.2.195_1.

Güler, K. (2015) 'Social media-based learning in the design studio: A comparative study', *Computers & Education*, 87, 192–203. doi: 10.1016/j.compedu.2015.06.004.

Haddad, E. (2010) 'Christian Norberg-Schulz's phenomenological project in architecture', *Architectural Theory Review*, 15(1), 88–101. doi: 10.1080/13264821003629279.

Hannon, A. (2014) 'Fleeting occupations: The "studio" as an extension of psychological inhabitation', *Journal of Visual Art Practice*, 13(1), 50–60.

Henshaw, V. and Mould, O.T. (2013) 'Sensing designed space: An exploratory methodology for investigating human response to sensory environments', *Journal of Design Research*, 11(1), 57–71.

Heschong Mahone Group (1999) *Daylighting in Schools. An Investigation Into the Relationship Between Daylighting and Human Performance*. Fair Oaks: Heschong Mahone Group.

Ingold, T. (2002) *The Perception of the Environment: Essays on Livelihood, Dwelling and Skill*. London: Routledge.

Ingold, T. (2011) *Being Alive: Essays on Movement, Knowledge and Description*. Abingdon: Routledge.

Kellert, S.R. and Wilson, E.O. (2013) *The Biophilia Hypothesis*. Washington, DC: Shearwater.

Lave, J. and Wenger, E. (1991) *Situated Learning: Legitimate Peripheral Participation*. Cambridge: Cambridge University Press.

Malnar, J.M. and Vodvarka, F. (2004) *Sensory Design*. Minneapolis, MN: University of Minnesota Press.

Merleau-Ponty, M. (1962) *Phenomenology of Perception*. London: Humanities Press.

Moran, D. (1999) *Introduction to Phenomenology*. New York: Routledge.

Morrison, A., Rigney, L., Hattam, R. and Diplock, A. (2019) *Towards an Australian Culturally Responsive Pedagogy: A Narrative Review of the Literature*. Adelaide: University of South Australia.

Muhammad, S., Sapri, M. and Sipan, I. (2014) 'Academic buildings and their influence on students' wellbeing in higher education institutions', *Social Indicators Research*, 115(3), 1159–1178. doi: 10.1007/s11205-013-0262-6.

Murdoch-Kitt, K.M. and Emans, D.J. (2020) *Intercultural Collaboration by Design*. Abingdon: Routledge.

Nair, P. and Doctori, R.Z. (2019) *Learning by Design: Live Play Engage Create*. Bangalore: Education Design Architects.

Norberg-Schulz, C. (1980) *Genius Loci: Towards a Phenomenology of Architecture*. New York: Rizzoli International Publications.

Nussbaumer, L.L. (2014) *Human Factors in the Built Environment, Human Factors in the Built Environment*. New York: Fairchild Books.

Otero-Pailos, J. (2010) *Architecture's Historical Turn: Phenomenology and the Rise of the Postmodern*. Minneapolis, MN: University of Minnesota Press.

Özkan Yazgan, E. and Akalın, A. (2019) 'Metaphorical reasoning and the design behavior of "pre-architects"', *International Journal of Technology and Design Education*, 29(5), 1193–1206. doi: 10.1007/s10798-018-9485-9.

Pallasmaa, J. (2012) *The Eyes of the Skin: Architecture and the Senses*. Chichester: John Wiley & Sons.

Pigrum, D. (2007) 'The "ontopology" of the artist's studio as workplace: Researching the artist's studio and the art/design classroom', *Research in Post-Compulsory Education*, 12(3), 291. doi: 10.1080/13596740701559720.

Rasila, H. and Rothe, P. (2012) 'A problem is a problem is a benefit? Generation Y perceptions of open-plan offices', *Property Management*, 30, 362–375. doi: 10.1108/0263747 1211249506.

Relph, E. (2008) *Place and Placelessness*. London: Pion Ltd.

Saltmarsh, S., Chapman, A., Campbell, M. and Drew, C. (2015) 'Putting "structure within the space": Spatially un/responsive pedagogic practices in open-plan learning environments', *Educational Review*, 67(3), 315–327. doi: 10.1080/00131911.2014.924482.

Schwartzman, M. (2011) *See Yourself Sensing: Redefining Human Perception*. London: Black Dog Publishing.

Scott-Webber, L., Branch, J., Bartholomew, P. and Nygaard, C. (2014) *Learning Space Design in Higher Education*. Faringdon: Libri Publishing.

Seamon, D. (1996) 'A singular impact: Edward Relph's place and placelessness', *Environmental and Architectural Phenomenology Newsletter*, 7(3), 5–8.

Seamon, D. and Mugerauer, R. (2000) *Dwelling, Place and Environment*. Malabar: Krieger Publishing Company.

Sharp, J.G., Hemmings, B. and Kay, R. (2016) 'Towards a model for the assessment of student boredom and boredom proneness in the UK higher education context', *Journal of Further and Higher Education*, 40(5), 649–681. doi: 10.1080/0309877X.2014.1000282.

Slovic, P., Finucane, M.L., Peters, E. and MacGregor, D.G. (2007) 'The affect heuristic', *European Journal of Operational Research*, 177(3), 1333–1352. doi: 10.1016/J.EJOR.2005.04.006.

Steg, L. and de Groot, J.I.M. (2019) *Environmental Psychology: An Introduction*. Newark: Wiley & Sons.

Tuan, Y-F. (1977) *Space and Place: The Perspective of Experience*. Minneapolis: University of Minnesota Press. doi: 10.2307/2064418.

Vyas, D., van der Veer, G. and Nijholt, A. (2013) 'Creative practices in the design studio culture: Collaboration and communication', *Cognition, Technology and Work*, 15, 415–443. doi: 10.1007/s10111-012-0232-9.

Walter, E.V. (1998) *Placeways: A Theory of the Human Environment*. Chapel Hill: The University of North Carolina Press.

Wenger, E. (2000) *Communities of Practice: Learning, Meaning, and Identity*. New York: Cambridge University Press.

Woolner, P. (2010) *The Design of Learning Spaces*. London: Continuum.

Worum, H., Lillekroken, D., Roaldsen, K.S., Ahlsen, B. and Bergland, A. (2020) 'Physiotherapists' perceptions of challenges facing evidence-based practice and the importance of environmental empowerment in fall prevention in the municipality – A qualitative study', *BMC Geriatrics*, 20(1), 1–17. doi: 10.1186/s12877-020-01846-8.

6

FLEXIBILITY AND CAPACITIES TO ADJUST EXPERIENTIAL LEARNING, LEARNING SPACES, AND DESIGN EDUCATION

Introduction

This final chapter focuses on the 'brain' of design education; our inherent abilities to indicate our need for flexibility and the capacities to adjust sensory affect within experiential learning, learning spaces, and design education for engaged teaching and learning. This chapter unpacks approaches to experiential learning, first discussing flexibility in concept development, then play as experimentation, materiality, and creative mess. In design education, the ability to vary everyday routines means the student can spend time exploring new possibilities, materials, techniques, and processes to support their conceptual journey. Play narrows the field of sought-after resolutions to develop artefacts and systems through enacting the design process. Materiality and creative mess are tactile intimacies, applying modern, man-made, and natural materials in the design process, aligning to the students' specific methods of practice. Playing with and testing new experiences is critical for improvement and the exploration of material qualities and attributes, and the experimental linkages and differences the students come to recognise between these materials and methods. Then, the discourse moves into an examination of flexibility in design education and the need for elasticity between broader university learning structures and specialist design-based studio learning, suggesting how educators and students can be supported through mutual systems and structures.

Experiential learning in design education

Sensory affect, creativity, and construction in design education are intertwined. Creativity has long been recognised to invoke sensory experiences in design construction via varied analogue and digital practices, to produce specific design

DOI: 10.4324/9781003175988-6

intentions. The role of sensory affect in experiential learning is intricate and multi-layered within each design discipline and the signature materials used. These are becoming increasingly diverse across each student's playful interdisciplinary processes in their preferred specialism. As the boundaries between traditionally segregated design domains are now blurry (and indeed between art, design, science, technology, and biology among others), then design educators and students must be afforded the flexibility and the capacities to adjust sensory affect within their own experiential learning, learning spaces and studio teaching and learning, to make the most of their practice.

Therefore, an awareness of sensory affect and its known and emerging effects on experiential learning and learning spaces, as a fluid and evolving entity, can benefit educators and students who need to adjust to changes in their design process, practice, and pedagogies. Design studio learning has key values, properties, and signature approaches, which can develop and adapt from a physical educational environment to an online one (and vice versa), from a public place (such as a museum or gallery) to a home-based learning space. These flexible adaptations also extend to playful experimentation and material cultures in design-based experiential learning. This enables design educators and students to take a fresh look at their teaching, learning, and creative practice through the lens of sensory affect, adding knowledge to their expanding arena of existing and emerging knowledge, understanding, and skills. This chapter expands upon the necessary flexible, sensorial approaches to design-based experiential learning and its conceptual, playful, materialistic, and agile practices.

Experiential learning emphasises direct sense experience (Kolb, 1983). The theoretical foundations of experiential learning highlight a four-stage learning cycle; first encapsulating concrete experience, then reflective observation, followed by abstract conceptualisation and finally, active experimentation (Caner Yüksel and Dinç Uyaroğlu, 2021). Concrete experience necessitates intuitive, bodily feeling or sensing when learning from experience, and building on subjective and collective prior experiences in the creative process. Then, comes iterative reflection throughout experiential learning and the creative practice cycle; what worked and what didn't and why? As an influential tool in education, reflection is often overlooked when addressing the context and effectiveness of learning spaces despite being embedded in design education. Next, abstract conceptualisation and concept development in design and design thinking encapsulates the process of generating, developing, and refining ideas to produce one or more solutions to a design issue or problem. Abstract conceptualisation is a critical step in design education and practice. Within art and design education 'the role, legitimacy and accountability of artefacts in the creation and generation of knowledge' is central to design-based learning, production, and practice (McAra, 2019). As there are 'tacit, incomplete and uncertain elements to the practice of design' students initially develop concepts via experiential learning, and then reinforce the identification, understanding, and communication of their intended design ideas to others (Jones, 2015:1600).

Flexibility in concept development

In this conceptual process of developing ideas and resolutions, reflection-in-action is a necessary 'thinking and doing' cyclic approach for design educators and students. Subjective reflection is entrenched across teaching and learning inquiry, educational research and creative practice as educators deliberate on their preferred teaching approaches to design pedagogy and students consider their chosen methods to engage with their design specialism. Reflection-in-action permits educators and students to react and plan future actions as they make decisions and improvements, when iteratively engaging with experiential learning and their specialised learning spaces, basing these changes of direction upon judgements accumulated over time. In this way, design educators and students pay critical attention to their everyday actions as they participate in intuitive self-reflective inquiry to improve their own practice in a cycle of learning through experience (Sullivan, 2009; Marshalsey, 2017). Embodied knowing happens as design educators and students engage in reflection and affection as they become aware of sensory affect in the dynamic interactions between themselves, their experiential praxis, and their educational environment. In this way, educators and students can evaluate the impact of sensory affect on their present practice by actively experiencing their 'thinking-by-learning-through-reflection-on-doing' activities in their learning spaces. Reflective practice can enable design educators and students to learn from experience about themselves, their work, and the way they relate to home and work, significant others and wider society and culture. This approach provides strategies for design educators and students to bring thoughts and perspectives out into the open, and to frame appropriate and searching questions never asked before. For many years, it has been recognised that this awareness of conscious, embodied, and qualitative learning experiences arises via the perspective of being reflective practitioners (Schön, 1984; Moon, 2006). Depraz (2003) proposed that the basic structure of 'becoming aware' involves an iterative cycle of reflection and affection; providing relatively safe and confidential ways to explore and express experiences otherwise difficult to communicate and challenging assumptions, ideological illusions, damaging social and cultural biases, inequalities, and questions personal behaviours (Depraz et al., 2003; Bolton, 2014:3).

In concept development, strategies must be in place to afford flexibility and the capacities to adjust conceptual thinking during the students' design process. Educators respond to students concrete and abstract diversions and wayfinding; from conceptual inception and initial construction to the ongoing disregarding of weaker ideas, and embracing and refinement of stronger, concrete concepts in a complex landscape of production techniques. This cognitive flexibility – our ability to juggle multiple concepts at the same time – mirrors our ability to think and engage with several variable design-based ideas, projects, and creative briefs in the design curriculum at the same time. In design education, insufficient time is a critical factor in concept development today, as tighter project turnaround and faster deadlines squeeze the conceptual thinking allocation in favour of production time. Providing the time to think about the potential avenues instigated in the conceptual development phase of a project is a necessity that is often overlooked within formal timetable structures. Design itself is also experiencing this rapid shift in agility across ideation and production 'processes, are becoming more and more complex due to the digital transformation and the new technical possibilities of Industry 4.0' (Schneider et al., 2020:abstract).

Second, the ability and capacity to vary everyday routines means the student can spend time exploring new possibilities, materials, techniques, and processes to support their conceptual journey. Testing new experiences is critical for improvement. As educators and students seek out new experiences in teaching, learning, thinking, and making, this approach supports cognitive flexibility and expands experiential knowledge. Divergent thinking becomes apparent when enacting this free-flowing and fluid approach to design briefs and projects, as individuals and peer collaborators in design-based learning. As the boundaries of design thinking and making are pushed into new fields, then design realisation and therefore, signature studio learning becomes a necessary higher-order challenge – improving knowledge, understanding, and skills in design. Furthermore, setting non-medium-specific briefs, which are open to the design student's interpretation and creativity, are an example of a personalised and flexible approach to their contextual shifts in thinking and doing as learning. When briefing students, design educators might state a theme or concept but not the artefacts or systems final representative form. For example, brief students for projects focusing on design and refugee health, or design and the ageing population, or design and wellbeing in low socio-economic areas – but the solution for the theme should not be specified (e.g. a poster, product, or UX (user experience) app). This is where student ingenuity and creativity should flourish as they embrace abstract and then resolved conceptualisation of their preferred design solutions – let their minds wander to seek proposed creative answers for the issue at hand. As industry mass-production and/or mass audience are often concrete prerequisites of a design project these days and small-scale concept development is often overshadowed by large and complex systems design and development, then design education can still support a degree of playfulness and slower conceptual thinking and development. Serendipity and accidental creative and conceptual discoveries still have a part to play in contemporary design-based learning. In this way, exposure to new cultural, socio-economic, and societal shifts and trends the students may not have experienced before can extend and expand their experiential knowledge and practice – supporting their growth as socially responsible designers and global citizens transitioning out of higher education into the fast-flowing river of design industries. Engaging with these themes through the lens of sensory affect and the body, students' design empathy will emerge when understanding the critical issues of the world and what it means to be human today. As suggestions, further themes for flexible design concept development, based on current megatrends (the patterns and trajectories of the future, which shape the world we live in (Hajkowicz, 2015)) and preferred design futures could include:

- Design, sustainability, and the circular economy
- Design and health

- Design and space
- Design and indigenous populations
- Design and the ageing population
- Design, digital innovation, and disruption
- Design, biodiversity, habitats, and the climate crisis
- Design and economic resilience
- Design and the future of work
- Design and politics
- Design, inclusive, and diversified cultures
- Design and rapid urbanisation
- Design and population growth
- Design and social change
- Design and play
- Design and education
- Design, food, and resource scarcity
- Design and social interaction
- Design, security, defence, and conflict
- Design and consumer personalisation
- Design, transport, and human mobility

(Collated from texts by Hajkowicz, 2015; BlackRock Inc., 2018;
Tytler et al., 2019; Project Management Institute, 2022)

Play as experimentation

In design education, play is critical for the exploration of these conceptual themes, and the experimental linkages and differences between concepts and materials, their methods, and final forms. The materials in play serve two functions; to further development and to offer new perspectives in the exploration of the world (Montessori, 1970). Play narrows the field of the appropriate materials and sought-after techniques to develop the essential artefacts and systems for conceptual development.

As a term, critical play originated from gaming context and theory, and challenges the accepted norms to reshape practice in unrestricted ways (Flanagan, 2009). This strategy of conscious play-as-practice can inspire inadvertent discovery and serendipity. This may be realised in three different perspectives; a game could be critical in the literal sense – reaching judgemental or negative conclusions; critical – to analyse and scrutinise the merits and faults of a creative work and lastly, criticality suggesting a detailed and scholarly analysis and commentary (Flanagan, 2009). In design education, play or gamification can invoke thoughtful and speculative contexts to conventionally non-playful and serious topics, to provoke new concepts and solutions, individually or collectively. This investigative process challenges and engages the student to become skilled in their preferred design fields.

A fluid 'pedagogy of ambiguity' is found mainly in art and design education. These are the essential 'diverse wanderings' that function as purposeful, experimental play leading to deliberate and incidental experimentation and developing emergent objectives (Austerlitz et al., 2008). Open-ended practice and production is essential for creative experimentation and development in design education, and not constrained by rules or regulations, leading to intentional and accidental ideas and resolutions in the process. Tieben et al. (2014) highlighted the literature surrounding the benefits and importance of emergent playfulness and that being immersed in open-ended play feels safe and empowering to the design student. Tieben et al. (2014:351) identified three design values that are crucial in designing for 'playful persuasion'. These design values are (1) to elicit and seduce playful interactions, (2) to reinforce emergent play, and (3) to create playful activities that echo these values. Critical play, and its refined outcomes, specifically emerges from the learning space and context, which fosters unrestricted creative deviations, experimentation, and mess. This can lead to pushing the boundaries of existing practice, materiality, techniques, and illuminate new ways of working in design practice and education. Tsekleves and Darby (2020:49–66) made several recommendations in their chapter *The Role of Playfulness and Sensory Experiences in Design for Public Health and for Ageing Well*, which are also applicable to the context of design education today. These include:

1   Emphasising fun and tangible playful experiences through sensory interactions.

- Playful activities and experiences encourage the subjective creative expression of their users, which are generative and open-ended. Therefore, captivating user engagement and increasing the 'sense of joy, sensation and thrill'.
- Discovering via exploratory experiences and hence being encouraged to revisit and reflect on the design process, facilitating creative expression and stimulating sensory affect, intrinsic motivation, and achievement.

2   Engaging users with as many of the five senses as possible.
3   Use natural and fabricated material.
4   Facilitate and encourage movement and physical engagement.
5   Provide multi-stimulus feedback.
6   The design process should be inclusive and accessible by everyone who uses the learning space, offering participation to every person, with an ease of use of all analogue and digital resources and machinery.
7   The design process should result in the creation of an artefact or system that creates a visual or cultural link with the place in which it is installed or the experiences it offers.
8   Exploration and experimentation in design studio learning are inherently social activities; 'Connectedness forms one of the key values for humans, as we are social beings'.
9   Physical, cognitive, and emotional.

- Collaboration reduces cognitive load and increases feelings of sensation, fellowship, sympathy, and accomplishment.

(Tsekleves and Darby, 2020:49–66)

Materiality

> *Haptic engagement is close range and hands-on. It is the engagement of a mindful body at work with materials and with the land, 'sewing itself in' to the textures of the world along the pathways of sensory involvement.*
>
> (Ingold, 2011:132)

Playing with materials in the studio turns ideas into works. Materials move from being innate and obscure to ideas and constructions to refined design outcomes. The sensory modality of touching and working with materials affects the mind and body 'In our imagination, the object is simultaneously held in the hand and inside the head' (Pallasmaa, 2012:14). Fundamental design-based learning processes range from craft-based, slow approaches using natural and found materials towards the contemporary trends of faster, man-made 3D printing and additive manufacturing. Drawing as a central studio technique has also changed in nature from mark-making using paper and pencil to drawing on digital tablets with stylus to potentially, drawing in the air next? However, the concept of mark-making remains the same and while experimenting in sketchbooks is central to the materiality origins of the design studio, there are now many different methods to do so. In terms of creativity, touch screens are the new tools replacing paper and pen despite many arguing for the sanctity of conventional sketchbooks. Since the introduction of digital production into higher education in the 1990s, technological innovation such as the internet and cloud-based working has driven the dominance of TEL in education, more generally – and writing and drawing is one evolving example. The boom in digital practice within society and its influence on higher education has meant information about the world is mainly relayed through touching screens, smart phones, and computers daily (Howes, 2005:30; Facer, 2011). Yet, craft and conventional print-based techniques have made a resurgence and the need for analogue processes (such as letterpress) are now in greater demand alongside digital means, not only in education but also in the wider community. Increasingly, blending digital technology with conventional, natural materials has emerged; 3D printing of clay is an example. Nonetheless, thinking through the hands is a key value when exploring the materiality of design practice and in the range of materials to which students can construct 2D, 3D, and 4D maquettes, design interfaces, and prototypes, and when using a variety of resources, scales, and aesthetics.

Material trajectories allow us to stay connected with design studio learning through history and as design education evolves into a future entity – never losing its values through time. Additionally, materiality and material cultures can foster nostalgia with memory-laden journeys and leave imprints of those who have gone before: objects left behind, a build-up of paint in the sink, work on the walls, or drawers filled with wooden and lead letterpress typography, among others. Malafouris (2013) describes this as the ontology of material signs and traces. Time shapes the values of specialised studio learning spaces and the material cultures embedded there from the past, present, and into futures iterations of design education. The open-ended journey of material cultures also forms and evolves the interactions between each design educator and students over time. These progressive interactions also occur between students and their artefacts; in their material engagement with what they produce (the interaction of people and 'things' in the specialised studio learning spaces); 'The inseparability of thought, action, and material things' (Malafouris, 2013).

The choice of, and accessibility to, materials in design education and its learning spaces must be diverse to meet individual and collective needs. It is known that design education encapsulates a wide range of creative disciplines within a variety of spaces and resources adapted for fashion, textiles, graphic design, interaction design, or product design among others. These disciplines can be divided into screen-based or technology-supported fabrication cultures and hand-driven, craft-orientated, maker-based cultures. Of course, overlaps can occur in the design process, and through the experimentation and development stages. Students will be drawn to certain processes and techniques, depending on their intuitive affinity with preferred materials, as materials impress the human mind and body (Lupton and Lipps, 2018). This is due in part to being drawn to the choice of material by degrees of touch – translated as roughness or smoothness and reflected in the properties of the surface, object, technique, resource, or material. Every educator or student encounters materials in the design studio, often by the hands but also via eyes, ears, nose, and skin.

Material experiences can differ when students work with diverse materials and their associated resources, when engaging in design education. Consider sinking into the soft furnishings of sofas and bean bags in learning spaces, working with type-setting materials and print machinery or within a 3D digital lab. Materials and material cultures, and their production techniques, can transform the sound or feel of a design studio or a learning space and hands-on analogue and digital practice can invite an embodied response. Not every material is physical, yet light (natural or artificial/digital), air (warm or cold), sound (such as music, ambience), and smell (aromatic or nostalgia-invoking) are materials too. Today, many objects and structures in design education are made from natural materials are designers and students strive to solve the problems of our planet through sustainable initiatives and materials. Students should be encouraged to explore the endless boundaries of materiality. Future-focused examples can be seen in the text, *Radical Matter: Rethinking materials for a sustainable future*, which includes waste, repair, natural assets, insects, and hair among others as future design materials (Franklin and Till, 2018).

Creative mess

Artists make visible their materialistic process more than designers do and this influences the practice of design students, who initially assume they will be sitting at a dry desk all day when enrolling in higher education. Creative mess is often thought to be an additive component of creating art, yet design mess is seen as subtraction – removing material to reveal prototypes or the final design solution when making. Being tidy can reflect the expectations of societal norms, although designers and students may need a neat, orderly space to begin or continue their creative process. Even though they may be naturally tidy people, they still make a mess, but this is often hidden within the digital artboards of software platforms, such as Adobe Illustrator® or Miro®. In the digital sense, we save these design files as technological scraps and multiple 'versions'. Digital mess is less visible and more challenging to keep neat, as a lack of organised, and multiple tiers of administrative files and irrelevant naming conventions and folders can be framed as untidiness in this context.

Mess is a necessary output of any creative process involving materials, yet perhaps 'mess' is the wrong linguistic term for this context, denoting unorganised waste and leftovers. Mess – in the creative experimental, active process of design practice and education – may represent disorder and the specific leftovers from material or technical investigation. However, without degrees of creative mess, resolution cannot be found in the design journey. It is critical that students are allowed to experiment, develop, take risks in their learning journeys, and feel few inhibitions when creating process-driven mess. I encourage design educators and students to use any surface, material, process, and space they wish, externalising the proceeds of a student's subjective cognitive thinking and hands-on doing. But I am talking about non-digital mess here; visible and easier to clean and tidy. This could be 3D printing waste, discarded paper, offcuts of wood, metal or composite materials and prototypes, wet mess from ink, paint and spraying, and other forms of thinking that has a disorderly yet visible footprint in the design process; "the presence of messiness in someone's space actually means the individual is open to seeking 'new directions'" (Dunn, 2013:online).

In summary, design students should be allocated space for creative mess on their personal workstations and their communal work areas; and to be encouraged to take responsibility for the tidiness either during or at completion of their processes in their private and shared areas in learning spaces. However, mess is different from grime and dirt built up over time – no-one likes to work in these conditions, and the creative process has no connection here. Occasionally mess does become offensive through powerful or bad odours, rotting materials or the scale of one student's mess encroaching on other students' spaces for working, and not cleaning up a communal work area, which leaves this resource unusable for the next student. When deadlines are looming, this is disrespectful to others in the same situation. Cleaning up others unnecessary mess such as mouldy studio coffee mugs is also another horror (I believe every design studio learning space hosts at least one culprit). Yet, the capacities to be either physically messy or digitally messy, on small and large scales should be afforded to all design students, no matter what the discipline. Tidy graphic design or messy print-making design, neat digitally created experience design or wet illustration and machined 3D or CNC printing, all educators and students in design education should be supported in their experiential learning and process through creative mess tolerance – by the institution and estates governance, mainly.

Flexibility and capacities to adjust design education

In design education, there is a pedagogical gap that exists between broader university learning structures, systems, and spaces, and the requirements of specialist design education in higher education. Within a geographically and digitally dispersed Co[D]P, design students are now tasked with taking ownership of their own practice-based learning journeys to a greater degree than ever before (Wenger, 2000). Several recent studies have surveyed the design education sectors' pivot to online education, and the mixed responses by design educators who are unsure if they want to do so on a permanent basis (driven by the unfamiliarity of numerous digital platforms and the time involved to convert lesson planning to online delivery) and the ongoing effects on student engagement. Wragg (2020) examined the current social realities of design education and the effects of transitioning from a physical space to the widespread acceptance of online platforms. Wragg (2020) also describes the evolution of the traditional studio and the notion that students' attendance, time and interaction has declined, despite the preferences of on-campus design students to engage with a physical learning space. The online studio can produce new opportunities for social and dynamic engagement across 'a collection of boards, walls and threads that enable students to actively engage in the same types of activities that would be undertaken in a physical studio on-campus' (Wragg, 2020:2293). Yet, until now educators have been deliberately reluctant to embrace the technological and pedagogical characteristics of online design education, despite students' further need for a flexible workaround to their jobs and responsibilities. Dreamson (2020) advises meta-connective pedagogy as the solution to student engagement within online design education. That is, conventional studio learning is not lost, yet it is changing and the experiential learning journey, critical to design education and student engagement, must remain at the forefront of this evolution.

In either physical, blended, or online forms of design education, educators and students should be allowed to embrace the flexible use of formal and informal, group and individual activities in their preferred approaches and platforms to teaching and learning. There is a conformity for design education to fit into higher education systems and structures, which doesn't always align well with the parameters of a rigorous design education. University institutions should support the degree programs that involve day-to-day creative practice and empower educators and students to devise their own preferred paths in design-based practice and culture without pressure. Flexibility to work with and across university systems and structures should also be self-driven by design educators and students in terms of time, locations, arranging their practice and resources in their specialised learning spaces. Educators and students should be afforded the flexibility to create the conditions they need, to support their design-based teaching and learning practice and processes. In addition, design curriculums in higher education should aim to be broad across human-centred design, sustainability, social-responsibilities, and socio-cultural contexts. Students graduating expertise portfolios should aim to reflect who they are as a designer across these topics and may not be necessarily situated within a distinct specialism or framework, but instead reflect their conceptual and technical design interests, reflecting the fluidity of design today.

Access to wide-ranging specialist and non-specialist facilities should be provided and with open-ended time to design, to reflect chosen interests and to promote interdisciplinarity. If curriculum timetabling is rigid, creativity cannot gain momentum and design students are forced to adhere to small pockets of time, in which nothing much is produced. Indeed, physical, blended, and online learning spaces must be always accessible to design students and there should not be dogmatic barriers to engagement, such as locked doors and inoperable resources. Ownership of physical learning spaces and workshops on campus is often tightly controlled (generally, for all the right reasons) yet frequently, this is to the point of exclusion as hierarchies of power keep students away from the very learning spaces they need. I have seen a lack of engagement in students who are defeated by a lack of trust in them that they can't operate machinery efficiently, even with instructional training and safety accreditation fulfilled. Failure is learning and these barriers should be dissolved or mediated.

In addition, and in support of access and trust, every design student ought to be allocated a personal workstation or desk regardless of their year group, and close to their preferred specialised learning spaces and resources. Allocating formal, communal creative learning spaces and assigning a personal desk space to individual students can foster a closeness in the community and means that they are more likely to implement strategies to engage with their Co[D]P, specialised studio learning and design education. The visibility of shared work-in-progress and networking across and between year groups are critical social and progressive components of design education. Therefore, there should be large-scale flexible learning spaces provided for the production and experimentation of messy or clean large-scale work, for example, textile design wall-hangings or digital projections. Furthermore, in formative and summative assessment submissions students should be given the flexibility and choice to select their preferred formats: from digital presentations to the presentation of artefacts or as an embodied performative display. A 'broadening out' of staff overseeing courses and overlapping in the development and managing of the design curriculum itself, as a form of collaborative working, which can involve professional design partners (physically and online), can expand the guiding framework needed to support students' diverse interests.

Students should have access to communal facilities and designated working and social spaces for opportunities to mix with all year groups in their design education and beyond, overlapping and networking across their interests together, online, and offline. The networked rhizomes entrenched within design-based teaching and learning can bring together individuals, social clusters, year groups of students, practices, shared knowledge, and the crossing of disciplines and interests. Non-teaching breakout areas are fluid spaces where collegiality is buoyed and progress is discussed over tea, lunch, and restful breaks, and for students to convene together in relaxing settings during pauses in formal pedagogy. Often, unplanned yet rich peer learning occurs in these types of spaces as students meet and discuss project briefs and assessment while drinking, eating, and resting – normally before or after timetabled classes. The breakout space at HDK-Valand, at the Academy of Art and Design in Gothenburg, Sweden is situated within the broader Masters students studio (Figure 6.1). This breakout space functions as an informal space on the fringes

FIGURE 6.1 Informal breakout space at HDK-Valand, Academy of Art and Design, Gothenburg, Sweden.

Source: © Lorraine Marshalsey.

of a formal design studio learning space within the architecture. Its location meant gatherings were visible to the broader studio community who could dip and out as they wished – to quickly make a hot cup of coffee, microwave lunch or to voluntarily contribute to a spontaneous discussion happening over time in this space, regularly overflowing into insightful peer learning discussions. I am particularly drawn to this idea of the rich, flexible opportunities present here, moving back and forth between informal and formal learning, purely due to the proximity to others and inclusive location to the studio.

Similarly, the Parlour within Queensland Collage of Art, Griffith University at the Gold Coast campus in Queensland, Australia, offered comparable activities (Figure 6.2). This informal Parlour was situated in a transit corridor, surrounded by wood-working and 3D-printing workshops and seminar rooms. Over time, and since its inception, the Parlour essentially became a student-led meeting and workspace, an individual and communal student workplace, a lunch space, a breakout space from the workshops and seminar rooms and as a visible space for spontaneous interactions among the users, mostly known to each other. Design educators would also periodically host small breakout groups here and freely encounter students working here. This space was open and used by students all year round and it was common to see students using this space outside of timetabled trimesters, without

FIGURE 6.2 The Parlour, Queensland College of Art, Griffith University, Gold Coast, Australia.

Source: © Lorraine Marshalsey.

restrictions. The flexible layout meant furniture could be dragged together to form grouped settings or spread out for individual use. The high tabled area was used for laptop work and as a lunch table. In addition, I once observed a wood-bending steam machine being wheeled into the Parlour through the large roller doors for a specialist class. This wood-working technique meant product design students could learn the hands-on practicalities of making wood pliable when it is exposed to steam, via a guest lecture.

In seminar rooms, it is becoming more common to see moveable furniture present in contemporary learning spaces. This is largely due to the success of manufacturing companies, who develop the latest furniture for learning spaces across early years, primary, secondary, and higher education institutions. Despite the portable nature of wheeled chairs and tables, the immovable nature of the surrounding learning space facilities – the fixed nature of the screens still positions the lecturer at one podium computer to the left of this image – can cause engagement issues (Figure 6.3). A carpeted seminar room often has multiple, fixed screens, and speakers hanging from the ceiling. Students twist in their chairs to view the small screens and when educators use this space, they are inclined to use the technology offered. Wall space is often limited in learning spaces with a small whiteboard and a magnetic board visible on a moveable partition. Room-dividing partitions, separating this learning space from the neighbouring one, are heavy to move and can only be moved by authorised technical staff. The sensory affect impact of learning spaces like these, speaks only of dry-based, tidy, short-term, and impermanent design pedagogy. In summary, learning space and the associated furniture in these spaces should be easily adjustable, moveable, and transportable,

FIGURE 6.3 Formal learning space at Queensland College of Art, Griffith University, Gold Coast, Australia.

Source: © Lorraine Marshalsey.

FIGURE 6.4   Sofas in a design-based learning space.

Source: © Lorraine Marshalsey.

for example, wheeled chairs, tables, dividing screens, storage, resources, lighting, and so on. I see more potential for design-based teaching and learning in this learning space if it had less 'office' furniture and had zones to work in, for individuals and teams. It would be better if this learning space had mobile TEL, which could be wheeled to any corner, with large wall and floor space for working on instead and lightweight, flexible partitions to divide the space ad hoc depending on the activities taking place there. Design-based learning spaces and their associated contents and resources should be entirely comfortable yet flexible enough to support engagement in across formal and informal gatherings, for example, can the students decide if they prefer formal critiques to be held in and around informal sofas instead? Informal settings, such the sofas seen in Figure 6.4, can facilitate formal teaching and learning activities such as critiques and group work, and articulate a feeling of less pressure to 'perform' for design educators or students, while supporting movement in and around the space. When chairs are always positioned the same way at tables, then this suggests 'first come, first served' when design students select the best seat for that class's activities (and preferably, to be situated near a laptop charging point). Layouts should be flexible and adaptable in every learning space – design-based or not.

Conclusion: foregrounding experiential learning, learning spaces, and design education through the lens of sensory affect

This book has argued for the importance of enabling appropriate experiential learning and learning spaces, through the lens of sensory affect, to address the challenges and trends facing design education today. The first half of this book set the scene and defined sensory affect, experiential learning, learning spaces and design education, alone and in combinations of each other. First, the discourse exposed the imbalance between the needs of signature design studio pedagogies and wider university structures and systems and how this has contributed to the current pressures bearing down on design teaching and learning in higher education today. Despite the complex terminology, modalities, and models of contemporary experiential learning and learning spaces, 'webs of stickiness' can be constructed, identifying, and revealing the optimal conditions for engaging design educators and students.

Second, this book has illuminated the need to be aware of what it is to be human today and why we need to listen to the body for guidance and direction in education, more broadly. Sensory affect (those experiences detected through the body) is an approach highly relevant to our engagement with the vast complexity and inconsistent landscape of design education today. Sensory design can reach beyond purely thought to connect bodily experience to concrete experience, the abstract and conceptual development of design practice in education, as the senses work in tandem to establish deeper levels of cognition and communication between the body and mind. The broad discourse of the senses in design and design education of the past and present clearly frames this need for an awareness of sensory affect in experiential learning and learning spaces today. 'Then and now' blends with the technological innovation of the future to emphasise the central sensory and experiential discourse of this book, and as higher education continuously evolves and transforms in this post-digital and pandemic age.

If the key trends in design and education include the senses, embodiment, emotional design, and personalisation in design and education then why aren't these critical aspects at the forefront of our thoughts in learning spaces (Waldrip et al., 2016; Bennett et al., 2020; France, 2020)? Thinking-through-the-body responses means design educators and students will be empowered to develop the tools needed to become aware of their chosen methods of location, learning, and practice, and of how their sense of place is influenced by sensory affect. When we listen to the body for direction, we can be empowered to adjust sensory affect, and the sensations and perceptions arising from our active senses, in and across experiential learning and learning spaces, shaping our subjective and creative actions. In a diverse framework of corporeal experience, our bodies, learnings, and spaces, become one intertwined cycle of experience. Gendlin and his notion of the *Felt Sense* supported this enhanced body-space awareness and reinforces the externalisation (in words) of body-space engagement. In the provision of 'becoming aware', design educators must also consider including sensory-based teaching practices, embodied pedagogies, and BBL in design education today.

The impact of sensory affect on learning spaces, the social, cultural, and relational interactions present, the planned design curriculum and associated pedagogies, and the experiential learning of design practice has significant, tangible influence on reflective teaching and student engagement. Becoming aware of the experiential influence of sensory affect, using bodily navigation, will strengthen those teaching and learning in design education today. A conscious recognition of sensory affect will allow design educators and students to engage better with their educational contexts – at university, online and at home – using selective attention and situational responsiveness to the conditions present in these settings (Schwartz and Krantz, 2016). Foregrounding an awareness of sensory affect through bodily experiences will aid and/or challenge educators and students to act on the following responses in design studio education:

- The effects of *selective or divided attention*, allowing educators and students to focus on one or more sources of stimulus when many sources are present, therefore, supporting engagement.
- The effects of *stimulus salience*, when objects in the immediate surroundings attract educators and students' attention and interrupt engagement.
- The effects of *attentional capture*, when a dominant stimulus causes educators and students to transfer attention to that stimulus rather than a preferred one and interrupting engagement.
- The effects of *inattentional blindness*, when educators and students fail to engage with, or perceive, visible yet unexpected objects in the immediate surroundings and interrupting engagement because of a lack of attention.

(Schwartz and Krantz, 2016:232–239).

The latter half of this book turned thoughts about sensory affect into action. The explicit approaches to unlocking better conditions for teaching and learning can only occur through design educators and students lived experiences and sustained by three central themes, composed of *all-surface use, empowerment,* and *flexibility*:

1 Surfaces, materiality, and experiential learning were explored via *all-surface use* in physical, specialised, online, communal, legacy, and outdoor learning spaces and teaching strategies.

2 Environmental *empowerment* was addressed through a sense of place, environmental stressors, restorative environments, and structures of shared power in the Co[D]P. Diagnostic methods and strategies were recommended to identify and address sensory affect in design-based learning spaces, within several key themes and empowering the 'things' we feel, embody, nurture, and believe in as human educators and students.

3 Then, *flexibility;* the capabilities of choice and our inherent abilities to indicate our need for elasticity to adjust sensory affect within experiential learning,

learning spaces and design education for engaged teaching and learning in higher education. Approaches to experiential learning, concept development, then play as experimentation, materiality, and creative mess were unpacked as agile necessities in design-based learning.

Learning spaces are evolving in parallel with the rapid development of new technological tools, processes, and pedagogical practices in education. Students do not work entirely on campus anymore and student engagement must be rethought in terms of the multitude of places students learn in design education. Learning spaces today are accessed by students working from a distance (at home, café, parklands, library), when travelling (train, plane, driving, cycling), when working around family commitments, housemates, share-houses and employment, when on campus, when working purely online (locally and globally) and when opportunistic ad hoc spaces for studying present (under the stairs, a park bench, sitting on the floor or a corner of a hall in the university). Educators and students may perceive a sense of place differently in the variable landscape of learning space design today. A range of studies cited in Holtham and Canienne (2014:232–233) provided a definitive set of guidelines of learning space design from several perspectives, which I have expanded upon to support this narrative of *all-surface use, empowerment*, and *flexibility* in contemporary design education:

- Design spaces for multiple uses, with integral flexibility in each space to accommodate simultaneous and successive lessons, current and emerging pedagogies, and design practice.
- Design spaces which will not date quickly, and which can be adapted with ease to enable the space provision to grow and reconfigure over time.
- Design spaces to energise and inspire creative thinking and doing, inspiring educators, and students.
- Design spaces using the vertical and horizontal dimensions and functions of each space. Use an all-surface mindset to create learning spaces, which embody a humanised perspective.
- Design spaces to foster support, empowerment and control to educators and students in relation to the functions and features of the spaces.
- Design spaces to maximise the potential of different students' learning styles, educators' pedagogical approaches and active, experiential learning.
- Design spaces to support different purposes such as co-operative learning and collaboration among students, forms of enterprise education and the associated curriculum activities taking place.
- Design spaces to host and blend analogue and digital resources, merging craft and technology across online and face-to-face interactions to maximise the abilities and needs of all educators and students.
- Design spaces to facilitate and encourage ownership of these spaces to the students so that they may form an attachment and a sense of place when learning.
- Design spaces to comfortably foster a sense of physical and mental wellbeing.

- Design spaces to be aesthetically pleasing but not to the detriment of function, use, comfort, fitness for purpose, population, light, temperature, and acoustics.
- Design spaces to create, maintain and enable flow by providing the affordances for educator and student engagement, in relation to warmth, natural light, space to work, access to kitchens and sustenance outlets, wi-fi, private and reflective spaces, accessible writing surfaces on tables, walls and floors and the inclusion of sofas in formal learning spaces.
- Design spaces to promote equity and inclusive practices across cultures, talents, and to address physical challenges.
- Design spaces to foster engagement, interaction, and feedback between educator and student.

To summarise, under the three themes (*all-surface use, empowerment,* and *flexibility*), the discourse of this book has dynamically embraced sensory affect in experiential learning, learning spaces, and design education through reflective teaching approaches, methods, and strategies in higher education. The purpose of this book was to systematically examine potential solutions to two differing, yet related challenges in design education today: first revealing the disparity between the needs of design education and those of wider university structures and systems in higher education. Second, this book has foregrounded the need to be aware of what it is to be human today and how to listen to the body for direction in the repertoire of physical and digital learning spaces on offer, to support reflective teaching and student engagement today. The answer is to create positive, reflective teaching strategies, flourishing learning experiences and to manipulate learning spaces, through practical sensory affective approaches and actions, in a time of economic, technological, political, environmental, and educational change in higher education.

References

Austerlitz, N., Blythman, M., Jones, B.A., Jones, C.A., Grove-White, A., Morgan, S.J., Orr, S., Shreeve, A. and Vaughan, S. (2008) 'Mind the Gap: Expectations, Ambiguity and Pedagogy Within Art and Design Higher Education', In Drew, L. (ed), *The Student Experience in Art and Design Higher Education: Drivers for Change.* Cambridge: Jill Rogers Associates Limited, pp. 125–148.

Bennett, D., Knight, E. and Rowley, J. (2020) 'The role of hybrid learning spaces in enhancing higher education students' employability', *British Journal of Educational Technology,* 51(4), 1188–1202. doi: 10.1111/bjet.12931.

BlackRock Inc. (2018) *What are megatrends? BlackRock, Inc.* Available at: www.blackrock.com/sg/en/investment-ideas/themes/megatrends.

Bolton, G. (2014) 'Reflection Practice: An Introduction', In *Reflective Practice: Writing and Professional Development.* London: Sage Publications Ltd, pp. 1–24.

Caner Yüksel, Ç. and Dinç Uyaroğlu, İ. (2021) 'Experiential learning in basic design studio: Body, Space and the design process', *International Journal of Art and Design Education,* 40(3), 508–525. doi: 10.1111/jade.12364.

Depraz, N., Varela, F.J. and Vermersch, P. (2003) *On Becoming Aware: A Pragmatics of Experiencing.* Amsterdam: John Benjamins Publishing Company.

Dreamson, N. (2020) 'Online design education: Meta-connective pedagogy', *International Journal of Art & Design Education*, 39(3), 483–497. doi: 10.1111/jade.12314.

Dunn, D.S. (2013) Creative mess, Creative clutter, *Psychology Today*. Available at: www.psychologytoday.com/au/blog/head-the-class/201309/creative-mess-creative-clutter.

Facer, K. (2011) *Learning Futures: Education, Technology and Social Change*. Abingdon: Routledge.

Flanagan, M. (2009) *Critical Play: Radical Game Design*. Cambridge: MIT Press.

France, P.E. (2020) 'Reclaiming personalized learning: A pedagogy for restoring equity and humanity in our classrooms', *Corwin*. doi: 10.4135/9781544360652.

Franklin, K. and Till, C. (2018) *Radical Matter: Rethinking Materials for a Sustainable Future*. London: Thames & Hudson.

Hajkowicz, S. (2015) *Global Megatrends: Seven Patterns of Change Shaping Our Future*. Victoria: CSIRO Publishing.

Holtham, C. and Canienne, A. (2014) 'Collective Learning Spaces: Constraints on Pedagogic Excellence', In Scott-Webber, L. et al. (eds), *Learning Space Design in Higher Education*. Faringdon: Libri Publishing, pp. 225–240.

Howes, D. (2005) 'Skinscapes: Embodiment, Culture and Environment', In Classen, C. (ed), *The Book of Touch*. Oxford: Berg Publishers, pp. 27–40.

Ingold, T. (2011) *Being Alive: Essays on Movement, Knowledge and Description*. Abingdon: Routledge.

Jones, D. (2015) 'Reflection-in-action and Motivated Reasoning', In Zande, R.V., Bohemia, E. and Digranes, I. (eds), *Proceedings of the 3rd International Conference for Design Education Researchers*. Aalto: Aalto University, pp. 1599–1615. doi: 10.13140/RG.2.1.2642.5440.

Kolb, D.A. (1983) *Experiential Learning: Experience as the Source of Learning and Development*. Upper Saddle River, NJ: Financial Times/Prentice Hall.

Lupton, E. and Lipps, A. (2018) *The Senses: Design Beyond Vision*. New York: Princeton Architectural Press.

Malafouris, L. (2013) *How Things Shape the Mind: A Theory of Material Engagement*. Cambridge, MA: MIT Press.

Marshalsey, L. (2017) *An investigation into the experiential impact of sensory affect in contemporary communication design studio education* (Thesis). The Glasgow School of Art. Available at: http://radar.gsa.ac.uk/5894/.

McAra, M. (2019) 'Modelling experiential knowledge ethically: An Artefact-based approach to visually documenting a participatory design process with young people', *International Journal of Art and Design Education*, 38(3), 583–598. doi: 10.1111/jade.12242.

Montessori, M. (1970) *The Psychological Background of the Montessori Material Within the Setting of the Prepared Environment*. Amsterdam: Association Montessori Internationale.

Moon, J.A. (2006) *Learning Journals: A Handbook for Reflective Practice and Professional Development*. London: Routledge.

Pallasmaa, J. (2012) *Encounters: Volume 2: Architectural Essays*. Helsinki: Rakennustieto Publishing.

Project Management Institute, I. (2022) *Global Megatrends 2022*. Newtown Square: Project Management Institute, Inc. doi: 10.1071/9781486301416.

Schneider, D., Fröhlich, T., Huth, T. and Vietor, T. (2020) 'Design for flexibility-evaluation interactions between product properties and production processes', *Procedia CIRP*, 91, 814–818. doi: 10.1016/j.procir.2020.02.240.

Schön, D.A. (1984) *The Reflective Practitioner: How Professionals Think in Action*. London: Basic Books.

Schwartz, B.L. and Krantz, J.H. (2016) *Sensation & Perception*. Thousand Oaks, CA: Sage Publications Ltd.

Sullivan, G. (2009) *Art Practice as Research: Inquiry in Visual Arts*. Thousand Oaks: Sage Publications Ltd.

Tieben, R., Sturm, J., Bekker, T. and Schouten, B. (2014) 'Playful persuasion: Designing for ambient playful interactions in public spaces', *Journal of Ambient Intelligence and Smart Environments*, 6(4), 341–357. doi: 10.3233/AIS-140265.

Tsekleves, E. and Darby, A. (2020) 'The Role of Playfulness and Sensory Experiences in Design for Public Health and for Ageing Well', In Ian Heywood. (ed), *Sensory Arts and Design*. London: Routledge.

Tytler, R., Bridgstock, R., White, P., Mather, D., McCandless, T., Grant-Iramu, M., Bonson, S., Ramnarine, D. and Penticoss, A.J. (2019) *100 jobs of the future*. Available at: https://100jobsofthefuture.com/.

Waldrip, B., Yu, J.J. and Prain, V. (2016) 'Validation of a model of personalised learning', *Learning Environments Research*, 19(2), 169–180. doi: 10.1007/s10984-016-9204-y.

Wenger, E. (2000) *Communities of Practice: Learning, Meaning, and Identity*. New York: Cambridge University Press.

Wragg, N. (2020) 'Online communication design education: the importance of the social environment', *Studies in Higher Education*, 45(11), 2287–2297. doi: 10.1080/03075079.2019.1605501.

INDEX

For Product Safety Concerns and Information please contact our EU
representative GPSR@taylorandfrancis.com
Taylor & Francis Verlag GmbH, Kaufingerstraße 24, 80331 München, Germany

www.ingramcontent.com/pod-product-compliance
Lightning Source LLC
Chambersburg PA
CBHW070335270326
41926CB00017B/3877

9 781032 008264